WALK ROME

An in-depth guide to walking Rome

Walk along with a native Roman to explore the Eternal City at your own pace with clear routes, historical context, and timely information.

Carlo Mignani

Betsy Schad Mignani

Contents

WALK ROME 1

Overview of the seven walks...............................3

WALK ONE - The Heart of Rome.........................5

The Killer Artist – Caravaggio's Rome 27

WALK TWO - Ancient Origins............................29

Cosmatesque Decoration 42

Rome's Origins 59

WALK THREE - Imperial Rome...........................61

Julius Caesar 89

WALK FOUR - Rome Opens to the World 91

Fountains of Rome...108

WALK FIVE - The Vatican..................................111

Michelangelo in Rome.......................................135

WALK SIX - Baroque Rome 137

Rival Geniuses Bernini and Borromini...........167

WALK SEVEN - The Symbolic Center...............169

The Medieval Landscape 190

SHORT VISITS 192

USEFUL INFORMATION 194

The Legacy of Rome 198

A brief overview of Rome's artistic periods.................200

A short history of Rome....................................203

Preface

I was born and raised in Rome and after living in the US for several years and memories of my youth fading, I found myself walking my city as a tourist. The guidebooks that I used tended to concentrate mostly on the main attractions and showed a disconnect with the rest of the city. I knew there is so much more in Rome to explore. This led to the idea to write a more varied and interesting guidebook: Walk Rome.

Rome has grown over many centuries, sometimes in a haphazard way, and any given location may exhibit layers from many different periods. One of the goals of this book is to give just enough background to further understanding of the historical context and significance of each featured attraction.

Carlo Mignani

Acknowledgements

Thanks are due to family and friends who have used and commented on early versions of this book during its long journey. Their suggestions and feedback have been greatly appreciated. In particular, Christine and Andrea Meloni, Helen and Michael Meredith, John and Amelia Schad, Giulio Ciuffa, Katherine Meredith and Jim Cantwell.

Special thanks to Christine Meloni for her careful editing.

Photographs

All photographs are by the authors, with the exception of a few generously provided by the following: Anthony Galizia, Silvia Mignani, Peter Ognibene and Matt Ognibene

All drawings and maps are by Betsy Schad Mignani

WALK ROME
Seven walks for seven hills

Why walk in Rome

Rome is a city to explore and to enjoy by walking. The climate is mild and the weather is good, the days of rain are relatively few. The best months to visit are in May and June, and in September and October, when the weather is more enjoyable and the sites are less crowded.

Why I decided to write this book

I was born and raised in Rome. After living in the US for many years with memories of my youth steadily fading, I found myself walking the city as a tourist. The guidebooks that I used were superficial and tended to concentrate only on the main attractions. I knew there is so much more in Rome to explore in this continually evolving city. To consolidate our research, my wife and I went to Rome several times, walking those streets, visiting personally the monuments, museums, stores, and restaurants that we suggest, and recording our observations.

Description of the walks

We have divided the tourist center of Rome into **seven parts** (not corresponding to the seven traditional hills). For each area we suggest a route that goes by the main attractions and many other interesting but less known places. The first page gives an overview. **Each walk** has a main **map** that details the recommended route and the location of the attractions, monuments, churches, subway stops, and information kiosks. Along the way we point out nearby eateries, art expositions, wine bars, pubs, the best ice cream shops, interesting stores, Internet cafes and more.

Rome has grown over many centuries, sometimes in a haphazard way, and any given location may exhibit layers from many different periods. One of the goals of this book is to give just enough background to further understanding of the **historical context and significance** of each featured attraction. Historic events of the last 3000 years, curiosities and unusual facts are described in **shaded boxes** scattered throughout the book. At the end of each walk is a **list of nearby restaurants**, showing the type of cooking and the average price. Relax, slow down, observe and immerse yourself in this fascinating city. There are so many corners in Rome worth exploring and savoring at your own pace like a good bottle of wine.

This book is perfectly suitable if you want to **explore Rome on your own**. What you see is presented in an understandable historical context. It is a cross between a standard guidebook and a tour with a guide, but you choose your own time and pace. In addition we give you clear routes to follow, a lot of timely and continuous on the spot information, and flexibility of action for fantastic days, romantic evenings and an unforgettable vacation.

How to use the walks

While each walk is planned for a full day, walking at a moderate pace and stopping frequently, it could take two or three days. It is up to you to personalize them according to your preferences. We also suggest **other areas to explore** and **shopping zones**.

If you are visiting Rome for the first time and have time, follow more faithfully the streets advised. **If, however, you only have a few days,** use the parts of the walks that cover the main attractions. See the section "Short visits. You will reap the most benefit if you try to read this book before you arrive in Rome.

Best museums Three museums should not be missed: the **Vatican Museums** (Walk 5), among the most important in the world, **Galleria Borghese** (Walk 6), with its numerous works by Bernini, the best representative of Roman Baroque, and **Palazzo Massimo** (Walk 6), which houses excellent archeological artifacts from ancient Rome.

Best panoramic views
You can see panoramic views from the top of Saint Peter's dome, from the terrace of Castel Sant'Angelo, from the Campidoglio (Capitoline Hill), looking at the Forum and from the Campidoglio terrace café, atop the Palatino and from the Pincio. At the top of Castel Sant'Angelo in particular there are numerous signs pointing to the important monuments. It might be a good idea to take some of the walks first before enjoying the panoramic views. That way you can recognize and relate better to what you are seeing.

Best picturesque neighborhoods to stroll around at your leisure: the small streets of the picturesque medieval Trastevere (Walk 2), the characteristic Monti quarter in the Suburra behind Via Cavour (Walk 7), the Jewish ghetto (Walk 7), and the Borgo, just outside the Vatican (Walk 5).

Best shopping Small shops abound in the area around Via dei Giubbonari, Largo Argentina and the Pantheon (Walk 1) and Via Cola di Rienzo (Walk 5). Many of the streets in the area of Piazza di Spagna (Walk 4), between Via del Corso, Via Trinità dei Monti, Tritone and Piazza del Popolo are artistically interesting and host stores from the premium fashion houses.

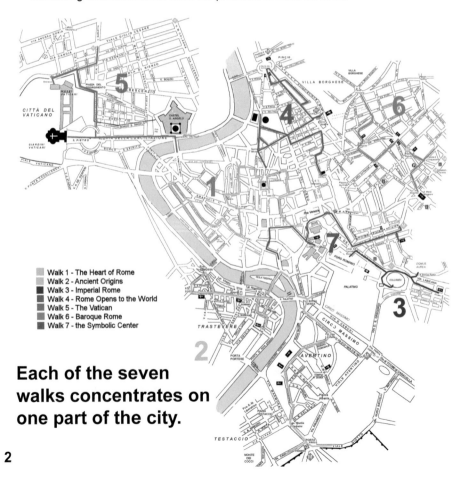

Walk 1 - The Heart of Rome
Walk 2 - Ancient Origins
Walk 3 - Imperial Rome
Walk 4 - Rome Opens to the World
Walk 5 - The Vatican
Walk 6 - Baroque Rome
Walk 7 - the Symbolic Center

Each of the seven walks concentrates on one part of the city.

Overview of the seven walks

Each walk concentrates on a section of the city, indicated by the small maps.

Walk 1 - the Heart of Rome

is a tour through the center of Rome, and contains the most important monuments, such as the amazingly preserved ancient **Pantheon**, the lively Baroque **Piazza Navona** with the Four Rivers fountain by Bernini, and the popular **Campo de' Fiori** plaza with its daily market. It explores Baroque and Renaissance areas.

Walk 2 – Ancient Origins

takes you from the unique **Piramide** and **Porta San Paolo** set into the ancient **Aurelian Walls**, up the Aventine hill to one of the earliest Christian basilicas, **Santa Sabina**, then to the area around the **Bocca della Verità** where early Roman temples coexist with medieval churches. Continue over millennia-old bridges across the **Isola Tiberina** to the picturesque medieval **Trastevere** quarter, with its typical shops and restaurants.

Walk 3 – Imperial Rome,

starts at the **Colosseum**, the largest amphitheater built in ancient times. The **Domus Aurea** is Nero's Golden House, with large underground rooms and remaining fresco decoration. Its excavation in the 1500's inspired Renaissance artists. Go underneath **San Clemente** for a trip through history to see several levels of construction from the pre-Christian era, through the Middle Ages to the current church. A complete tour of the **Roman Forum** follows.

Walk 4 – Rome Opens to the World

visits the **Piazza di Spagna**, a mecca for tourists and artists for centuries, the surrounding high fashion stores and the **Trevi fountain**, where you may want to toss a coin. **Via del Babuino** and **Via Margutta** still retain the characteristic atmosphere that attracted Italian and foreign poets and artists. **Ara Pacis** and the **Mausoleum of Augustus** represent the beginning of the imperial period.

Walk 5 – the Vatican.

Saint Peter's Basilica and **Piazza San Pietro** are the highlights. The vast **Vatican Museums** contain art from ancient to modern. Renaissance masterpieces include the **Sistine Chapel** with Michelangelo's frescoed ceiling and the Last Judgment, plus Raphael's frescoes in the **Stanze di Raffaello**. Down by the river is the ancient **Castel Sant'Angelo**, originally a mausoleum, then a fortress and refuge for the popes, a high security prison and now a museum.

Walk 6 – Baroque Rome

showcases many of the great artist Bernini's masterpieces. Begin in the **Galleria Borghese**, then walk down the iconic **Via Veneto** to visit Baroque churches by Borromini and Bernini. Pass by the **Quattro Fontane**, **Piazza della Repubblica** and then the museums in the ancient **Diocletian Baths**, the largest ever built, finally, **Palazzo Massimo**, bursting with ancient sculptures, tablets and mosaics.

Walk 7 – The Symbolic Center,

the political and religious center of ancient Rome, reveals Michelangelo's **Piazza del Campidoglio**, with the **Capitoline Museums** and a panoramic view over the Roman Forum. Explore the remains of other **Imperial Forums** and the multilevel **Trajan's Market**, and then head over to the **Jewish quarter**, on the way stopping at the charming **Fountain of the Tortoises**.

WALK ONE - The Heart of Rome

The jewel of the historic center is the **Pantheon**, the most studied and copied building in the world. It represents the height of Roman engineering and its enormous importance is clear considering that its dome is larger than that of Saint Peter's Basilica and is the widest span built before the nineteenth century. The historic center is usually considered the area between Via del Corso and the Tiber, as opposed to the ancient Roman center, the Forum, described in Walk 3. The streets are frequently narrow and without sidewalks and can change names from one block to the next. The palaces and streets date from the Middle Ages to the nineteenth century.

Two historic periods can be easily discerned. The **medieval** zone from Via del Corso to the Tiber and north of Corso Vittorio Emanuele II is mainly evident in the area west of Piazza Navona. The other area, instead, has a more **Renaissance** character, extending south of Corso Vittorio Emanuele II, and includes **Via Giulia**, the most important street of the 1600's. **Piazza Navona**, with its fountains and festive atmosphere, is a magnificent example of Roman Baroque, while the nearby Piazza **Campo de' Fiori** represents the authentic character of old secular Rome. The walk also includes the church **Il Gesù**, Sant'Ignazio's trompe l'oeil effects of perspective and other churches that reflect the character of the Counter Reformation and the beginning of the Baroque period. The **Pasquino** statue was a place for people to leave anonymous notes, expressing their opinions when doing so overtly could land them in jail.

In this walk:

1 The **Gesù**, the model church of the Counter Reformation, whose style was spread throughout the world

2 **Palazzo Doria Pamphilj** and **Galleria Pamphilj**

3 Piazza and Church of **Sant'Ignazio** with its "false" dome

4 **Piazza Colonna** and the Marcus Aurelius Column

5 The **Pantheon**, the building most admired in history

6 The charming **elephant** by Bernini in front of **Santa Maria sopra Minerva**

7 **San Luigi dei Francesi** with paintings by **Caravaggio**

8 **Palazzo Altemps**, a museum with ancient sculptures

9 Borromini's Church of **Sant'Ivo** with its curious spire

10 **Piazza Navona**'s splendid atmosphere by Bernini and Borromini

11 **Pasquino,** the original "talking statue"

12 **Sant'Andrea della Valle**

13 **Teatro di Pompeo** where Julius Caesar was assassinated

14 The picturesque atmosphere of **Campo de' Fiori** with its lively market

15 The imposing **Palazzo Farnese**

16 The Renaissance area of **Via di Monserrato**

17 **Via Giulia** with its interesting fountain Il **Mascherone**

18 **Palazzo Spada** where a special effect of perspective can be seen

In this walk you will also find ...
The best ice cream in Rome in the area around the Pantheon

At the end of the walk, see *The Killer Artist – Caravaggio's Rome*

Starting point: The Pigna fountain at Piazza Venezia

Begin from the fountain La Pigna that is found at the corner of Piazza San Marco and Via San Marco, near Piazza Venezia.

Take Via San Marco and go right on Via dell'Aracoeli, where you will see the church called Il Gesù on the right.

The water of **La Pigna** (the pinecone fountain) is drinkable and, like all the other fountains and fontanelle (small black street fountains), is constantly flowing and of good quality. The Romans and hundreds of millions of tourists have been drinking this water for more than 2000 years and it is perfectly safe. It is still possible to discern different tastes of water from the various aqueducts. When two Romans want to meet in the center, this is a place often used for appointments.

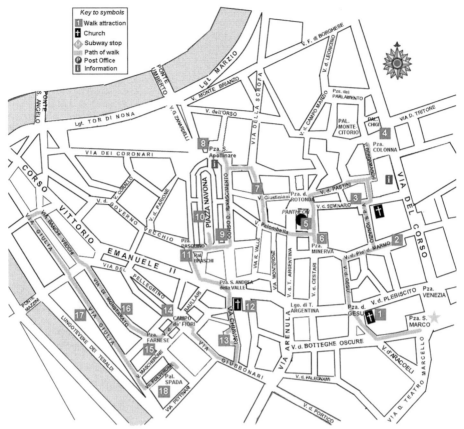

Map for Walk One

1. Il Gesù, Piazza del Gesù 1, is the mother church of the Jesuit order. In the 16th century, the Protestant movement emerged with an emphasis on simplicity of structures and on personal responsibility. Il Gesù, on the contrary, is decorated in a purposefully opulent manner to try to emphasize the importance of the church and the clergy. This is emblematic of the opposing movement, the Counter Reformation. The interior design represents a change from earlier churches. Columns and aisles were eliminated and the transept shortened so that the faithful, positioned in the dark nave, could see the raised, illuminated altar from any point. The single long nave made processions more dramatic.

It was the model for the Jesuits' churches, reproduced all over the world. Although built between 1568 and 1578, several years before the beginning of the new style, the interior decoration of Il Gesù is Baroque, done between the seventeenth and nineteenth centuries. We can characterize the typical Jesuit churches and others of the Counter Reformation, including Sant'Andrea della Valle (See #12):

> The plan is a Latin cross, that is, one arm longer and a dome over the intersection.
> The emphasis on the displayed art is on mystical themes in opposition to those frequently almost pagan during the Renaissance.
> Gilded decoration especially on the vaults and domes. It is real gold leaf, beaten thin.
> Decorative elements include stucco decoration, painted white or gilded.

Decorative elements include stucco decoration, painted white or gilded. An example in the Gesù is the dance of the putti (cherubs) above the arches of the chapels. (See left).

From Piazza del Gesù take Via del Gesù and then go right on Via Pie' di Marmo.

Try the wine-bar Enoteca Corsi at Via del Gesù 87 for a light and quick meal.

A large **marble foot**, from which the street takes its name, is situated at the intersection of Via Santo Stefano del Cacco and Via Pie' di Marmo. (Pie' is a shortened form of *piede*, foot, and *marmo* means marble). When you get to the intersection look right. The experts say it is from the late imperial period, but they do not know who is depicted. In the sixteenth century, the marble foot was placed on the street that now bears its name.

*Ditta G. Poggi, Via del Gesù 74, sells a wide variety of **art supplies**, from 1825. Trinity College, Via del Collegio Romano 6, is an **Irish pub.***

Walk down Via Pie' di Marmo to Piazza del Collegio Romano, where you find the Palazzo Doria Pamphilj and the Galleria Doria Pamphilj.

2 Palazzo Doria Pamphilj and the **Galleria Doria Pamphilj** are at Piazza del Collegio Romano 2. http://www.doriapamphilj.it/

The novelty of the palazzo is that each of its four facades is different. Begun in 1505, it is one of the most impressive in the city, and the exteriors were built by several architects over a period of about three centuries. In the eighteenth century the side facing Via del Corso was redone in the Rococo style. Observe the contrast between the vivacious Palazzo Doria Pamphilj and the dull Palazzo Odescalchi near the intersection of Via del Corso and Via Lata. Numerous royal rooms were used for receptions and parties by the European nobility. Since the Pamphilj family still lives there, you may visit the palazzo only in the mornings.

Inside is the **Galleria Pamphilj**, begun in the 1600's by Donna Olimpia, which today is the largest private collection still owned by Roman nobility. The exhibit is on the first floor (above the ground floor), the so-called "piano nobile" or "noble floor" and contains works by Raphael, Titian, Guercino, Guido Reni, Bernini, Velasquez and Rubens, among others. Three masterpieces by Caravaggio enrich the collection: *The Flight into Egypt, John the Baptist* and *The Penitent Magdalene*. (See the list of Caravaggio paintings in the article at the end of the walk.)

The fountain called **Il Facchino** (the porter) (see right) is from the sixteenth century and is set into the wall on Via Lata, which is between Piazza del Collegio Romano and Via del Corso. It represents a man holding a barrel, but instead of wine, it contained water. This is another of the famous "talking statues." (See Pasquino later on this walk).

At Via del Corso 320, the **Museo del Corso** holds **art exhibitions.**

From Piazza del Collegio Romano, take Via di Sant'Ignazio up to Piazza Sant'Ignazio.

Near number 42, above the street, notice the **arch** (at left) that united the Jesuits of Sant'Ignazio (Saint Ignatius Loyola) with the Dominicans of the nearby church of Santa Maria sopra Minerva, allies in the Counter Reformation. Along the street you may see a large, mysterious letter "**L**," now rather faded, at about 12 feet up. It is toward the end of the wall on the side of the church, almost to Piazza Sant'Ignazio, between 2 white pilasters. This was the way in which, during the 1800's, it was indicated where to put the streetlights. The "L" meant *luce* (light) or *lampione* (street light); it is the last remaining of these indications.

A Tuscan restaurant, Il Buco is at Via di Sant'Ignazio 8.

3 Piazza di Sant'Ignazio

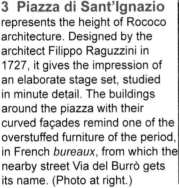

represents the height of Rococo architecture. Designed by the architect Filippo Raguzzini in 1727, it gives the impression of an elaborate stage set, studied in minute detail. The buildings around the piazza with their curved façades remind one of the overstuffed furniture of the period, in French *bureaux*, from which the nearby street Via del Burrò gets its name. (Photo at right.)

The best effect is from the steps of the **Chiesa di Sant'Ignazio**. This church was named for Saint Ignatius Loyola, founder of the Jesuit order. It is among the largest churches in the capital, after the three large basilicas of San Pietro (Saint Peter's), San Paolo (Saint Paul's) and San Giovanni (Saint John's). Begun in 1626 in the early years of the Baroque style, the building, as the Gesù, is the product of the rigid canons of the Counter Reformation, while the interior, initially sober, was replaced with the richness of Baroque decoration. (For more about the architectural style see Il Gesù, number 1.) Observe the frieze of stucco angels and the enormous frescoes.

The Jesuit Andrea del Pozzo painted The Entrance of Saint Ignatius to Paradise on the **ceiling**. Under the dome, there are paintings of biblical scenes such as David and Goliath and Samson and the Philistines. The dome's ceiling is distinguished by a magnificent "trompe l'oeil" effect, produced by the frescoes which give the impression of being much higher. The **dome** is not real; the effect of height is produced by the frescoes.

9

There are two white stones on the floor, down the middle of the nave, indicating the best vantage point to observe this original creation. Realistic painted columns and figures stretch the illusion of height.

From Piazza di Sant'Ignazio take Via del Burrò, on the left, to Piazza di Pietra. The building on your left is the Camera di Commercio (Chamber of Commerce) .

At Piazza di Pietra, you can see 11 enormous Corinthian **columns** from the period of Hadrian, about 145 AD, attached to the side of this massive building, which is the Chamber of Commerce and was formerly the *Borsa*, the Roman stock exchange. (See left)

Go down Via dei Bergamaschi to Piazza Colonna.

4 At Piazza Colonna rises the **Column of Marcus Aurelius**, erected in honor of the emperor after his death, which occurred during a campaign near Vienna defending the frontier, in 180 AD. It is composed of 28 cylinders, one on top of another, that evoke in bas-relief the wars of Marcus Aurelius against the Germans and the Sarmatians, (people from an area that today is part of Poland). About twelve feet wide and 138 feet high, a spiral staircase once allowed visitors to reach the summit. Originally a statue of the emperor was placed at the top, substituted later by one of Saint Paul.

The **fountain** in the piazza was erected in 1577 on a design by Giacomo della Porta, famous for designing many of the fountains around Rome. Two groups of dolphins decorate the marble basin. For many years the fountain was besieged by a sea of cars parked around it and was not very visible. Now with the no parking law the entire piazza has reassumed the original character.

*Nearby, in the Galleria Alberto Sordi, is <u>La Rinascente</u>, a department store. Underground, in the basement is a section of the **ancient Acqua Vergine aqueduct** . <u>Giolitti</u>, a very good **ice cream** café, many think the best in Rome, is in Via Uffici del Vicario 40. From Piazza Colonna, go past Montecitorio and Giolitti is on the left. The nearby Via di Campo Marzio has locally owned **boutiques**.*

Palazzo Chigi overlooks Piazza Colonna. It was built in the sixteenth and seventeenth centuries and contains the office of the Prime Minister of Italy and the seat of the government. Next to Palazzo Chigi is the **Palazzo di Montecitorio**, (at right), built by Carlo Fontana on a design by Bernini, which is the seat of the Camera dei Deputati, the House of Representatives. In the center of the piazza is an Egyptian obelisk brought to Rome by Augustus (reigned 27 BC – 14 AD) to be the gnomon for a large sundial, unfortunately gone now. The shadow of the obelisk fell on a marble meridian line on the pavement to indicate noon each day. Part of the meridian line has been found under a building on Via di Campo Marzio. (See Walk 4). The **covered gallery** containing shops on the other side of Via del Corso was Galleria Colonna, but is now renamed Galleria Alberto Sordi for the famous Roman comic actor.

Go back on Via Bergamaschi, turn right, pass through Piazza di Pietra, take Via dei Pastini and you come to Piazza della Rotonda and the Pantheon.

The area between Piazza Colonna and the Pantheon has some good **leather** *stores for bags and wallets, artistic papers, and jewelry. Each of the local bars near the Pantheon is good for a* **sandwich***, coffee or just to drink something and relax at an outdoor table.* <u>Fiocco di Neve</u> *(snowflake) in Via del Pantheon 51 is also a good* **ice cream** *shop.*

Continue up Via del Pantheon to Piazza Maddalena for a break and then come back to the Pantheon.
Restaurant tables line the sidewalks and just beyond Via delle Coppelle is <u>Della Palma</u>*, a large* **ice cream** *store that also has many other special sweets. The area is also known for especially* **good coffee***:* <u>La Casa del Caffé Tazza d'Oro</u>*, Via degli Orfani 84 at the corner of Via dei Pastini and* <u>Caffé Sant'Eustachio</u> *(considered by many the best in Rome) in Piazza Sant'Eustachio 82 a couple of blocks west of the Pantheon.* <u>Enoteca Spiriti,</u> *Via di Sant'Eustachio 5 is a* **wine bar** *with abundant portions and tables outside.*

5 The Pantheon was built by emperor Hadrian between 119 and 128 AD over an older temple from 27 BC that had been erected by Marcus Agrippa, as the inscription above the entrance indicates. It is the largest, oldest and best-preserved monument from ancient Rome. Dedicated originally to all the gods, it is astounding in its grandeur and simplicity. Circular and square forms are used in a harmonious manner.

Construction was made possible by the technical advances of the arch and dome and the Roman invention of concrete. This was a mixture of lime, pozzolan (a pinkish volcanic material) and water with the addition of aggregate that could vary from broken bricks, gravel, pieces of travertine or tuff, according to the weight and consistency desired. The dome has stood up for 19 centuries without the use of a steel armature as current building codes would require. Several cracks in the dome have been observed but the structure does not seem affected. To allow the concrete to cure properly, construction proceeded at increments.

The Pantheon and Piazza della Rotonda

What was the secret?

Modern concrete would not last 2000 years. The extraordinary strength and durability of Roman concrete is due to the specific properties of the materials and the methods of construction. The particular chemical reaction of the materials produced a hard mixture capable of expanding to hold the pieces of rock together. The best results were obtained when moist lime and pozzolan were used with a minimum of water and this mixture was pounded into a layer of rocks. Pressing the mixture reduced the quantity of water necessary which, if too much is used, results in weakening the structures. This tamping action also produced a greater cohesion of the material.

The ancient concrete used for seawalls and harbor piers is stronger today than when it was first mixed 2000 years ago. Scientists are discovering now that when seawater percolated in the tiny cracks in the concrete it created tobermorite crystals, which are now prized for industrial applications. This ancient formula could still be useful in human history. It could protect the coast from advancing seawater.

The sphere of the **dome** fits perfectly into the cylindrical base. It has the same dimensions in height and width. An enormous sphere of 43.5 meters (143 feet) in diameter would fit inside perfectly. To reduce the weight of the dome, the builders used heavier materials at the base and progressively lighter toward the top. The walls are 20 feet thick and the dome, which at the base has the same thickness, is gradually thinner toward the center, with a series of seven step rings, until it measures only about 5 feet thick at the top The concrete at the highest part of the dome incorporates 9 inch pieces of tuff, a light and porous volcanic material. Support for the dome is provided both by the thick walls acting as a buttress and by the inclusion of arches within the walls.

These are easy to spot on the exterior, and are typical of construction from that period. It is thought that the formation of the concrete dome was done on a wood structural support. This dense forest of wood extended all the way to the top and was tightly tied together.

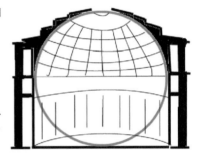

With no windows, the **oculus** at the top of the dome is the only opening where light enters. Rays of sun passing over the floor of colored marble circles and squares produce a truly magical effect.

The **coffered ceiling** has an aesthetic purpose, to emphasize the size of the dome, but the increased open spaces also serve to lighten the weight. The columns and wall decoration, often in yellow and precious marbles, are original, as is the floor. It is the only Roman monument to have maintained, for two millennia, the same function for which it was originally built. It was despoiled only twice. Constans II, emperor of the eastern empire, in 663 removed the gilded bronze tiles from the roof, which were replaced with lead plates. Almost a thousand years later, in 1625, Pope Urban VIII of the Barberini family had the bronze that covered the ceiling of the portico removed and melted down to build the baldacchino for the Basilica of Saint Peter.

Pasquino (see number 9) took the opportunity to sound his opinion and wrote: "What the barbarians didn't do, the Barberinis did." An exaggerated affirmation in relation to the Pantheon, but it clearly expressed the treatment of many ancient buildings in Rome.

Ancient astronomy
The building was designed in a north-south direction, but with a slight variation, it is thought for astronomical reasons. The sun's rays that come through the oculus at noon at the summer solstice (the 21st of June) hit the center of the entrance. It seems probable that in ancient times the oculus was used also for astronomical observations.

The **dome** of the Pantheon, larger than that of Saint Peter's, was the largest span built before the nineteenth century. It has been studied and used as inspiration by innumerable artists and architects all over the world. Brunelleschi studied it before building the Duomo of Florence, as did Michelangelo for the construction of the dome of Saint Peter's.

It greatly influenced the architects of the neoclassic period. Just think of Saint Paul's in London, or the Supreme Court building and the Jefferson Memorial in Washington, D.C. and many other public buildings, churches and museums.

Consecrated as a church in 609 AD it was thus saved from the fate of the buildings in the Forum, the Colosseum and the Baths of Caracalla where, during the centuries, construction materials were plundered to build the palaces and piazzas of Rome. With the intervention of the church, any stone removed from the Pantheon would be a mortal sin, so it was left relatively intact.

In the sixteenth century, in the portico, the first modern art exhibits were held. The **tombs** of the kings Vittorio Emanuele II, who unified Italy, and Umberto I as well as those of the artists Raphael, Annibale Carracci and several other famous persons and artists are here. At the third niche from the left, with the statue of the Madonna and Child, there is a bust of Raphael and his tomb is just below, where he is buried along with his fiancée.

Raphael's tomb

Raphael's tomb
The artist was interred in an ancient sarcophagus, situated in the 3rd chapel on the right. His tomb is inscribed in Latin: "Here lies Raphael; while he lived, Mother Nature feared to be outdone; and when he died, she feared to die with him."

Renaissance and Baroque buildings surround the piazza. The **Fountain in Piazza della Rotonda** was designed by Giacomo della Porta in 1575. The basin is square with round bows on the sides, which are echoed in the steps surrounding it. It has an eclectic style. The formal basin contrasts with the almost grotesque masks and with the upper, more Baroque part. An obelisk was added in 1711, giving the fountain an appearance similar to the Fountain of the Four Rivers in Piazza Navona.

A curious fact noted by the nearby residents is that sometimes, for no apparent reason, the water jet increases considerably, and the waters rise in a part of the basin. The piazza is a pedestrian zone, picturesque and relaxing without the noise and pollution of traffic. It is very pleasant to sit at a table in a café in this unique atmosphere with the splashing of the fountain and the Pantheon in the background.

Go around the Pantheon and along Via della Minerva to Piazza della Minerva.

6 Piazzale della Minerva holds the charming sculpture of a small **elephant**, (photo below) which supports an Egyptian obelisk found near the ancient temple of Isis. It was designed by Bernini, but sculpted by Ercole Ferrata in 1667. The elephant was chosen because it represents piety and wisdom. The nearby Domini-can monks did not like Bernini's design because they worried that the elephant could not support the obelisk. To satisfy these unfounded fears, Bernini added a large marble saddle. The nearby Dominicans were considered somewhat arrogant and rigid, even by some Popes; some scholars have seen the position of the elephant as a playfully irreverent joke against them. With the back side of the animal facing the Dominicans, Pope Urban VIII would have had Bernini elegantly and artistically express what he thought of some of their positions.

Santa Maria sopra Minerva is the most "Gothic" church in Rome (photo), even though from the outside it does not seem to be that style. Inside there are also decorative elements from other periods. It was founded in the eighth century on top of the ruins of a temple to Minerva and rebuilt in the present form in 1280. The thirteenth century austerity was transformed by a restoration in 1850. Numerous paintings, sculptures, frescoes and reliefs are displayed, including works by Michelangelo, Giacomo della Porta, Filippo Lippi, Carlo Maderno and projects of Sangallo.

To the left of the altar are the tomb of the 15th century painter Fra Angelico and a statue begun by Michelangelo, **Christ Risen** (*Cristo Risorto*). The bronze loincloth was added during the Baroque period.

Outside, on the wall of a building, on the right facing the church, is a **plaque** commemorating the Roman sojourn of the French writer Stendahl, who loved Italy.

On the façade of the church itself, on the right side, several **plaques** indicate the level of the Tiber, recorded during floods over the years. Lines extending from fingers indicate the flood level. The last was in 1870, after which the fledgling nation enclosed the river in its embankments. Imagine how deep the water must have been in the nearby Pantheon!

> On the two parallel streets which lead from the Pantheon to Largo Argentina, Via dei Cestari and Via di Torre Argentina, there are several shops selling **religious articles.** Going around the Pantheon in Via della Palombella 28, <u>Mancini Leather</u> sells **leather** articles for travel, notebooks and umbrellas.

> Continue around the Pantheon on Via Palombella, then right on Via della Dogana Vecchia to Piazza San Luigi dei Francesi.

> At Via della Scrofa 31, <u>Volpetti</u> is a good **gourmet deli**, open also in the evening. At Via della Scrofa 65, <u>La Città del Sole</u> has a large selection of **toys and games**, many also in English. The store is very close to the church of San Luigi dei Francesi.

7 San Luigi dei Francesi is the church of the French community in

Rome. It was built between 1518 and 1589 with artistic contributions by Giacomo della Porta and Domenico Fontana. It contains three large paintings by **Caravaggio**, who is famous especially for his use of *chiaroscuro*, or strong lights and shadows. In a chapel on the left of the main altar, dating from 1598 to 1601, they recount the life of Saint Matthew. On the left in the chapel is "The Vocation of Saint Matthew," in the center, "Saint Matthew and the Angel" (shown right) and on the right "The Martyrdom of Saint Matthew." Paintings by Domenichino, Guido Reni and many others and memorial tablets by Chateaubriand are also displayed, and there are references to several famous French personages. Interest in Caravaggio has blossomed in recent years, so there are sometimes crowds. (More about Caravaggio at the end of the walk.)

> Take Via della Scrofa, go left to Piazza Sant'Agostino then walk through Piazza delle Cinque Lune to Piazza Sant'Apollinare where Palazzo Altemps, one of the four parts of the Museo Nazionale Romano resides.

8 Palazzo Altemps is located just a 2 minute walk from Piazza Navona

and 5 minutes from the Pantheon and is less crowded than most. http://archeoroma.beniculturali.it/en/museums. Rent the English headphones for an instructional visit. **15**

The beauty of the 15th century palace competes with the numerous works of ancient art for your attention. For a long time it was only open to scholars but now it has been restored and is open to the public. In more than 30 rooms and an attractive courtyard, there are frescoes and Greek and Roman sculptures that date from the first century. The main attraction is the Ludovisi collection. Masterpieces include:

- The *Ludovisi Ares*. The sculpture representing Mars or Achilles is a Roman copy of a Greek original, restored in 1622 by Bernini.
- The *Ludovisi Throne*, including the Birth of Aphrodite in the Room of the Stories of Moses. It is a Greek original from the 5th century BC.
- The group *Galata Killing Himself after Killing his Wife* was commissioned by Julius Caesar to celebrate his victory over the Gauls and installed in the garden of his villa on the Quirinal Hill.

Some are copies of Greek originals that have been completely lost. Palazzo Altemps is a part of the Museo Nazionale Romano, together with the Terme di Diocleziano (Baths of Diocletian) in Piazza della Repubblica, Palazzo Massimo which faces Piazza dei Cinquecento and Crypta Balbi on Via delle Botteghe Oscure.

> *From Piazza Sant'Apollinare, cross Piazza delle Cinque Lune and turn right on Corso Rinascimento. Sant'Ivo is on your left just past Via degli Staderari.*
> *A McDonald's is at Piazza delle Cinque Lune 74..*

Bee, eagle and lion papal insignias in the courtyard of the Church of Sant'Ivo

Changing times
It is difficult to believe, but the Church of Sant'Ivo became a storage depot for the Alessandrina Library in 1870. Restored in 1926 it was reconsecrated and again open to the public.

9 The Church of Sant'Ivo lies inside the Palazzo Sapienza which, until 1935, was the site of Rome's University, founded in 1303. (The sign outside says "Archivio di Stato") In the courtyard the several papal insignias (eagles and dragons for the Borghese family, bees for the Barberini) attest to the construction during the reigns of several popes. Look up to the third level from inside the courtyard.

Borromini had to adapt to the limitations of the site: to build the chapel in the courtyard that was part of the Sapienza. He wanted to honor the Barberini family, repeating the emblem of the **bee** in the plan of the church, in parts of the vault, and in the spire made in the form of a bee stinger.

The soaring lantern leads to a **spiral** that climbs to the sky in the shape of a flame, a globe, a dove and finally a cross. (Binoculars give you an advantage). When entering, the light streaming from the big windows forces you to look up. If you thought that the Baroque architectural style was overly elaborate or excessively ornamental, you are forced to reconsider when visiting this jewel. Here the style is essential, dynamic without affectation.

Sant'Ivo offers naturally a spiritual connection that is more difficult to reach in other churches. Notice how much movement Borromini was able to create, combining concave and convex surfaces on the walls, even though there are almost no decorations or colors. Borromini's San Carlo alle Quattro Fontane (Walk 6) exhibits similar characteristics.

This unique **steeple** is visible from several points nearby; the best is in Piazza Sant'Eustachio. It is also easy to make out from the panoramic terrace of the Vittoriano (Walk 7).

> *Cross Corso Rinascimento and take Via dei Canestrari to Piazza Navona.*

10 Piazza Navona has a strange effect on people. Its festive atmosphere makes people feel serene and smile. It was built on the ancient Domitian stadium which could hold 30,000 spectators. The surrounding buildings were built over the bleachers and its ruins are still visible underneath the church of Sant'Agnese.

Although the shape of the piazza suggests that horse races were held here, the central spine that would be typical of a hippodrome has not been found. The name "Navona" comes from "*Circus agonalis,*" or competition arena, which then was transformed into "in agone," then "nagone" and finally "Navona."

In ancient times, the Domitian stadium was also used for mock naval battles. The arena, that is the current piazza, was filled with water and war ships representing the various noble families challenged each other in battle, goaded on by the spectators. The piazza was associated through the centuries with games of all types, sports competitions, theatrical shows, horse races, gymnastics, celebrations, and later fireworks and festivals. It maintained its festive character now expressed through the Baroque style that pervades it.

The **Fontana del Moro**, (the Moro Fountain), (detail above at right) in the southern part of the piazza, was built by Giacomo della Porta in 1576. Nearly a century later, in 1654, the central statue, which represents an Ethiopian struggling with a dolphin, based on a design by Bernini, was added. The artist enclosed the entire fountain in a low pool whose borders faithfully repeated the shape of the Della Porta basin.

The **Fontana di Nettuno**, (the Neptune fountain), (photo next page) furthest to the north, was also originally by Giacomo della Porta and dates from 1574. The artist constructed the basin, but it remained without decoration for three centuries until 1873 when the Neptune statue was added, followed by the horses, sirens and dolphins. As you can see, Della Porta made the basins of the two fountains identical.

17

La Fontana di Neptune   *A view of Piazza Navona*

The **Fontana dei Quattro Fiumi** (the Fountain of the Four Rivers) in the center of the piazza is by Bernini, (photo below) executed between 1648 and 1651. The four rivers depicted in the main central fountain represent the **Nile**, the **Ganges**,

Rio de la Plata and the **Danube**. Each river is connected to a continent and a typical animal: the Nile by a lion, the Ganges by a serpent, the Rio de la Plata by a fantastic armadillo-like animal and the Danube by a horse. Note especially that the statue of the Nile has his head covered because in the seventeenth century the source of the river was not yet known. The two emblems above the figures contain a dove, the symbol of Pope Innocent X who commissioned the fountain. A gilded bronze dove was also placed at the top of the obelisk

Starting in 1652, occasionally the **piazza** was transformed into a lake. The mouth of a large fish in the Fountain of the Four Rivers, on the western side, the side near the church, is the only drain for the water. During summer weekends, the drain was plugged and the entire area was flooded to give some relief from the summer heat to the local population.

The spacious piazza, well defined by the buildings that delimit it, the Baroque works of Bernini, Borromini, Della Porta and many others, the sound of the water, the art vendors and the incessant movement of the people constitute a unique setting. The golden sunlight of late afternoon emphasizes the contrasts and accentuates the architectural details of the fountains and the surrounding buildings. .

In the Fountain of the Four Rivers, the figure that represents La Plata has his hand raised, according to legend, to block from view the Church of Sant'Agnese designed by Bernini's rival, Borromini. The rivalry between the two artists was well known. However this hypothesis would seem to be unfounded since the façade of the church was not built until 6 years after the fountain.

On the piazza, during December, booths pop up to sell toys and Christmas decorations in a festival atmosphere, together with various artists selling their works. The Christmas holidays extend to January 6 when, in all of Italy, during the festival of the Befana, children receive gifts.

Underground, 15 feet below the piazza, ruins of the ancient Domitian Stadium, UNESCO Heritage site, can be visited. Entrance at Via di Tor Sanguigna 3. Audio tours are available.

The church of **Sant'Agnese in Agone** with its magnificent and scenographic façade by Borromini adorns the piazza. Its dome gives the impression of resting directly on the façade. When you enter the church, however, it becomes evident that the dome is at least four yards behind it. When you come back and check the distances, only then you will realize that you are faced with a "trompe l'oeil," a perspective trick of Borromini. (See Palazzo Spada, number 18). Classical music concerts are held periodically.

The baroque **Palazzo Pamphilj** (now the Brazilian embassy) flanks the piazza. In the grandiose project of Pope Innocent X, the Palazzo Pamphilj would have constituted a regal palace. Piazza Navona would have been an external courtyard. The Palazzo was designed by Girolamo Rainaldi and several of the frescoes were done by Pietro da Cortona.

A good spot to observe the unique atmosphere of the piazza is from an outside table at the famous bar Tre Scalini, *where, if you like chocolate* **ice cream**, *order the* **tartufo**, *their specialty. On the same side of the piazza,* Ai Tre Tartufi *is a "newcomer" from 1896 that also serves the unique ball of ice cream. Be aware that you are paying for the atmosphere as well as the taste! Take a look at* Al Sogno *at number 53, a* **toy** *store that has dolls, stuffed animals and* **pinocchios**.

Cross Piazza Navona and head south, turn right and take Via del Pasquino to Piazza Pasquino.

11 Pasquino. In this funnel-shaped piazza, where several streets come together, attached to a wall of Palazzo Braschi you will find the very eroded torso and head of **Pasquino**, one of the famous "talking statues."

The pontifical state, headed by the pope for many centuries, controlled most of central Italy. Obviously it found itself exercising, besides spiritual power, also the executive, legislative and judicial. Because of its authoritarian nature, a lay opposition could not express itself. In spite of that, the voice of the people found a way to be heard by anonymous and satirical comments that were left attached to certain statues. The most famous of these was Pasquino.

This mutilated torso, dating from ancient times, is thought to have been of Menelaus dragging the body of his son Patroclus, according to Greek mythology. There are several stories about the origin of Pasquino, but the most plausible is the following. Near this ancient half-buried statue, in the fifteenth century, a certain tailor named Pasquino had his shop. Here writers, prelates and gentlemen met to order clothes, converse on recent events and chat.

19

Pasquino was particularly witty and humorous and able to generate pungent and satirical comments in verse.

After the tailor's death, in order to repair the road, the old statue was dug up and leaned temporarily by his shop. People began to jokingly declare that Pasquino was back, so the statue took on his name. From that moment on every satirical verse or epigram that an anonymous author wanted to leave was attributed to Pasquino. From this we got the word *pasquinade*.

Church and State
In the twenty-first century, in the west, we take for granted the separation of the Church from the State. In other cultures today and in Europe in the past, it was not always thus. The Church in Italy for many centuries wielded both spiritual and temporal power in a territory that included Rome and central Italy.

Later, these pungent comments were left on other "talking statues," such as the Babuino in Via del Babuino (Walk 4), Marforio in the courtyard of the Capitoline Museum (Walk 7), il Facchino in Via Lata (this walk), Madame Lucrezia in Piazza San Marco near the entrance to the church (Walk 7), and Abbot Luigi, Piazza Vidoni, to the left of the church Sant'Andrea della Valle. Frequently conversations between the statues were carried on for days, each responding to comments on another.

Regarding the accusations that Alexander VI became pope thanks to raging corruption, echoing the themes of the new Protestant movement:

ALEXANDER SELLS THE KEYS, THE ALTAR, CHRIST;

HE WHO FIRST BOUGHT THEM HAS A GOOD RIGHT TO SELL

The catalyst was the licentious life, the scandalous nepotism and the bad government of Pope Alexander VI (1492-1503). Of him Pasquino said:

TARQUINUS THE SIXTH (KING). NERO THE SIXTH (EMPEROR). THE SIXTH NOW (ALEXANDER VI). ALWAYS UNDER THE SIXTH IS ROME RUINED

Pope Paul IV (1555-59), in the climate of the Counter Reformation, expanded the powers of the Inquisition, the right to use torture and had the Jews confined to the ghetto. Commenting on his work Pasquino said:

CHILDREN, LESS JUDGMENT AND MORE FAITH, COMMANDS THE HOLY OFFICE.
AND REASON LITTLE, FOR AGAINST REASON THERE IS THE FIRE.
AND KEEP YOUR TONGUE IN ITS POST FOR PAUL LIKES A LOT HIS ROAST.

The day Paul IV died, the people of Rome rebelled. The palazzo of the Inquisition was burned and his statue on the Campidoglio was destroyed and thrown into the Tiber.

Many popes felt profoundly offended by these epigrams. In particular Hadrian VI was very close to throwing the statue of Pasquino into the Tiber and Paul III repeatedly tried to have him silenced by passing severe laws prohibiting pasquinades. During the years there were many attempts to catalog at least part of these satirical comments but they were sharply fought by the Church. The collection of epigrams was systematically burned, and merely being found in possession of a copy could risk your life.

An Insalata Ricca *restaurant in Piazza Pasquino 72 offers a variety of* **salads**. Cul de Sac, *in Piazza Pasquino 73, has many types of* **wine**. Abbey Theatre, *Via del Governo Vecchio 51, is an* **Irish pub**. Il Piccolo, *Via del Governo Vecchio 74, is a* **wine bar** *and night club.*

*Along Via del Governo Vecchio are also several **local boutiques**. La Montecarlo, Vicolo Savelli 13, has **pizza** and rapid service. To get there from Piazza Pasquino take the second left off Via del Governo Vecchio.*

From Piazza Pasquino, take Via San Pantaleo, Piazza San Pantaleo, and go left on Corso Vittorio Emanuele II up to Piazza Sant'Andrea della Valle.

12 The Church of Sant'Andrea della Valle.

This area in ancient times was a valley where water from the Viminal and Pincian Hills collected. In this lake, as the historian Tacitus recounted, Nero liked to ride around in a boat made of ivory and gold.

The church was designed by Giacomo della Porta but the façade and the dome were built by Carlo Maderno, probably with help from Borromini. Sant'Andrea della Valle, together with the Gesù and Sant'Ignazio constitute magnificent examples of the Counter Reformation and the beginning of the Baroque period. Of interest is the Cappella Barberini that Cardinal Maffeo Barberini, who was later to become Pope Urban VIII (1623-1644), had built in 1604. It is one of the best early Baroque works in the city. Giacomo Puccini set the first act of his opera *Tosca* in this church.

The lantern above the **dome** which, at nearly 265 feet high, is the second largest next to the one atop Saint Peter's, is the first true work of the young Borromini.

Numerous other artists contributed to the construction of this church. Carlo Rainaldi finally received the job of continuing the construction, but he was not able to modify the work of Maderno, which he did not like. He decided to add two angels to the façade. Giacomo Antonio Fancelli sculpted one, but he was criticized by many, including the pope. He was also not content with his payment and for this he refused to do the second.

The façade remained with only one angel, whose wings are opened but attached and almost stuck to the wall. This did not escape notice by the pungent comments of Pasquino who jabbed:

I'D LIKE TO FLY LIKE A BIRD ON THE WING
BUT INSTEAD TO THIS WALL I HAVE TO CLING.

On the left side of the church is the Roman statue of **Abate Luigi** (Abbot Luigi), another of the "talking statues." It depicts a Roman in a toga and was found under the foundation of a nearby palazzo. During the years it was decapitated by vandals, or, as Pasquino would say, it has "lost its head" several times, but promptly replaced with another from the city warehouse. No one knows why it is called "abbot" but the name has stuck.

*Another Insalata Ricca restaurant is at Via dei Chiavari 85. At Via dei Chiavari 34 is Antico Forno Roscioli for good **pizza** by the slice.*

Walk down Via dei Chiavari. Go right on Largo del Pallaro and continue on Via di Grotta Pinta, which loops back to Via dei Chiavari.

13 Teatro di Pompeo. Via di Grotta Pinta forms a curve because the buildings were constructed on top of the ruins of bleachers of the **Teatro di Pompeo** (Pompey's Theater), built between 61 and 55 BC by Pompey, son-in-law and often political ally of Julius Caesar. Both were extremely ambitious and their lives were inextricably intertwined. The informal alliance of Pompey, Caesar and Crassus, the so-called **triumvirate**, was able to keep the peace. But after the death of Pompey's wife Julia (Caesar's daughter), and of Crassus, conflict seemed inevitable. After the Senate ordered that the two armies disband, Caesar took as an excuse the refusal of Pompey to let his army go, to declare war and cross the Rubicon with the famous saying "the die is cast." Caesar defeated the enemy in several battles that led finally to the death of Pompey. Shortly before leaving for another military campaign, this time against the Parthians (Iran), he was assassinated by a group of senators on the Ides of March (March 15) 44 BC. Ironically, the senators chose the Teatro di Pompeo for the **assassination**, in which Brutus, Caesar's adoptive son, participated, and it is said that his body fell not far from a statue of Pompey. For more details see the article on Julius Caesar at the end of Walk 3.

> *Continue down Via dei Chiavari to Via dei Giubbonari, then go right to Piazza Campo de' Fiori.*
>
> *In Via dei Giubbonari and the nearby streets you can shop at reasonable prices for* **clothing, leather and shoes.** *Along Via dei Giubbonari you can get good* **snacks and Jewish specialties**. Open Baladin, *Via degli Specchi 6, has a vast assortment of* **beers**.

14 Campo de' Fiori takes its name from its origin as a flower meadow sloping down to the Tiber. (*Campo* means field, *fiori* means flowers). Today it is one of the most picturesque piazzas and evokes the vibrant authentic character of old Rome.

There is a **market** every day and the whole area has a popular and secular character. At Via del Biscione 76 is one of the oldest hotels in Rome, built with materials taken from the ruins of the Teatro di Pompeo. The clients could be witness to unusual spectacles from their windows. In fact, the piazza was one of the sites for corporal punishments and executions.

In the center of the piazza is the monument to **Giordano Bruno**, (photo next page) who was burned here as a heretic in 1600, partly for claiming that the sun was just another star with the planets, including the earth, revolving around it. It is a powerful symbol of freedom of thought and dissent. The monk was a Dominican who had been a teacher at the Sorbonne.

His experience was a dramatic example of the atmosphere of intolerance that accompanied the Counter Reformation. His trial lasted seven years and included interminable interrogations, threats and torture of every kind and finally he was condemned to die by the judges of the Holy Office as an unrepentant heretic. The monument was erected in 1889 by promoters of freedom of thought after the unification of Italy, during the period when the Pope took refuge in Saint Peter's.

A palazzo in Vicolo del Gallo close to Campo de' Fiori has an unusual emblem inserted in the wall about 10 feet up. This in the 1500's was the "Locanda della Vacca" managed by Vannozza Cattanei, the lover of Cardinal Rodrigo Borgia, who then later became Pope Alessandro VI (Alexander VI). She gave birth to 4 children by Borgia: Lucrezia, Cesare, Giovanni and Gioffre. (See Walk 5, Castel Sant'Angelo).

Other Victims
As you can see at the base of the monument dedicated to Giordano Bruno, he was not the only one to suffer death as an "enemy of the Faith." Other cases of intolerance characterized the polarized and ruthless climate of the Counter Reformation by means of imprisoning, torture to obtain repentance and condemning to death.

Museo Barracco, Via dei Baullari 1, offers various **exhibitions.**

At Vicolo del Gallo 14 is Forno Campo de' Fiori *for pizza, biscotti, cakes and bread. In Via dei Baullari 4 is* Il Fornaio, *a good place for* **pizza** *by the slice, cookies and sweets.* Hostaria Farnese *on Via dei Baullari 109 also has* **pizza**. The Drunken Ship, *Piazza Campo de' Fiori 20, is a bar and pub.*

Cross Piazza Campo de' Fiori, take Vicolo dei Baullari and you come to Piazza Farnese.

15 Palazzo Farnese. "The die" is the nickname for this attractive Renaissance palace, the most prestigious of the Roman palazzos. It has been the site of the French embassy since 1871; it is not usually open to the public. The French government pays a nominal figure every 99 years. Sangallo designed it and completed most of the work from 1515 to 1545; however, it was then finished by Michelangelo and Della Porta. The travertine marble

Palazzo Farnese

Family Symbols
Often important families had their family symbols included in monuments and buildings. If you look carefully you can frequently see the bee for the Barberinis, the lily (fleur-de-lis) for the Farnese, the eagle for the Borghese family, a dragon for the Boncompagnis, stars for the Altieris and a falcon for the Falconieri family.

around the windows is thought to have been taken from the Colosseum. The two large granite tubs in front came from the Terme di Caracalla. In 1627 they became **fountains** with the addition of an elegant urn topped with a lily, the symbol of the Farnese family.

23

Walk to the right of Palazzo Farnese, and take Via di Monserrato, which passes by the small Piazza Santa Caterina di Rota.

16 Via di Monserrato. The house numbers on Via di Monserrato increase on the left and decrease on the right. Continue on Via di Monserrato where you will pass several palazzos from the sixteenth century, frequently with inner courtyards, among which are: **Palazzo Incoronati** at number 152, **Palazzo Fioravanti** at number 61 and on the left the L shaped **Palazzo Ricci**. In this area, while you are strolling, look up now and again because many of the buildings have terraces above, laden with a variety of plants, which give the street a distinctive tone especially with the play of shadows in the late afternoon sun.

The **Church of Santa Maria in Monserrato** gave the name to the street. This is one of the Spanish churches in Rome. Here, in the first chapel on the right, are the tombs of two Spanish Popes, Callistus III and Alexander VI. The famous Borgia Pope was transferred here after passing many years in an angle of the basement of Saint Peter's.

At number 42, about 12 feet up, there is a **plaque** set into the wall in honor of Beatrice Cenci. The noblewoman, with the complicity of her brothers, her step-mother and her lover had her violent and corrupt father killed, and made it look like an accident. They were found out, however, and tried and, in spite of public opinion in their favor (it is said that the father sexually assaulted the daughter), they were condemned to death and decapitated in 1599. As a symbol of rebellion against abuse of power, Beatrice was immortalized by several writers, among them P. B. Shelley *(The Cenci)* and Francesco Domenico Guerrazzi who wrote the novel *"Beatrice Cenci,"* and in numerous paintings.

Ancient plaque in Latin

Near number 145, where Via di Monserrato ends and Via dei Banchi Vecchi begins, there is a marble **sign in Latin** (right) ,on the wall, from the era of the emperor Claudius, circa 50 AD, which designated the perimeter (*pomerium*) of an ancient Roman neighborhood

At number 24 in Via dei Banchi Vecchi, on the left, is the **Palazzo dei Pupazzi**, the "puppet palace" with its elaborately decorated façade (detail left). Continuing on the right you see Palazzo Sforza Cesarini at number 118, built in the fifteenth century by Pope Alexander VI.

From Via dei Banchi Vecchi go left on Via dei Cimatori and then left onto Via Giulia.

17 Via Giulia was the most important street in Renaissance Rome. Pope Julius II, (1503-1513), from whom it gets its name, wanted Bramante to build it as a straight line. In the process of rationalizing the city, many existing medieval structures were knocked down. The pope was a patron of the arts and surrounded himself with artistic geniuses such as Bramante, Michelangelo, Sangallo, Raphael and many others. Not all the buildings along the street are from the Renaissance; some were built or renovated during the Baroque period, while others are from the nineteenth century. The house numbers are not always sequential.

At number 85 you may see inscriptions above the three windows on the second floor that read: "POS-SEDEVA" "RAF SANZIO" "NEL 1520" indicating that the artist **Raphael** (Raffaello Sanzio) owned this land and intended to build himself a house here.

At number 79 is **Palazzo Medici Clarelli,** also called "il Palazzetto" or the little palace, built in 1536 by the Florentine architect Antonio da Sangallo.

Near Vicolo del Cefalo, **Palazzo Sacchetti** at number 66 was built in 1542, so close to the river that it was frequently flooded. The church of San Biagio degli Armeni, commonly called "San Biagio della pagnotta" (*pagnotta* is a small loaf of bread), is right after Vicolo del Cefalo. It takes its name from the fact that the monks distributed bread (pagnotta) on the Saint's feast day, February 3. Saint Biagio was the protector of the throat.

Pope Julius II wanted a large court to be built here, but Bramante only had time to begin it. Thus, near number 62, there remains an unusual area of large

rounded blocks sticking out onto the street that the Romans have characteristically baptized "**the sofa**" of Via Giulia.

At 33 Vicolo del Gonfalone is the **Oratorio del Gonfalone** where chamber music **concerts** are held frequently. At Via Giulia 16, Palazzo Varese has an interesting internal courtyard. Just before the arch, near Palazzo Falconieri, there are signs that list **Borromini's works** of art and suggest a possible itinerary to view them.

Another quaint touch is the **Farnese arch** (left)**,** which was built as part of a project that would have connected Palazzo Farnese with the Farnesina on the other side of the Tiber by way of a bridge. The project was abandoned but the arch remains, and gives a romantic air to the street.

When you get almost to the end of Via Giulia you will see on the right a fountain with a large mask of ancient origin, **il Mascherone**. At the top of the fountain is the lily, the emblem of the Farnese family. In this area there are many fine antique stores and art galleries.

The Mascherone fountain was very popular because during some celebrations given by the Farnese family, instead of water, wine flowed out. One famous celebration in 1720 for the Gran Maestro of Malta had wine spewing out for 3 days.

The streets nearby are named frequently for the commercial activities that once took place there: Via dei Cappellari (*cappello* means hat), Via dei Baullari (*baule* means trunk), Via dei Chiavari (*chiave* is key), and Via dei Giubbonari (*clothing*).

18 Palazzo Spada and **Galleria Spada**. http://galleriaspada.beniculturali. it/. The Gallery contains, among others, works by Titian, Rubens, Guercino, Guido Reni and Andrea del Sarto. The palace, however, is famous for a conge-nial trick of perspective by Borromini. Cardinal Bernardino Spada (1594 – 1661) gave Borromini the task of creating an atrium on the ground floor going from the library to the courtyard. The architect, in collaboration with the mathematician Fra Giovanni Maria da Bitonto who did the calculations, produced an incredible **columned corridor**, accentuating the effects of perspective by having the walls converge, the floor rise and the distance between the columns decrease. The

length of the area is only about 28 feet but the clever design makes it look like about 120 feet. At the end of the corridor is a small statue, less than 3 feet tall, which looks much larger because of the special effects.

The palazzo has an impressive façade, and inside, beautiful stucco decorations and statues of emperors. The palace itself may only be visited by guided tours. However, without getting a ticket, you can admire the **perspective** ruse from the court-yard behind a glass partition (left). Outside, look up to see a fine sundial.

The entire walk is about 5 km. (3.3 mi.). If time is short, do not miss the Pantheon, Piazzale della Minerva, and Piazza Navona. Note: At the end of Via Giulia, if you go toward the river and take Ponte Sisto, you will find yourself in Trastevere, which is described in Walk 2.

Walk One - The Heart of Rome

Additional Restaurants

Le cave di Sant'Ignazio, Piazza Sant'Ignazio 169, www.dasabatino.it. Cuisine from several regions and pizza. Tables outside in this unforgettable piazza. €€

Osteria dell'Ingegno, Piazza di Pietra 45, www.osteriadellingegno.com. Simple yet refined. €€

Armando al Pantheon, Salita de' Crescenzi 31, armandoalpantheon.it. Good Roman cooking. €€

La Rosetta, Via della Rosetta 9. larosettaristorante.it. One of the best seafood restaurants. €€€

Mastro Ciccia, Via del Governo Vecchio, 76, Tel. 6880 2108. Roman cuisine and pizza. €€

Pizzeria Baffetto, Via del Governo Vecchio 114, pizzeriabaffetto.it. All types of pizza Roman style. Wood fired oven. €

Ditirambo, Piazza della Cancelleria 74, www.ristoranteditirambo.it. Traditional dishes. €€

Grappolo d'Oro, Piazza della Cancelleria 80, www.hosteriagrappolodoro.it. Roman and regional dishes, with tables outside. €€

Trattoria Polese, Piazza Sforza Cesarini 40, www.trattoriapolese.com. You can eat outside under umbrellas, by candlelight. €

26 Hostaria Romanesca, Campo de Fiori 40, Tel. 686 40 24. Roman cooking. €

The Killer Artist – Caravaggio's Rome

Caravaggio stabbed and killed Ranuccio Tomassoni in Piazza San Lorenzo in Lucina over a bet on a ball court game during the night of May 28, 1606. Now the area is punctuated by expensive restaurants, trendy boutiques and excellent ice cream shops, quite safe due also to the sizeable presence by police protecting the nearby sites of Parliament and the Cabinet.

But in the 1600's at the time of Caravaggio, in spite of the numerous churches, Rome was quite a violent place, especially at night. The city was a magnet for adventurers, soldiers and pilgrims, likely to feed the growing prostitution market. It has been estimated that at the beginning of the XVII century 18% of the female population of Rome was involved in prostitution. Maybe Rome is the only city in the world to have a square dedicated to a "high level kept woman." Piazza Fiammetta was dedicated to Fiammetta Michaelis, the lover of several important Romans, among them Cesare Borgia, son of Pope Alexander VI (immortalized in *The Prince* by Macchiavelli).

A multitude of beggars roamed the streets day and night. Some, given the chance, ready to rob the unaware passersby, others so desperate that they could be easily manipulated into doing almost anything, and finally pilgrims who, having fulfilled their religious dream, were looking for money for their trip home.

Another characteristic of Caravaggio's Rome was the high frequency of corporal punishment and public executions, which drew large crowds. The executions were held on the other side of Castel Sant'Angelo or at Campo de' Fiori or Piazza del Popolo, where dead bodies frequently were left, exposed to popular curiosity.

The calling of St. Matthew

Two notorious public executions happened in Rome in this period and it is quite likely that Caravaggio saw them. In 1599, in front of a huge crowd, Beatrice Cenci and her stepmother Lucrezia were decapitated (see #16 Via di Monserrato), while her brother was tortured, drawn and quartered. One year later the philosopher Giordano Bruno (See #14 Campo de' Fiori) was condemned to burn alive in Piazza Campo de' Fiori as a heretic. At that time, the Church did not like that Henry IV of France had come to terms with the Protestants. So the frequency of executions in Campo de' Fiori near the French embassy, located then in Palazzo Orsini, increased, with the ambassador angrily complaining about the stench of those revolting spectacles.

Caravaggio had a short choleric temper and the testimony of his contemporaries and his long police record show it. He was often drinking and dining in dives with his rowdy friends, also artists, bodyguards, adventurers, many quick with the sword, where old jealousy and wounded egos could quickly ignite a confrontation. After the painter murdered Tomassoni, a dark character himself, he was forced to flee to Naples, Malta and Sicily. When he finally died at the age of 39 of exhaustion and fever, while trying to reach a ship that had sailed away with his painting, his face was horribly disfigured and his body bore the signs of his numerous brawls.

The artist painted what he saw around him and what he directly experienced: the dark alleys, the muggings, the executions and the wearing away of the body. For example, the extreme realism in the painting *David and Goliath,* with the head detached from the body and dripping in blood, was something that the artist must have witnessed firsthand.

The Death of the Virgin

Some of Caravaggio's paintings had been refused because he did not follow the artistic guidelines imposed by the church. This explains why "The Death of the Virgin" ended up at the Louvre and not in the Church of Santa Maria della Scala in Trastevere. This painting was commissioned by the Carmelite Fathers, but when they first saw it they were shocked. The Madonna is not idealized; nothing suggests heaven or God. She is in a far too earthly position with swollen feet, an enormous belly and ashen color, while the apostles around her show all the weight of their passing years. The Fathers feared that the model was a prostitute and wanted nothing to do with it. In fact, the model was quite probably Maddalena Antognetti, lover of several important people and maybe of Caravaggio himself.

The **master of chiaroscuro** depicted the common people and often the poorest, showing them accurately, getting older, dirty, and shoeless. He expressed a realism centuries ahead of his time that was in direct contrast with the idealized and ideological form of art that the Church, under pressure from the Reformation movement, was trying to impose.

Caravaggio was born Michelangelo Merisi in 1571 and died in 1610. Although his works are scattered around the world, a large number are here in Rome, both in museums and churches. Some of the greater concentrations are listed.

Caravaggio's works in Rome:

This Walk:
Galleria Doria Pamphilj: *Penitent Magdalene, Rest on the Flight into Egypt, John the Baptist*

San Luigi dei Francesi: *The Calling of Saint Matthew, The Martyrdom of Saint Matthew, The Inspiration of Saint Matthew*

Sant'Agostino: *Madonna of the Pilgrims*

Walk 4:
Santa Maria del Popolo: *The Crucifixion of Saint Peter, The Conversion of Saint Paul on the Road to Damascus*

Walk 6:
Galleria Borghese: *Young Sick Bacchus, Boy with a Basket of Fruit, Saint Jerome Writing, Saint John the Baptist, David with the Head of Goliath, Portrait of Pope Paul V, Still Life with Fruit on a Stone Ledge, Madonna and Child with Saint Anne (Madonna de Palafrenieri)*

National Gallery of Ancient Art, Palazzo Barberini: *Judith Beheading Holofernes, Narcissus, Saint John the Baptist in the Desert, Saint Francis in Meditation*

St. Jerome Writing

Walk 7:
Capitoline Museums: T*he Fortune Teller, Saint John the Baptist*

WALK TWO - Ancient Origins

In this walk, we trace the evolution of the city from humble origins to the grandiose creations of the imperial period. We look at the ancient **Aurelian Walls** that protected the city and **Porta San Paolo**, one of the gates. The once populous neighborhood of **Testaccio** has become a trendy area, especially for young people. It contrasts with the quiet residential **Aventine Hill** graced with some of the oldest churches.

In the area around the **Bocca della Verità**, where it is thought that the first Roman settlements were formed, pagan and Christian structures that span more than 2500 years coexist harmoniously. Not far away, on the Palatine Hill, according to legend, Romulus founded Rome in 753 BC. Archeological research has ascertained the presence of human settlement from at least the tenth century BC. This is the area where simple shepherds, by means of diplomacy, planning, wars, and a "can do" mentality, were able to create a republic (*res publica*) that lasted 500 years, and then maintain a vast empire. The astonishing achievements of the Roman civilization are at the base of western democracies. See "The Legacy of Rome" at the end of the book. **Circo Massimo** and the **Baths of Caracalla** take us back to the imperial period. The walk ends with the **Isola Tiberina**, its ancient bridges and the numerous narrow streets of the picturesque, medieval **Trastevere** quarter.

In this walk:

1 Rome's Defensive Walls (Mura), the ancient city walls protecting Rome since the third century from increasing threats of invasion
2 The **Piramide**, the exotic tomb of Caius Cestius and **Porta San Paolo**, a well-preserved portal in the walls, also site of a WWII battle **29**

3 The **Protestant Cemetery** where the English poets Keats and Shelley are buried and the **Testaccio** neighborhood

4 The quiet **Aventine** hill with the ancient churches of **Santa Sabina** and Sant'Alessio, the Villa dei Cavalieri di Malta and the mithraeum of Santa Prisca

Cosmatesque polychrome marble, used to decorate many medieval churches

5 **San Saba**, the "piccolo Aventino," considered the eighth hill of Rome

6 **Terme di Caracalla** (Baths of Caracalla), a major imperial bath complex

7 **Circo Massimo** (Circus Maximus) a stadium with a capacity of more than 300,000 persons

8 The historic area around the **Bocca della Verità,** with arches, temples and churches

9 The picturesque **Isola Tiberina**, with ancient bridges still functional

10 Quaint **Trastevere**, Santa Maria in Trastevere, restaurants and shops

11 The church of **Santa Cecilia**, the patron saint of music

12 **Santa Maria in Trastevere**, an example of the unique medieval style
See the article at the end of the walk describing Rome's origins.

This walk passes through the Aventine Hill area and Trastevere

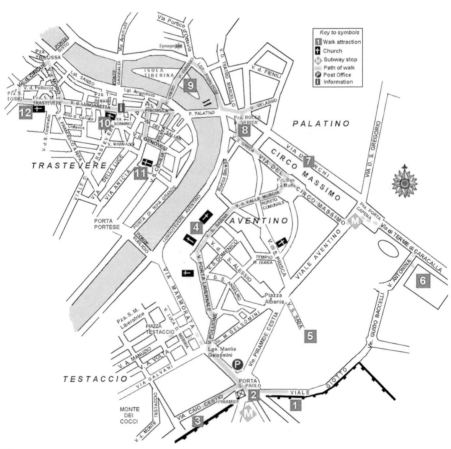

In this walk you will also find …
   The most picturesque areas for walking: Trastevere and the Aventino
   The best areas for dining: Trastevere and Testaccio
   The most historic and suggestive: around Piazza Bocca della Verità
   Several examples of Cosmatesque decoration on church floors and walls

Starting point: Piazza Porta San Paolo (Metro Piramide)

When you come out of the Metro station Piramide, you find yourself facing a large cobblestone piazza divided by Porta San Paolo. The part to the south is called Piazzale Ostiense and the northern part is Piazza di Porta San Paolo. Across the piazza you see the Aurelian Walls which follow to the right, while on the left you see Porta San Paolo with its two cylindrical towers, and finally still further to the left is the Piramide, attached to the other section of the walls. Walk over to the beginning of Viale Giotto to observe the walls more closely

Behind the train station is Eataly, *a large collection of restaurants and shops. See their website:* http://www.eataly.net/it_en/shops/rome

The Piramide and Piazza di Porta San Paolo

1 Rome's Defensive Walls (Mura).
Protective walls of varying heights and lengths were built during the centuries, corresponding to the size the city had attained. The first walls surrounded the original settlement on the Palatine hill. No remains have been found since the entire Palatine Hill was later the residence of the emperors who, for centuries, built and demolished at their leisure.

The **Servian Walls**, (Mura Serviane), according to tradition, were built by Servius Tullius, the sixth king of Rome, in the sixth century BC. It is quite probable that the Romans had defensive walls since the sixth century BC, given that many nearby cities had them then. So far, however, the only remaining walls date from the fourth century BC. The square blocks of volcanic tuff two feet thick came from a quarry near the city of Veio just 12 miles north of the city, conquered by the Romans in 396 BC. About 7 miles long, 30 feet high and 13 feet thick, the walls surrounded over 1100 acres. They discouraged Hannibal from attacking Rome directly when he invaded Italy with his elephants and devastated the Italian countryside.

After the victory over Carthage (second century BC), the defensive walls were no longer needed since the republic had no powerful enemies. Five centuries later, after some barbaric tribes crossed the Alps, the emperor Lucius Domitian Aurelian quickly ordered a wall 12 miles long around the city, to include the seven hills, Trastevere and part of the Janiculum Hill. The Aurelian Walls (Mura Aureliane) that you see in this piazza (photo at right) were built between 271 and 275 AD, and raised and reinforced during the fourth and fifth centuries, the late imperial period, when the defense of the city became a high priority.

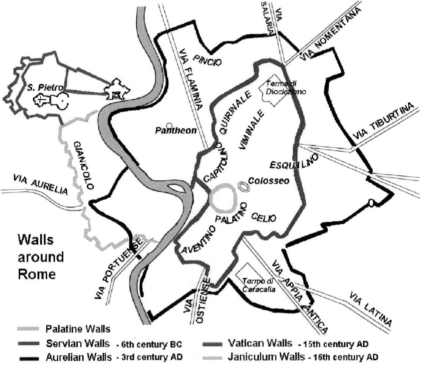

Walls around Rome

Palatine Walls
Servian Walls - 6th century BC
Aurelian Walls - 3rd century AD
Vatican Walls - 15th century AD
Janiculum Walls - 16th century AD

Originally the Aurelian Walls were from 18 to 24 feet high, and about 11 feet thick. The general Stilicone of Vandal origin was able to convince the emperor Honorius (395-423) to increase the height and thickness of the walls but it did not prevent the sack of Rome by the Visigoths in 410.

During the era of the popes, in the ninth century the Leonine Walls were erected after Arab raiders from North Africa sacked Saint Peter's, and lastly in the fifteenth and sixteenth centuries the Vatican Walls (Mura Vaticane) and the Janiculum Walls (Mura Gianicolensi) were built. There are sections of the Servian Walls still visible in many places.

If you want to see more of the fortifications, walk up Viale Giotto, keeping them to your right. There are openings for archers at regular intervals, often in good condition, and the towers that accommodated the catapults and other war machines are still visible. The walls opened by way of the main gates, such as Porta San Paolo.

Continue on Viale Giotto for an alternate route to the Terme di Caracalla. One of the characteristic fontanelle (drinking fountains) with the markings "SPQR" is at about 100 yards before the stairway opened in the wall. The popular name for these fountains, "nasoni" derives from the Italian word for nose, "naso."

Café du Parc in the Parco della Resistenza dell'8 Settembre on the other side of the piazza has numerous tables outside, with a nice view of the ancient monuments. The 8th of September in 1943 was the date that the armistice with the Allies became public and the beginning of the resistance against the Germans.

Head toward Porta San Paolo almost in the center of the piazza

A Missed Target

Walking east, after about 500 yards from Piazza Porta San Paolo the Aurelian Walls are interrupted by a staircase. The two areas, above and below, were separated for 17 centuries until a bomb from an American plane, destined for the nearby Ostiense railway station during World War II, created an opening. This made it possible to erect a stairway. Everything that is ancient is untouchable. In fact, during the construction of the subway there were continual interruptions and delays for archaeological inspections. That stretched the deadline with considerable frustration of all the parties involved. Even now, still hidden under the city, there is an incredible quantity of archeological artifacts. This was the subject of several wonderful scenes of Fellini's film "Roma."

Porta San Paolo is from the fourth century. Part of the Aurelian Walls, it was later remodeled with additions in several periods. The cylindrical towers date from the time of Honorius (395 – 423 AD).

From the gates (*porte*) in the walls, goods and persons funneled into and out of the city. **Porta San Paolo** gets its name from the Basilica of San Paolo, which is situated about 1 ½ miles to the south on Via Ostiense. It resembles the fortifications that were built all over Europe up to the late Middle Ages, that is, about 10 centuries later.

For a long time, during the imperial period, the population of Rome was around a million people. With the port of Ostia only about 12 miles away, these gates on the southern part of the city were the busiest. Traffic jams occurred then with carts as they do today with cars. To remedy the situation, Julius Caesar prohibited carts from entering the city between dawn and sunset, with the exception of those carrying construction materials. The incessant noise of the iron-rimmed wheels on the stone pavement must have been insufferable, especially at night, for those who lived near the most traveled roads. We know of several ordinances that tried to control this type of noise pollution. The traffic was, in fact, prohibited near residential streets during the night to allow the inhabitants some sleep.

Roman Cities

During its expansion, Rome found itself maintaining garrisons in the new territories. Camps were typically constructed in strategically important areas, possibly near water sources, and initially started by means of two large intersecting streets, one east-west and the other south-north. The surveyors, architects and specialized craftsmen of the legions created many towns from scratch. This was the start of London, Manchester, Mainz, Lyon, Canterbury, Exeter and many English cities ending with "-cester" , which comes from *castra*, or military camp. Other areas, which already had settlements, grew considerably larger with the commerce resulting from the military presence. This was true for Paris, Cologne, Salzburg, Worms and others.

The road system

The vast road system goes back to the republican era (second and third centuries BC). Especially the consular roads like Appia, Cassia, Aurelia, and Flaminia that led to the distant provinces constituted a level of complexity only reached again by twentieth century highways. These ancient Roman roads were planned in a straight line; it is likely the general course was plotted using the stars. They required enormous collateral projects. Swamps had to be drained, bridges raised to span valleys and huge amounts of rock and dirt had to be removed.

The modern road and railway systems in many countries have been superimposed over the strong foundations of the ancient Roman road network.

The ancient road surface still visible in places

When the legions occupied new territories, they continued to build and expand the roads maintaining contact between Rome and the provinces. About 60,000 miles long, the **road system** extended from Britain in the north to North Africa and from Spain to the Black Sea. Troop reinforcements, supplies of arms, and the "necessities" of Roman life such as food, wine, mail, clothing, shoes and nails, could now be sent to the frontiers in record time. As with the current relationship between industrialized and developing countries, both Rome and the provinces benefited from the increased commerce.

The improved communications and commerce favored the process of urbanization that the Romans wanted. It was very difficult to trade with nomadic or sparse populations. Substantial business deals were possible only when a territory reached a certain population density, had a tax system and courts to guarantee respect for laws. To accomplish this, the Romans built a large number of villages and encouraged the local people to become town dwellers. The streets of these new towns soon filled with the amenities typical of other Romanized cities such as baths, amphitheaters, modern houses, a variety of stores and temples.

Along Via Appia Antica

Walk toward Piazza di Porta San Paolo and see how Via Marmorata narrows between the Piramide and Porta San Paolo. From three or four lanes, it shrinks to only room for one or two cars. As you go around in the city, you realize that this is not unusual. Ironically the Romans, even though they were famous urban planners, (in fact they founded or planned the growth of many cities in Europe, North Africa and the Middle East), they were never able to plan Rome itself, which grew organically. Thus, the needs of modern traffic require patience and a compromise with the ancient.

Roads and Words

Along the roads every 6 or 16 miles there was a station where the official couriers could rest and change horses. Nearby, inns grew up where travelers could stay the night. Similarly, places to eat and drink used by travelers and later by the locals, *tabernae*, were added, from which derived the word "tavern." The word "highway" comes from the upper raised part, compared to the surrounding land, of the ancient Roman roads that had become characteristic of the English panorama. The word "street" comes from the Latin "*strata.*"

The first ancient highway

The roadway of Appia Antica (the old **Appian Way**) was shaped like a "donkey's back," that is, sloping down on the sides, to favor the draining off of water. The roadbed was about 13 feet wide to allow the passing of two wagons traveling in opposite directions. A ditch about three feet deep was excavated to form the foundation. Layers of four distinct types and sizes of rock were built up. One layer was stone and lime, while the upper layer, the "pavimentum," was very hard "silex" stone. On the sides were pedestrian walkways, wider than the road itself, which allowed for foot traffic. Extending for 380 miles to the port of Brindisi, it was of enormous importance for connecting Italy with the people of the eastern Mediterranean. This engineering masterpiece was conceived by Appius Claudius in 312 BC and he chose to be buried along his road.

An optional side trip will let you walk on the ancient city walls

The **Museo delle Mura (Museum of the walls)** at Via di Porta San Sebastiano 18 is best reached by taxi or public transportation. http://www.museodellemuraroma.it/en/informazioni_pratiche/orari_e_indirizzi/. It examines the walls in detail and shows the history of brick defensive construction. At about one and a half miles east from Porta San Paolo, along the walls, it is on three floors with access to a terrace and a tower. Normally you can pace on the walls as the soldiers did so often long ago and get a good view of the unusual green slice along the Appian Way. The area surrounding the Appian Way near the city has been declared protected, an oasis of green, banning construction. Parts of the original roadway survive, and scenes from the past can easily be imagined.

Ascending the stairs to the "control room," through a glass opening you can see the gigantic door and the iron gate (portcullis) that was raised and lowered between grooves in the stone. A lot of information is available about the walls.

Porta San Sebastiano was, in the 1930's, the residence of Ettore Muti, one of Fascism's high officials. Here Muti was most concerned with finding the privacy it afforded him, as someone in the higher echelons, to entertain numerous lovers. A flamboyant character, tall, and robust, he had a tumultuous and adventurous life and enjoyed speeding around in his Maserati 2300. A daring pilot in the African Campaign, at the command of an armored unit, he was among the first to enter the city of Madrid during the Spanish Civil War and later the royal palace of Tirana in the Albanian War. In the confusing period right after the arrest of Mussolini by the king in the summer of 1943, Muti was assassinated in mysterious circumstances, during the night while being arrested.

2 Piramide (M) When you walk on the piazza, what draws your eye is a small, perfect pyramid. No, you did not take a wrong turn and end up in Egypt. This is the very original sepulcher that Caio Cestio, a very rich man who had occupied several important political offices, wanted erected for himself. In his will he required that his heirs must build this tomb within one year in order to receive their inheritance. His will is engraved on the eastern side of the monument, (to the right in the picture) which is entirely of marble and which reminds us of the Egyptian pharaohs' tombs.

Ancient guides, medieval paintings and frescoes show that several pyramids dotted the city, demonstrating the fascination with Egypt after it was conquered in the first century BC. One pyramid near Castel Sant'Angelo was standing intact until 1499. The materials from these structures were reused for other buildings during the years. For centuries and still today, Romans have considered the sunken area around the Piramide as a humane place for stray and unwanted **cats** to roam free.

The Piramide of Caius Cestius, built in 12 BC is 88 feet high and each side is 72 feet. The frescoed interior chamber measures 19 by 13 by 15 feet high. In the third century it was incorporated into the Aurelian Walls and, because of that, it is still intact.

To the left of the pyramid, on the wall, are **plaques** commemorating events from the **Second World War** in Rome. The large one is in memory of the First Special Service Force of the United States and Canadian troops in the Italian campaigns, including Rome and Anzio. Another reminds us that here, in Piazza di Porta San Paolo, the first battle between the Italians and the German troops took place. On September 8, 1943, the Cassibile Armistice between Italy and the Allies, signed on September 3, was made public in a radio broadcast by General Eisenhower. An hour later the general Pietro Badoglio, who had been appointed prime minister after the king had arrested Mussolini on July 25, 1943, confirmed the end of hostilities.

While the king, the government and the high command were escaping, the Italian army and people were left without clear instruction.

Here in the piazza, on September 8, some Italian units, together with the local population, fought a 3 day battle against the Germans who were advancing up Via Ostiense to occupy Rome. As the plaque reminds us, several hundred Italians died, among them 50 women. So, more than 17 centuries later, the walls rendered a last glimmer of protection to the city.

The 8th of September is remembered in Italy as the beginning of the resistance to the Nazis and Fascists and of the civil war that lasted until the liberation of Italy, April 25, 1945.

A plaque commemorates the entry of US and Canadian troops on June 4, 1944 to liberate Rome.

Go around behind the Piramide and take Via Caio Cestio

Traveling Cats

The Egyptians were the first to domesticate cats. From 6000 BC to 2000 BC cats went from being semi-wild, as occasional guests in human settlements, to being pets. Arriving in Rome on trading ships, they later spread through Europe with the expansion of the Roman Empire. Around 100 AD cats were commonly kept in Roman homes. Their natural independence and detachment made them symbols of freedom. The goddess of freedom, Libertas, was often depicted with a cat at her feet.

3 The Protestant Cemetery, Via Caio Cestio 6, in reality is the non-Catholic cemetery, (Cimitero Acattolico) where a number of foreigners and non-Catholic Italians are buried. If the gate is closed, ring the bell. Among the more famous interred here are the **English poets** John Keats and Percy Bysshe Shelley. Julius Goethe, the son of the writer Johann Wolfgang von Goethe, political theorist Antonio Gramsci, and author Andrea Camilleri are also buried here, as are the German landscape painter Heinrich Reinhold, Italian novelist Carlo Emilio Gadda, Scottish anatomist John Bell, and many others. This is a little oasis of peace and serenity. The ever-present cats, abandoned to the confines of the Piramide, also wander around the cemetery; they are in good physical condition since there is an association that takes care of them.

Tombs of Keats and Severn

Retrace your steps and head left on Via Marmorata.

On the other side of the street there is a large **Post Office**.

Continuing on Via Marmorata, once you pass Largo Manlio Gelsomini, you can choose to explore Testaccio or go directly to the Aventine Hill.

Volpetti Più at Via Alessandro Volta 8, near the corner of Via Marmorata, is a good **tavola calda** *that offers, besides pizza by the slice, lasagna, salads and vegetables. A few steps away, at Via Marmorata 27,* Volpetti's *window displays irresistible Italian and foreign gastronomic products. For a quick lunch full of fantasy and fantastic food,* Pizza Trapizzino, *in Via Giovanni Branca 88, has pizza, supplì, but try the* **trapizzini** *which are white pizza cut like a pocket filled with delicacies.*

Testaccio. This neighborhood takes its name from the Monte Testaccio, an artificial hill more than 100 feet high and about a half mile around, formed since ancient times by the continual accumulation over the centuries of *testae*, fragments of terracotta amphorae used as containers for transport. For this reason, the hill is frequently called by its popular name Monte dei Cocci or mountain of shards. In an early attempt to control trash, local people continued during the centuries to bring broken dishes and pots of earthenware. Via di Monte Testac-

cio goes all around the Monte dei Cocci. Here many clubs and restaurants have been carved into or opened at the foot of the hill.

From the large port at Ostia, small ships brought goods up to the shores of the river at Testaccio where they were stored in large warehouses or taken directly to the wholesale markets. Traces of these ancient buildings are visible in Via Rubattino, Via Florio and Via Branca. Ruins of ancient structures are still visible from the Ponte Sublicio bridge looking toward the edge of the Tiber just under the embankments. (Photo at left) . **37**

Several discotheques are located on Via di Monte Testaccio: the oldest and most famous Akab, at number 69, Radio Londra at 67, Lucy Club at 53, L'Alibi at 44, and Big Bang at 22. The historic restaurant Checchino dal 1887, $$$, Via di Monte Testaccio 30 has its wine cellar dug right into Monte Testaccio.

Scrap Cuisine?

From ancient times, local inns have also used parts of the cow we normally throw out. From 1890 to 1965 the city's slaughterhouse was located here.

The abundance of scraps promoted the development of this characteristic Roman cuisine that used also the tail, tripe and other parts. Several restaurants were instrumental in interpreting this type of cooking, as Ristorante Checchino dal 1887 which is located in Via di Monte Testaccio, just outside the entrance of the old slaughterhouse. Today the old building holds part of the Museo di Arte Contemporanea, a contemporary art museum. The main building of the museum is located in Via Reggio Emilia 54.

The Testaccio neighborhood has no compelling attractions and thus does not attract many tourists. Since most of the restaurants and pizzerias cater to locals, some are open only in the evening. The buildings, characteristic of the late 1800's, include, especially toward Via Marmorata, large palazzos that imitate the style of the late Renaissance. Walking along Via Marmorata, look up on the Aventine hill where you can get a glimpse of the walls, gardens and religious buildings that we can visit next.

Testaccio does not have its popular character anymore, but has evolved, welcoming the Architecture department of the University of Rome, the European Design Institute and a part of the Museum of Contemporary Art of Rome and so many good restaurants, discotheques and establishments that on Saturday evening it is difficult to find a place to park.

*At Piazza Santa Maria Liberatrice, at the corner of Via Mastro Giorgio is a large **ice cream** shop. Giolitti, at Via Amerigo Vespucci 35 offers a more genuine experience. Da Oio a Casa Mia, Via Galvani 45 is a typical Roman trattoria. La Creperie, Via Galvani 11, offers, in addition to a regular menu, more than 100 types of **crepes** and gallettes with international dishes. For wine and beer, L'Oasi della Birra, Piazza Testaccio 38, and On the Rox, a bar and night club at Via Galvani 54.*

On the other side of the Tiber, passing over Ponte Sublicio and immediately left under the arches, the **Porta Portese** market is open only Sunday mornings. This is one of the largest open-air markets in Europe, where they sell everything from clothing to electronics to postage stamps. Test your bargaining skills, and, due to the incredible crowd, especially during the summer, think ahead about protecting your wallet.

Coming back to Largo Manlio Gelsomini (this is the only street to take you up to the Aventino) proceed on the rather steep uphill of Via Asinio Pollione. Staying to the left, continue on Via di Porta Lavernale. Just before getting to Piazza Cavalieri di Malta, on the left is the "modern" church of Sant'Anselmo.

4 Aventino (Aventine hill). To get an idea of the atmosphere of quiet opulence and serenity of times gone by, visit the Aventine. The tranquility of the area, especially toward the top of the hill, the presence of religious buildings, the high walls of protection and the telecameras often present, give you an idea of the search for privacy and security of the residents. The serene atmosphere and silence could not be more different from that of the nearby

38 trendy Testaccio.

It is the most southerly of the original seven hills of Rome and it is thought that the name came from the king of Alba Longa, Aventino, who was hit by lightning and was buried here. On the Aventino are some of the most ancient churches in Rome.

The modern **Church of Sant'Anselmo** at the end of a tree-lined lane on Via di Porta Lavernale, is part of a Benedictine monastery. Often during the evening service it is possible to hear their choir singing traditional Gregorian chants.

The first clocks
The Benedictine order, founded in the sixth century, emphasized activity at all times: "Idleness is the enemy of the soul." They felt it was their duty to use time efficiently because it belongs to God. Their desire to regulate monastic life led them in the 12th century to construct a device to ring bells calling them to prayer at the 7 devotional periods of the day. Soon, the new merchant class welcomed the idea and clocks began to appear in cities.

At first, clocks had no dials, only sounding a bell at intervals. The word clock comes from the Middle Dutch word for bell. Later, in the sixteenth century dials appeared and by the eighteenth, the second hand was introduced. The schedule widely used in mills and then in the industrial revolution would not have been possible without the clock.

Continue on Via di Porta Lavernale until you get to Piazza Cavalieri di Malta

On the Piazza is the **Villa dei Cavalieri di Malta**. Together with the palazzo on Via Condotti and the House of the Knights of Rhodes near Trajan's Market, this is part of the Sovereign Military Order of Malta, (See Walk 4 for more). Come across the piazza to the northwest side, up to the wooden doors at Piazza dei Cavalieri di Malta 3, and look through the large **keyhole.** Perfectly centered in the distance, flanked by manicured bushes, Saint Peter's dome appears.

Continue along Via di Santa Sabina and right away on the left is the Chiesa di Sant'Alessio

The **Chiesa di Sant'Alessio**, at number 23, is accessed through a courtyard and has a distinctive white façade. It was built in the fifth century on top of the house of Eufimiano, father of Alessio. As the story goes, to avoid having a marriage forced on him, Alessio decided to leave home and live as a pious ascetic. Many years later he returned and was not recognized by his father, who, however, let him live under the stairs like a homeless stranger. After his death a document showing his identity was found on his body. The statue of Saint Alessio in the chapel on the left of the entrance shows him in a pilgrim's clothing holding the document. The story was depicted in eleventh century frescoes in the old church under the Basilica of San Clemente near the Colosseo, (see Walk 3). The well from Eufimiano's house is still functional and is located between the nave and the left aisle. The wooden stairs where Alessio lived for 17 years are conserved above his statue in a crystal case (photo right).

Sections of the floor are in the Cosmatesque style, that is, geometric multicolored patterns in marble. Two columns in the choir also appear in that style. (See the description of Cosmatesque ornament after the Church of Santa Sabina.)

Continue on Via di Santa Sabina and still on the left is another very ancient church.

The **Chiesa di Santa Sabina,** a classical early Christian basilica, is one of the oldest churches in Rome. Tel. 06.579 401. Today the interior seems austere, but originally the faithful experienced a different atmosphere, since the walls were covered with colorful mosaics. Materials from pre-existing buildings and especially marble columns from the nearby Temple of Giunone Regina (Juno) were used in its construction. During the imperial period several houses of the nobility were

established in this area. Sabina was a Roman matron who lived here on the Aventine and had embraced the Christian faith. According to several sources she was martyred in 125 AD during the reign of the emperor Hadrian. In 422, about a century after emperor Constantine legalized Christianity, this church was erected on the remains of Sabina's house. It was built by the architect Pietro d'Illiria, a priest originally from Greece, remembered in the name of the small piazza near the entrance.

In 1219 the Church gave the building to the "order of the preachers" or the Dominicans. It was restructured by several artists in various periods, including Francesco Borromini in 1643, who gave it a decidedly Baroque tone.

The church was built in the **basilica** style, that is, a long building with a semicircular apse at the end. The interior is very simple. Twenty-four columns with Corinthian capitals separate the nave and aisles. A difference from the traditional basilica, however, is the use of large arched windows that the architect inserted in the upper part. Instead of glass, very expensive at the time, a type of marble-like stone, selenite, cut very fine, was used, which gave a unique quality to the light entering the windows. The building is oriented to the north so that the sun could penetrate during both the morning and afternoon from these windows.

Plan of a typical basilica with a nave, side aisles separated by columns and a semicircular apse. Usually used by Romans as a court and meeting place, in the Christian era basilicas were often transformed into churches.

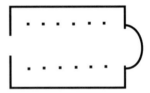

The eight columns in the atrium in front of the façade come from Roman buildings. A fairly dark portico covers the entrance to the church. The cypress **wood paneled doors** (left) are from the fifth century and on the remaining 18 panels are depicted scenes from the Old and New Testaments. During a restoration in 1836, in the panel that represents Moses parting the sea, above the door to the right, the face of the pharaoh who is about to drown was retouched to look like Napoleon. That attests to the strong emotions that the French emperor, no friend of the Church, (he had the pope arrested and brought to France in 1799), was able to generate even years after his death. The highest panel on the left has one of the oldest existing representations of the crucifixion.

Inside, above the door, a **mosaic panel** remains, containing an inscription in blue and gold between two feminine figures. These are the only remains of the magnificent mosaics that at one time decorated much of the interior. Under the main altar lay the remains of Pope Alexander I, one of the early bishops of Rome, martyred around 116.

Around the year 800, Pope Leo III ordered changes, including the addition of the **choir**, a low marble wall to separate the clergy from the congregation. Although later removed, parts of it, with various Christian motifs in bas-relief, have been inserted into the walls as decoration. Pope Sixtus V (1585 – 90) had the church renovated according to the style that was coming into fashion, the Baroque. In this period, the windows were walled up. About two centuries later, during the Napoleonic era, the church was used as a stable and suffered more damage.

Mocking art

One of the earliest known representations of the crucifixion is in the form of graffiti mocking the new religion. An ass-headed naked man is crucified backwards while one of the faithful is depicted in an adoring position at the level of his posterior. A Greek inscription says, "Alexamenos adores his god." This graffiti was discovered among the palaces of the emperors on the Palatine Hill. Early Roman Christians were reluctant to express it artistically because they had lost relatives and friends to this form of capital punishment.

The basilica is rich with religious history, among which is the cell where San Domenico di Guzman, the founder of the **Dominican order,** lived. The Dominican order naturally left an imprint on the interior art. One of the most interesting tombs is that of a lay woman, Stefania dell'Isola. She is depicted holding the book of the rule of the lay Dominican movement with both hands over her breast.

During this past century Santa Sabina has been restored substantially to the level of its first 500 years, including carefully redoing the windows with thin translucent panes of stone restoring to the interior the unique ancient atmosphere.

The Dominicans

Saint Dominic, born Domingo de Guzman of a Spanish noble family, was ordained an Augustinian monk in his native Spain. Having distinguished himself for his discipline and call to service, in 1205 he was sent to Languedoc in France to preach to the Albigensian heretics, who had been winning many followers. After about ten years, together with other volunteers and wishing to form a preaching order, he went to Rome to seek permission from the Pope. In 1218 he received approval and was given Santa Sabina. His order was called the "Order of Preachers" but soon became known as the Dominicans. Using Santa Sabina as a base, the last years of his life were spent all over Italy and Europe organizing and establishing friaries. He died in Bologna in 1221.

Coming back out of the church, on the right, a **cloister** with alternating double columns adds to the medieval atmosphere.

Archeological **excavations** have brought to light remains of the Servian Walls from the fourth century BC which protected the young city. Directly under the church of Santa Sabina a small republican temple from the third century BC has been found whose columns have been incorporated into the structural walls. Also found are a house from the fourth century AD with streets and, below, rooms of the Roman period of the first century BC.

Cosmatesque Decoration

Walking around Rome and visiting churches, let your gaze fall occasionally to the ground beneath you. Inside many of the ancient churches, you will see the distinctive floors created by a group of Italian artists from the later Middle Ages called the Cosmati. These multi-colored geometric designs ornamented not only floors, but choirs, columns and exterior elements.

The term Cosmati refers to several families of artists, of which one, the Cosma, has given its name to the group. They worked mainly in the central part of Italy, especially in Rome and nearby regions, in the twelfth and thirteenth centuries. At that time, the popes were promoting a rebuilding of Rome's churches to restore the grandeur of ancient times. Being surrounded by classical ruins and Byzantine influences, the Cosmati were able to create geometric designs with an amazing variety and precision. They placed small triangles and rectangles of colored stones and glass in defined areas, usually bordered by white marble. The most used colors were green and red, although the natural colors of yellow and other earth toned stones increase the diversity in the designs. The small sizes of some of the pieces is due to the fact that they were reusing fragments of ancient materials.

On vertical surfaces, mosaic bands may curl around columns or border an arch. Inside the church, strips of geometric designs, usually stars, form borders around choirs or pulpits. Frequently the

floor of the central nave is decorated with large red porphyry circles surrounded by curved bands of geometric patterns. The surrounding spaces are filled in with sections of varying designs, again separated by strips of white marble. Visiting the churches on our walks you will see many of these examples. The condition of the floors in the churches varies, as some have seen significant restoration.

A colorful section of the floor of San Clemente

Cosmatesque decoration on the columns

Red and green are frequently used. Example of Santa Maria in Trastevere's floors which have been restored

On leaving Santa Sabina, go to the left toward the lovely **Parco degli Aranci** (Park of the Orange Trees, also called Parco Savello). On the left of the entrance a **fountain**, with an ancient mask set into a niche, spouts water into a trough. From the park you have a beautiful view of part of Rome.

For many young people, an invitation to go walking in the park means that the relationship is getting a little bit more serious.

From this point you may proceed directly to **Circo Massimo**, number 7, by taking Via di Valle Murcia, or take an optional route to visit Santa Prisca, San Saba and the **Terme di Caracalla.**

To go to Circo Massimo, continue on Via di Santa Sabina, which becomes Via di Valle Murcia, you will pass the City Rose Garden, which deserves a visit in season. Keep going to the Piazzale Ugo La Malfa, pass the monument to Giuseppe Mazzini, who, in the nineteenth century, was instrumental in the unification of Italy. Finally in front of you is the wide area of the barely delineated Circo Massimo and behind it, the Palatino (Palatine hill) with the ruins of the imperial palaces. Cross Via del Circo Massimo with care. *Skip ahead to number 7, Circo Massimo.*

The *optional loop* will take you to visit Santa Prisca, San Saba and the Terme di Caracalla. To do so, proceed down Via di Santa Sabina and turn right on Via Alberto Magno, turn left on Via Eufimiano, cross Largo Arrigo VII and on the left side of the beginning of Via di Santa Prisca is the church, set back from the street and accessed by a ramp.

Santa Prisca. This narrow church tucked between two larger buildings was built around the end of the fourth century near the house of the couple Aquila and Prisca, here on the Aventine Hill. Drapery merchants from Turkey, they converted to Christianity and befriended Saint Paul in Corinth and Saint Peter in Rome. Their home here on the Aventine Hill became an "*ecclesia domestica*" or a household place of worship. Here, legend says, the Apostle Peter would have baptized people utilizing the concave section of a capital, which is now to the right of the entrance. Above it, the twentieth century sculptor Antonio Biggi included a small bronze work of Jesus receiving baptism by John the Baptist.

Church documents tell also of a 13-year-old girl, also called Prisca, who was martyred under the emperor Claudius for refusing to worship the statue of Apollo and insisting in the Christian faith. This explains the two different stories depicted inside the church. The main picture over the altar by Passignano from the end of the 1500's represents Prisca, the mature wife of Aquila, being baptized by Saint Peter. In contrast, the Fontebuoni frescoes around the main altar refer to the transport of the young martyr's remains by Pope Eutychian (275-283).

Underground excavations have brought to light an extraordinarily complete **Mithraeum**, a place of worship for the god Mithras. This cult was very popular in the early days of Christianity. At least three other rooms have been recovered, one used by the Pontifex and the ministers to don the sacred liturgical vests for the procession and sacred functions. It is open to the public the 2nd and 4th Saturday of the month. To visit, make a reservation at the Sovraintendenza Archeolo-   **43** gica di Roma: https://www.coopculture.it/en

Continue down Via di Santa Prisca, cross Viale Aventino and walk uphill on Via di San Saba.

5 San Saba.

The neighborhood of **San Saba**, sometimes called the "piccolo Aventino" is also considered the eighth hill of Rome. As with many neighborhoods of the city, San Saba was for centuries self-contained. People usually did not feel the need to go to other neighborhoods.

The center of social life for **San Saba** was the main square, Piazza Gian Lorenzo Bernini on top of the hill, with its daily open market, bar, movie theater and the walled enclosure of the church. Until the 60's, a yearly procession wound through the narrow streets of the San Saba neighborhood and terminated in the church courtyard.

Perched on top of the hill is the church of **San Saba**, curiously showing its back to the main square, Piazza Gian Lorenzo Bernini. The monastery of San Saba was founded here in the seventh century by monks fleeing the Arab invasion of Jerusalem. Saba was one of the main exponents of monasticism in the east. Today's church is the result of a reconstruction in the mid twelfth century and gives its name to the entire neighborhood.

Straight up Via di San Saba, at the first intersection take a few steps through a column-edged arch.

The strong wall on the sides of the entrance, the hidden courtyard and the smooth façade itself show the characteristics of a **fortified church**. The builders clearly kept in mind the possibility of attacking enemies and the necessity for defense.

The main entrance is in a brick portico under an arched loggia. Many archeological finds from the old complex and nearby area are on display on the portico walls, including several sarcophagi, marble altars and medieval bas-reliefs. One wall displays terracottas showing emblems of the builders. On the left, the bottom of the stairs indicates the ground level of the original church, which was built on the house of Saint Silvia, the mother of the future Pope Gregory I (590-604) who gave his name to the famous Gregorian chants.

Fourteen granite columns, with varying capitals, support arches that separate the nave from the two side aisles; all three terminate in apses. A curious fourth aisle, shorter, maybe originally a portico, extends along the left side. Here thirteenth century **frescoes** depict the life of San Nicola di Bari, the 4th century bishop of Myra who is known now as **Saint Nicholas** or **Santa Claus**. The legend says that a poor man had three daughters but no money for their dowries. San Nicola is said to have gone to the poor man's

The characteristic octagonal baldacchino of San Saba. Note the sheep, in the apse fresco, representing the 12 apostles.

house during the night and thrown three purses filled with gold coins through the window. One of the panels of the fresco shows the money being thrown into the house where the three young girls are sleeping (photo next page). Colorful Cosmatesque marble inlay graces the **floor** and also adorns a panel on the right wall. The main apse frescoes, showing the 12 apostles as men and also as sheep under a large Christ figure recall the mosaics of many medieval churches such as Santa Maria in Trastevere (see #12). Even though the artist is unknown, it has been dated to the early Renaissance, around 1465.

The peaked wooden roof with exposed beams fosters the perception of height. A baldacchino with an octagonal colonnaded roof hovers above the altar. The sacristy and its corridors also display interesting frescoes and artifacts that belonged once to the original oratory of Saint Silvia.

Come back down Via di San Saba, turn right on Viale Aventino (pass the Metro stop Circo Massimo) go right through Largo Vittime del Terrorismo and continue straight on Via delle Terme di Caracalla, having the athletic track on your right.

*There are several places for a **snack** on Viale Aventino near the FAO. (United Nations Food and Agriculture building). At Piazza Albania 5 on the corner with Viale Aventino there is one of the several small Insalata Ricca restaurants, scattered around the city, which serve a variety of **salads** among other things.*

6 Terme di Caracalla (Caracalla Baths) These are the best preserved imperial baths in the city. Located between Via delle Terme di Caracalla and Via Baccelli, they operated from 217 AD until 537 AD. Today we might describe it as a cross between a spa complex and a campus, and a tourist has

to enter to really appreciate its enormous size. It could be used all year round by men and women, but especially in the summer it allowed the Romans to cool off and relax without leaving the city. They could swim, exercise, take a steam bath, receive a massage, eat, do research in the libraries, meet with friends and acquaintances, or simply relax in the pleasant gardens. Laid out over several acres, the complex included dressing rooms with **mosaic floors**, which

can still be seen, two large gymnasiums, a series of pools with water at different temperatures, shops, an auditorium, hairdressers, restaurants and libraries. The buildings were also covered in marble and adorned with many of the best sculptures of the period.

Three pools were standard, one hot (furnaces sent hot air under the floor), one warm and one cold. Inviting gardens with porticos flanked a Latin library and a Greek library. Up to 1600 people at a time could bathe, and it was the second largest complex of the kind of ancient Rome, after the Baths of Diocletian. (Terme di Diocleziano) By the year 410 AD 11 imperial baths, 926 public baths and 1212 public fountains in the city were at the disposal of the Romans. **45**

In several places the buildings were over 100 feet high and they were famous for the richness of their decoration. Today, just sections of the two levels above and two below ground remain, which challenge us to imagine the original splendor.

There were 3 different levels **underground**. Wood on carts pulled by horses was continually delivered through curving underground tunnels. Twenty-five furnaces were worked by 10 people each, producing hot air, hot water and steam, delivered through a network of pipes. These levels also included service areas and a mithraeum, perhaps the largest space for the worshippers of Mithras, a Persian god popular from the first to the fourth century.

A mosaic fragment from the baths

The baths were used until 537 when the Goths, after invading the empire, cut off the water supply during the siege of Rome. During the following centuries the area was used as a cemetery and later provided services for the poor. After the tenth century the complex was abandoned and the materials were used for new constructions, as was often the case with ancient Roman buildings. Priceless archeological treasures went to adorn piazzas and palaces. Two large gray granite basins went to adorn Piazza Farnese in 1612.

Cosimo de' Medici had a granite column transported to Florence for the Piazza della Santissima Trinità, while other artifacts are on display at the Museo Archeologico di Napoli. The Belvedere Torso sculpture was transferred to the Vatican Museums and the beautiful multicolored marble floor was sent to the Quirinale, now the official residence of the President of Italy.

The baths were used from 1938 for many years for summer opera performances such as Verdi's *Aida*, but were interrupted for archaeological considerations. They have restarted and the baths are now used both for opera and other musical concerts in the summer.

The Terme di Caracalla served as inspiration for New York's Pennsylvania Station and Chicago's Union Station.

Retrace your steps to Via delle Terme di Caracalla, go through Largo delle Vittime del Terrorismo and cross the street to take Via del Circo Massimo.

While you are walking along Largo delle Vittime del Terrorismo with the white modern building of the FAO (UN Food and Agricultural Organization headquarters) on your left, looking straight ahead you can see the cupola of Saint Peter's on the left and the characteristic roof of the Synagogue on the right. They appear at the same level and of the same size but that of course is a trick of perspective due to their relative distances.

7 Circo Massimo (Circus Maximus) (M) is situated in a natural valley between the Aventine and Palatine hills. According to tradition, it was founded by King Tarquinius Priscus in the sixth century BC and initially was nothing more than a hollow particularly suited to horse racing.

During the centuries wooden bleachers were added for the spectators, it was expanded and finally a masonry stadium was erected, until, during the reign of Trajan, it became the largest stadium of all time. At its apex, measuring about 600 yards long and 200 wide, it had a capacity of over 300,000 spectators. Construction began in about 326 BC and it was in use until the sixth century AD. The oblong track was in the center and the bleachers surrounded it, occupying also the sloping grassy area. Special imperial boxes at the base of the Palatine, near the middle of Via dei Cerchi, allowed the emperor to watch the spectacles without leaving his palace.

Chariot racing was the most popular sport. It spread even to the provinces, as evidence from a complete stadium recently excavated in Colchester in Britain has shown. People were as passionate about the horse races as today's fans are about football or baseball. The drivers of the chariots were often from the poorer classes and the sport was dangerous in that, in the heat of the competition, the chariot could easily overturn. In fact, forcing the adversary off the track or even to tip over was part of the spectacle.

There were usually up to 24 races in a day and during the breaks acrobats and actors entertained the crowd. The typical race consisted of seven laps, and betting was quite common. A magistrate started the race by dropping a white cloth. At the starting line 7 dolphin-shaped symbols were clearly visible in the center spine of the track. After each lap one was removed, indicating how many were left. The basic strategy of maneuvering to gain the inside position has not changed during the centuries. So the drivers had to be very skillful in handling the tight 180 degree curves at the end of the straightaway. To reduce the chance of being bumped off the chariot, the drivers often tied the reins very tightly to their body. When they were knocked off, to avoid being dragged by  the horses, they had better be ready to use a knife to free themselves!

Four **mosaic emblems**, each depicting a member of a team, were found in the imperial villa of Severus. The teams are easily identified by the color of their uniforms, green, red, blue and white. The mosaic is now visible in Room IX on the second floor of the Palazzo Massimo museum (see Walk 6)

In the midst of the clamor of the crowd, the emperor Nero, in his youth, competed in the games and, needless to say, was always the victor. The devastating fire of 64 AD during Nero's reign is said to have started in the densely populated wooden apartment buildings near the southern part of the Circo Massimo.

At the southern edge, near Piazza di Porta Capena, you may see some ruins of the **bleachers**. In this area, according to tradition, before the building of Circo Massimo at the dawn of Rome's history, the event called the "Rape of the Sabines" (really a kidnapping), that has been immortalized in countless sculptures and paintings, occurred when the followers of Romulus, the first king of Rome, raided the Sabines and carried off their women.

Proceed downhill on the Via del Circo Massimo and on Via della Greca to the Piazza Bocca della Verità.

8 Piazza Bocca della Verità. This area is one of the most evocative in Rome for the particular atmosphere created by the history, the architecture of such different periods surprisingly harmonious and by an air of mystery. Romulus, according to legend, founded Rome not far from here on the Palatine hill, where you can still see the remains of the imperial palaces. It seems probable that near here, on the slopes of the Capitoline, Palatine or Aventine hills, the first inhabitants decided to settle. These hills had the advantage of a favorable strategic position. From their heights, it was easy to control the surrounding area and were easily defensible in case of attack.

There is archeological evidence of human occupation from at least the tenth century BC. Try to imagine the river, just a few hundred yards away near the Isola Tiberina, without the embankments, with the water able to expand. Here was the easiest place to ford.

The fountain in Piazza Bocca della Verita' alongside the Tempio di Ercole

Santa Maria in Cosmedin, built by Pope Hadrian I in the 8th century, was given to the Greeks fleeing Constantinople. The elegant seven-tiered bell tower was added in the twelfth. Several ancient columns, inserted into the wall of the left aisle, remind us that it was built on top of an older construction from the Flavian era of the first century. The Gothic baldacchino is fairly rare for Rome. Old and varied columns line the nave, and the aisles are asymmetrical. Medieval frescoes, unfortunately badly worn, adorn some of the walls. In a small room on the right which doubles as a bookshop is a small framed golden mosaic of the Epiphany, which came from the old Saint Peter's Basilica, datable to 706 AD.

The beautiful **polychrome marble floor** from the twelfth century was made by a group of artisans named Cosma, or **Cosmati**, a family famous for its marble mosaic floors. (See Cosmatesque Decoration earlier) Other churches on this walk that have Cosmatesque floors are Santa Sabina, San Saba, Santa Maria in Trastevere and San Crisogono.

Outside, in the portico of the church, is a large round stone representing the face of a faun with an open mouth. This is the **Bocca della Verità**, or mouth of truth, which is believed to have been originally the cover of an ancient storm drain. Legend has it that he who swears falsely while having his hand in the mouth will have it bitten off. Although there are those who say that some priests, hearing a confession of culpability in confidence, passed on this information to the authorities, there is no documentation that hands were ever really cut off during Papal Rome.

However, it is thought that occasionally the Bocca della Verità was used as an instrument of pressure on a population often ignorant and superstitious. Some sources say that a priest hid behind it and with a stick hit the hands of those presumed to be liars. For a long time it has been used as a playful test for truthfulness among spouses and fiancés. You may recall a scene from the movie *Roman Holiday* where Audrey Hepburn and Gregory Peck try sticking their hands into the "mouth." At some times there may be lines of people waiting to try their luck and especially to take a photo.

Leaving the church, the **fountain** you see on the other side of the street was erected in 1717 and represents two tritons holding a large shell. The curving and almost Baroque style of the fountain is a counterpoint to the classic and more austere ancient and medieval creations nearby.

On coming out of the church, go to the right about 100 yards and on the right you will see a strange arch.

The arch is called **Arco di Giano (Arch of Janus)** from the fourth century. Coming near, you see immediately that it is not a classic arch, but a massive square structure with four intersecting arches, one on each face. It is not a triumphal arch but had a practical use, since it served to protect the meat merchants from the weather.

The Cloaca Massima (Rome's main ancient storm drain) passes under it.

Go up the stairs on the left to see the church San Giorgio in Velabro and the Arco degli Argentari,

The Arco degli Argentari (Arch of the Silversmiths), (photo next page) more than an actual arch, is a monumental portal to the Foro Boario, which was the first forum of Rome, the meat market. This small arch, attached to the church **San Giorgio in Velabro**, was constructed in 204 AD in honor of the emperor Septimius Severus by the bankers and merchants of the zone. The church has a portico and the bell tower is from the twelfth century. The Arco degli Argentari is decorated with bas-reliefs of emperor Caracalla and Septimius Severus and his wife. You can notice, on the inside panels, areas which had represented Caracalla's brother and wife were chiseled out to remove any trace after he had them assassinated.

49

The Arco degli Argentari

Looking in a northeast direction, the ruins of the Roman Forum are visible, which we will visit extensively in Walk 3. Walk around this area as much as you like and then retrace your steps.

Go back and walk across the piazza to the rectangular Temple of Portunus and then to the round Temple of Hercules (Vesta)

The temples of Portunus and of Hercules, so close to the river Tiber, were built on high bases to withstand the frequent flooding. The area of the temples, when flooded, produced conditions similar to the tidal high water experienced in Venice.

The rectangular **Tempio di Portunus** (Temple of Portunus) is also called Fortuna Virile. Dating from the fourth century BC, it was restructured in the second and first centuries BC. It was dedicated to Portunus, the god of ports and rivers. In this area, in fact, on the banks of the Tiber, the first port of Rome developed. During the Middle Ages this temple, as many others, was consecrated as a church for Santa Maria Egiziaca, a saint of the fifth century. Born in Egypt she was a courtesan in Alexandria but, after converting, she escaped to the desert and spent the rest of her life in penance. She is the patron saint of prostitutes.

The circular **Tempio di Ercole (Temple of Hercules),** called erroneously the

Temple of Vesta for a long time because of its similarity to a round temple of that name in the Roman Forum, is from the second century BC. It was dedicated to Ercole Vincitore (Hercules Victor), the god of the oil merchants. A portico of twenty Corinthian columns surrounds the central cella. In the 12th century the temple was also consecrated as a church. This perfectly preserved monument was one of the first constructed completely in marble imported from Greece. The roof, lost during the centuries, was redone in modern times.

Head uphill behind the Temple of Hercules, cross Lungotevere Pierleoni and walk on the sidewalk by the banks of the Tiber River.

On the left bank near the Tempio di Ercole, looking down, the **Cloaca Massima,** inserted in the embankment of the Tiber, empties through three concentric arches. This is an underground drain, still operating, which goes back to the time of the king Tarquinius Priscus, that is, the sixth century BC. It collects water from the Palatine and Capitoline hills and passes under the Roman Forum, the Arco di Giano and under the piazza in front of San Giorgio in Velabro. It might be hard to see because of the bushes (photo next page).

Walk on the sidewalk along the river toward the island.

Walking along the sidewalk by the river the beautiful plane trees with their hanging branches form a pleasant arched effect. Just before you reach Ponte Fabricio, on the right is the Jewish quarter and you can easily see the large synagogue, the ruins of the Portico d'Ottavia and the restaurant Giggetto. Here this walk meets up with Walk 7

9 Isola Tiberina. If you look out from the banks of the Tiber, you notice a bend and, further down, the picturesque small island called Isola Tiberina. In Roman times, Trastevere was connected to the rest of the city by way of numerous bridges, almost like today. Look down from the banks or from Ponte Palatino on the side toward the island, and you can see, parallel to Ponte Palatino, the remains of the ancient **Ponte Rotto** (broken bridge) (at right) from 142 BC. As the name suggests, only a part of this bridge, the first bridge built using stone arches, remains.

Evolution of the arch

The arch was the Romans' most important development in architecture. With ensuing experience their engineers pushed forward to create the vault and the dome. These elements were used extensively, combining stone and concrete for constructing bridges, aqueducts, basilicas, stadiums and palaces. The Pantheon represents the apex of this evolution. Some bridges and aqueducts built with this technology are still functional, not only in the city but in other parts of the ancient Roman empire. Examples are the magnificent Pont du Gard aqueduct in Provence (which gets its name from *provincia*). Two constructions in Spain are in good condition: a half mile long bridge with sixty arches above the Guadiana river and the famous Alcantara bridge, 600 feet long with six arches 148 feet high. The architect of the latter in 105 AD left an inscription that is still visible that says "I built a bridge that will last for centuries." And so it did. Only after the eighteenth century, with the Industrial Revolution and the production of steel, was the stone arch surpassed with the use of new materials and technical advances.

Isola Tiberina suggests the shape of a ship in the middle of the Tiber river

Two bridges connect the island: **Ponte Fabricio** (photo below) and **Ponte Cestio**. Reach Isola Tiberina by way of Ponte Fabricio, which dates from 62 BC, the oldest completely original bridge still intact and operational. Isola Tiberina is not a natural island. It did not exist in antiquity and there is evidence that it was formed originally by the accumulation of ballast from ships anchored at the nearby port. Later, just below the level of the water of the river, solid rock has been found on which Isola Tiberina was built.

The island has been associated with healing and religion from the earliest times. Here in the third century a temple in honor of Aesculapius, the god of medicine, was erected. On the same site the church of San Bartolomeo was later built. Since 1538 the northern section was the site of the hospital Fatebenefratelli (do-good-brothers), still operating today. The shape of the island suggests a ship and, during the centuries, blocks of travertine were used in the prow and stern to accentuate this figure. A tall obelisk (later removed) was erected in the center to suggest a mast, while the two bridges suggested moorings.

The southern part of the island is occupied by the church of San Bartolomeo, which dates from the tenth century. The tower is from the twelfth, while the façade is of the Baroque style. You come off the island using Ponte Cestio, on the right bank of the river, thought to have been built in 46 BC but completely reconstructed in 1892.

In the summer, there is a lot of activity on the island, including an open-air cinema and exhibits.

> *Once you have passed over the island, you will find the medieval Trastevere quarter with several unusual piazzas and picturesque alleys mixed with restaurants, trattorias and attractive shops. Another option is to go toward the Jewish quarter where you may find a variety of good restaurants. (The synagogue is only a few hundred yards along the Tiber, See Walk 7).*

> *From Isola Tiberina, exit using Ponte Cestio, cross Lungotevere and continue straight. In a few steps you will reach Piazza in Piscinula situated in the "quiet part" of Trastevere.*

10 Trastevere. (Pronounced "tras TEH veh ray"). Centuries of tearing down and reconstruction of buildings has generated the fascinating variety evidenced in this section of the neighborhood at the bend of the Tiber. This diversity is expressed in the different heights and ages of the houses and angles of the roofs, in the varied sizes of the entrances, stories and

windows, balconies and attics, in the sudden appearance of irregular little piazzas or a curve or narrowing of streets and numerous other details. **Viale Trastevere** divides the quarter in two distinct areas. The **southern part** is delimited by the bend in the Tiber and goes as far as Porta Portese where it connects by way of Ponte Sublicio to the Testaccio neighborhood described at the beginning of this walk. A labyrinth of small streets and buildings from the medieval period characterizes this area, which has a low population density. The rustic atmosphere and the silence that recall an earlier era are accentuated by the presence of numerous religious buildings. This area is typified by the zone around the church of Santa Cecilia and the small street, Vicolo dell'Atleta.

The **northern part** above Viale Trastevere extends from the base of the Janiculum hill (Gianicolo) to the Tiber and as far, by way of Via della Lungara, as the area around Borgo Santo Spirito where it connects with Walk 5, the Vatican. This area has numerous fascinating streets, most of the population resides here, and it is rarely quiet. For many decades it has attracted Italians and foreigners and it is dotted with many restaurants, eateries and tourist shops. Several of its streets have a quaint medieval tone. The differences in the two parts of Trastevere, the quiet south and the bustling north, are undoubtedly diminishing, but it is still possible to perceive them.

Trastevere means "on the other side of the Tiber" and in antiquity for many years it was not considered a part of Rome proper. In fact, the seven hills, where Rome originally was formed and spread out, are all on the other side of the river. The slopes of the nearby Janiculum hill have held dwellings since

ancient times. In this area the legendary Cincinnatus had his farm in the fifth century BC. The lower and flatter part near the river, however, with the nearby port, was not the best. It housed many apartments and cheap inns where malaria raged as a result of the frequent flooding of the river. On the banks of the quarter a river port was built, which easily connected with the large seaport of Ostia at only about 13 miles away, where sailors could embark for the farthest reaches of the empire.

A typical restaurant with outside tables in Via del Moro

The area was a magnet for new immigrants due to the business opportunities connected with the harbor. The population was often transitory and crime and prostitution quite high. In particular, here in the Republican period the oldest Jewish community in Europe was settled, and the first Christians as well, as the presence of numerous early Christian basilicas confirm.

The three churches of **Santa Maria in Trastevere**, **San Crisogono** and **Santa Cecilia** are of ancient origin. After the fall of the Roman Empire and the chaos of the barbarian invasions, the city, which at its height had reached a million persons, gradually emptied out, until it counted only a few thousand people during the Middle Ages. Trastevere followed this trend, the slopes of the Janiculum hill were deserted and the sparse population gathered along the river and around the three principal churches. The rebirth began in the eleventh and thirteenth centuries when the churches of Santa Maria and San Crisogono were reconstructed.

The Cistern Fountain

In the fifteenth and sixteenth centuries, the quarter was extended with new streets and buildings and finally even water was brought again, after having been cut in the 6th century by the Goths. The problem of the river flooding was finally resolved in the nineteenth century after the unification of Italy with the construction of the embankments.

53

Trastevere today is changed dramatically from the 50's and 60's. The original genuine and picturesque atmosphere has almost disappeared. The spontaneous character of the locals, who poured out onto the streets and restaurants in a noisy invasive way, shown in unforgettable scenes of films by Federico Fellini, has changed. Now it is impossible to find a Trastevere resident who boasts that he has never set foot in Rome. A new Trastevere has become more modern and cosmopolitan with the influx of newly arrived Italians and foreigners, with the shops and art galleries, and avant-garde shows.

Every year since 1535 the quarter celebrates the "Festa di noantri" or the festival of "us others," the word accentuating the distinction with "you others," inhabitants of other neighborhoods. The festival at the end of July includes concerts, sports competitions, other attractions, innumerable booths selling food, drinks and souvenirs and fireworks displays.

One of the best things for the tourist to do is to leisurely explore the streets and alleys, often without sidewalks, bask in the picturesque houses, the sudden narrowing of the road, the original windows, the mysterious arches, the attics, the stupendous balconies and terraces that, in summer, frequently overflow with flowers and plants.

Containing the Plague
One of the worst episodes in Trastevere's history happened with the arrival of the plague in June 1656. The epidemic was noted for the first time in an inn on Via Monte del Fiore. The authorities, in the night between the 23rd and the 24th of June isolated the neighborhood, at first with wooden gates and armed guards and later with walls. The windows of the houses that faced out were walled up. Isola Tiberina was transformed into a quarantined hospital and the plague continued for two years until 1658.

*Here, in Piazza in Piscinula 47, <u>Il Comparone</u> has a restaurant, a **pizzeria** and a bar with **ice cream** and outside tables that occupy much of the piazza. The restaurant <u>La Gensola</u> is in Piazza della Gensola, next to Piazza in Piscinula. The less expensive restaurant and **pizzeria** <u>Il Ponentino</u> is at Piazza del Drago 10.*

From Piazza in Piscinula take Via Titta Scarpetta, then turn left and immediately right on Vicolo dell'Atleta.

Vicolo dell'Atleta is the most picturesque in the neighborhood. Even if very short, the street widens and narrows, climbs and descends. At number 14 you are surprised by an unusual building from the thirteenth century, now a private residence, having an arched balcony. There is an inscription in Hebrew on the central column. It was a synagogue and reminds us that Jews were among the first inhabitants of the area and they have maintained a community here since republican times, that is to say, for more than 2000 years. On this street in 1849 the statue *Apoxymenos*, of an athlete cleaning himself, was found, thus giving the name to the street. It is now in the Vatican Museums.

At the end of Vicolo dell'Atleta turn left on Via dei Genovesi and then right on Via di Santa Cecilia. The street opens up at Piazza Santa Cecilia in front of the church.

For a quick bite, try the trattoria <u>Da Enzo al 29</u> at Via dei Vascellari 29. Via dei Vascellari is parallel to Vicolo dell'Atleta.

11 The Church of Santa Cecilia.

Originally built under Pope Pasquale I (817-24), the church displays small and large works of diverse styles and from almost every century. Notable are the quiet courtyard and the beautiful **medieval portico** from the twelfth century with columns from the Roman period and a rare mosaic frieze. The façade from 1741 is by Ferdinando Fuga. The Romanesque bell tower, one of the earliest, dates from 1113.

The church of Santa Cecilia, patron saint of music

The inside restoration in Baroque style was done in the eighteenth and nineteenth centuries. Above the central altar looms the magnificent **Gothic baldacchino** by Arnolfo di Cambio from 1293.

The tormented marble **statue of the saint** under the altar was sculpted by Stefano Maderno in 1614. The artist was able to see the amazingly well preserved remains of the saint when her tomb was briefly opened in 1599. According to legend, Cecilia and her husband Valerian were an affluent couple in ancient Rome, and were both prosecuted because they continued to preach Christianity even though the law prohibited it. Cecilia was condemned to die closed in her *calidarium*, that is the steam bath of her residence, a sentence

reserved for noblewomen. In spite of that, they say that she was able to survive for 3 days, singing in a beautiful voice, forcing her guards to finally deliver a mortal blow. She was repeatedly stabbed in the throat; for this, the saint became the patron saint of music.

Behind the apse a **mosaic** from the ninth century shows Cecilia and her husband Valerian together with Jesus. Paintings by Guido Reni adorn the calidarium complex where Cecilia was believed to be martyred and the Baroque Chapel of the Relics, under the church, by Valvitelli is from the seventeenth century.

The **Accademia Nazionale di Santa Cecilia** is one of the oldest musical institutions in the world. Officially founded in 1585, it has evolved over the centuries from an organization of largely "local" musicians to a modern academy and symphonic concert organization of international repute. Their large music complex in the northern part of Rome, offers a robust season of concerts.

> *Go back on Via di Santa Cecilia, turn left on Via Dei Genovesi and right on Via Anicia that becomes Via dell'Arco dei Tolomei. Go under the arch and turn left on Via della Lungaretta.*

Via della Lungaretta extends for about 700 yards and crosses the two areas of the quarter.

> *Take Via della Lungaretta and, after Piazza Sonnino, crossed by Viale Trastevere, begins the northern part of the neighborhood.*

La Fonte della Salute, *Via Cardinale Marmaggi 4, has **organic ice cream**, with tables outside.* Supplì, *Via di San Francesco a Ripa has very good **pizza by the slice and supplì**, rice balls. Also at Piazza Sonnino is a **Tourist Information Point.***

On Piazza Sonnino a medieval building stands out: the **Torre degli Anguillara**, also called the house of Dante since it now promotes the study of this poet. The fortress is from the twelfth century. It is easily distinguished by the picturesque crenellated tower and it used to include both houses and stalls. Close by is the medieval church of San Crisogono.

The **Church of San Crisogono**, Piazza Sidney Sonnino 44, (photo below) founded in the fifth century, was enlarged in the basilica format in the eighth and twelfth centuries and restructured in the seventeenth. The portico is from 1125 and the Romanesque bell tower from 1120. The ceiling is covered with painted incised wood coffers called "*lacunari*," and the multicolored marble flooring from the thirteenth century is one of the most beautiful in Rome of the "cosmatesque" style. Twenty-two ancient columns support the straight architrave. These same characteristics are in Santa Maria in Trastevere.

Of particular interest is the Chapel of the Santissimo Sacramento (Holiest Sacrament) by Bernini from 1641, to the right of the apse. The master of Baroque, in this case, was able to harmonize his work with the medieval tone of the church, creating one of his less exuberant creations. The early Christian basilica with traces of frescoes from the 8th and 11th centuries can be visited under the current church.

Continue on Via della Lungaretta to Piazza Santa Maria in Trastevere.

12 Piazza Santa Maria in Trastevere with its basilica is a lively and

attractive area. The basilica **Santa Maria in Trastevere** is probably the first official Christian church in the city. Emperor Alexander Severus (222 – 235) ceded the land to a group of Christians who then built a chapel. In 337 this was replaced by a church dedicated to Saint Calixtus who was martyred nearby. Later, around 1140, it was reconstructed as a basilica, the first church in Rome dedicated to the Madonna. During the years, five popes were buried here.

The Romanesque bell tower was added in 1143 and the portico, with 4 statues of popes, in 1702 by Carlo Fontana. Even though it has been heavily restored, the exterior, with its beautiful mosaics from the thirteenth century, is typical of the ornamentation of medieval Roman churches.

The façade mosaic features the Madonna and Child attended by seven women holding lamps. The small figures at Mary's feet represent the donors who paid for the mosaic. Most of the other medieval churches have been modified by the architects of the Baroque period, so that much of this uniquely medieval style of decoration has been lost.

Inside, the magnificent **gilded mosaics** that decorate the apse are from the twelfth century and depict Jesus and Mary surrounded by saints and proph-ets. On the left, Pope Innocent II, the donor, holds a model of the church. Below, the typical procession of sheep is symbolic of the twelve apostles.

Six 13th century mosaics that trace the life of the Virgin, flanking the windows, are by Pietro Cavallini. Along the nave 22 ancient columns of different dimensions, types of stone and colors came from various ruins, including the Baths of Caracalla. Domenichino created a ceiling of deep gilded coffers in 1617. As is common in many medieval churches there is a beautiful **marble floor** by the famous Cosmati family from the twelfth century. The good state of conservation is due to a restoration done in the 1800's.

On coming out of the church, go back a few steps on Via della Lungaretta. On the right is the picturesque Via di San Calisto. Turn left onto Via del Moro.

Il Forno, *Via del Moro 15, offers* **pizza** *by the slice, bread and sweet goods.* Pasticceria Valzani, *Via del Moro 37, at Via della Pellicia, is an old traditional* **pastry shop**. The Almost Corner Bookshop, *Via del Moro 45 at Via de' Rienzi is an* **English bookstore**. *At number 59 is* Polvere del Tempo, *a store with* **original items** *such as sundials, candles, hourglasses and leather covered books.* Officina della Carta, *Via Benedetta 26b, has traditional Italian* **paper** *and* **leather** *products.* Birreria Trilussa, *Via Benedetta 18, offers beer and* **pizza**. Hosteria del Moro, *Vicolo del Cinque 36, is a good* **trattoria** *with attentive and quick service.*

Continue on Via del Moro, go left on Vicolo del Cinque, then right on Via della Scala. Turn right on Via S. Dorotea and bear right to take Via Benedetta that takes you to Piazza Trilussa, where a statue of the Roman dialect poet Trilussa has been erected. Cross the piazza, cross Lungotevere, go to the edge and look over.

From here you have a good view of the river, the nearby **Ponte Sisto** and further away to the left Ponte Mazzini, and to the right Ponte Garibaldi. Ponte Sisto was built in 1475 by Pope Sixtus IV called the "papa tosto" or hard-headed pope by the Romans. The occasion was the Jubilee and the bridge was financed in part by taxes levied on courtesans, a business booming in Renaissance Rome. The rationale was to facilitate moving pilgrims from the left bank where most of the city was, including the seven hills, to the Vatican on the right bank.

An inscription at the end of the bridge toward the city reads: "You who pass here thanks to Sixtus IV, pray God that he will live long and enjoy the best of health." It continues that he had it redone "at his own expense and attention" and wished it to be renamed after him – the Sisto Bridge

Observe the "spurs" which facilitate the flow of water and also protect the pylons of the bridge. This area of the city, at only a few yards above sea level, is among the lowest in Rome and thus it was subject to periodic flooding. The circular hole in the highest central part of the bridge was used as an alarm signal for the population, advising them that the river had reached a dangerously high level.

> **Street Names**
> Via dei Genovesi was named for a group of sailors from the city of Genoa who settled in this area near the river port. Some of the names derive from the type of merchants or local artisan. For example, Via Scarpetta (scarpa = shoe), Via della Botticella (botticella = keg). Via in Piscinula (piscina = pool) comes from the presence of ancient baths in the area.

The entire walk from the Piramide to Isola Tiberina and the streets of Trastevere is about 4 miles (6.5 km.), including the loop to the Terme di Caracalla. If time is short, we recommend you not miss: **Piramide** and **Porta San Paolo**, **Terme di Caracalla**, the area around **Piazza Bocca della Verità** and **Via della Lungaretta**.

Walk Two - Ancient Origins

Additional Restaurants

Checchino dal 1887, Via di Monte Testaccio 30, http://www.checchino-dal-1887.com/ Only traditional Roman cuisine with one of the best wine lists in Rome. Between Via Nicola Zabaglia and Viale Campo Boario. €€€

Charro Café, Via di Monte Testaccio 73, 5783064. http://www.charrocafe.it/, Mexican cuisine. Six picturesque rooms dug into Monte Testaccio, "mountain of rubble," created by the accumulation over centuries of broken pots. €€

Da Bucatino, Via Luca della Robbia 84-86. http://www.dabucatino.it/. Typical Roman cooking, *coda alla vaccinara* (Ox tail), *bucatini all'amatriciana* (with spicy tomato sauce). €€

Enoteca Palombi - Oasi della Birra, Piazza Testaccio 38-41. Beers from all over the world and fine wines. Various types of *piadine* (white pizza with toppings of cheese or meats) and snacks. €€

Perilli, Via Marmorata 39. http://www.trattoria-romana.it/da/perilli/ Roman cooking. In continuous operation since 1911. Large portions in a lively atmosphere. €€€

Restaurants in Trastevere

Taberna Piscinula, Piazza in Piscinula 50, 5812525.
Creative pizzas with ingredients including chocolate or zucchini blossoms. €

La Gensola, Piazza della Gensola 15, http://www.osterialagensola.it/. 5816312. Sicilian style trattoria. Pasta with a variety of seafood, rolled meat dishes, fried seafood platter. €€€

La Fonte della Salute, Via Cardinale Marmaggi 4. Organic ice cream and frozen yogurt. €

Rome's Origins

The Italian peninsula was inhabited in prehistoric times by people living by hunting, fishing and gathering, clustered near lakes and rivers. The first villages were built toward the end of the Paleolithic period, about 10,000 BC. Successive waves of immigrants starting at least around 3000 BC pushed their way into Italy, first unsettling and then mingling with the original population that often still lived in caves. They came from southern Russia, North Africa via Spain, and central Europe.

Some of the new arrivals were quite advanced, preferred to live in open huts built on pilings, cultivated the ground, raised animals and wove cloth, but they especially knew how to work iron. Around the 9th to the 8th century BC other populations established themselves in Italy. The Gauls settled the Padana plains, then the Greeks and the Phoenicians established colonies in the south.

Models of early huts

The geographic location

Rome is situated in the fertile western part of the Latium valley, 15 miles from the sea where the Tiber snakes in a big bend. Here in ancient times, the curve provided an ideal place for landing ships. The area near the Isola Tiberina was also the first practical place to cross the Tiber River. The hills near the left bank, the Capitoline, the Palatine and the Aventine, are rather steep, easily defensible, and allow observation of potential enemy movement below. Furthermore, the river was an important route to bring precious salt, easily found in salt beds near the river delta, from the coast to the interior. In the ancient world salt was very valuable; sometimes soldiers were paid in salt (salary).

Eventually Rome became the biggest river port in Italy, where Etruscans from the north and Greeks and Phoenicians from the south traded goods among themselves and with the populations of central Italy. City-states flourished all over the Mediterranean basin between 1000 and 600 BC, and Rome followed the same trend. They were characterized by a small territory, limited population, a market, public places for worship and entertainment and, above all, fierce inde-

pendence. The typical city-state included an urban center, often protected by walls, and the immediate countryside. From a few acres on the Palatine Hill, it took Rome about 3 centuries to extend its territory to include Veio in 396 BC just 12 miles north of the city. The photo shows excavations on the Palatine which demonstrate early occupation.

City-states could have the most diverse forms of government, from tyranny to democracy to communism, where the citizens participated accordingly. Rome started as a kingdom and then evolved into a republic for about 5 centuries before becoming an empire for another 5 centuries. Ideally located at the intersection between culturally different populations, and on the natural salt route between the sea and the interior and as a river port, Rome grew with commerce to become a powerful city.

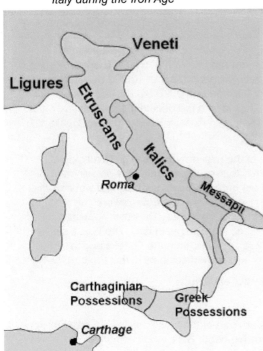

Veneti

Ligures

Etruscans

Italics

Roma

Messapii

Carthaginian Possessions

Greek Possessions

Carthage

Recent archeological excavations.

Archaeological coring drills down deep below the surface to bring up a cylindrical core of earth. This method allows examination of the geological layers with minimal disturbance of the terrain. It has been used in the area of the Roman Forum in 1985 by Albert J. Ammerman, an environmental archaeologist.

It was commonly believed that, to make room for the Forum, the buildings occupying the area were razed to the ground. The study of the underlying soil, however, has permitted the formation of a new explanation of the origins of the Forum.

It has been established that, in the pre-republican seventh century BC, in the valley between the Capitoline and Palatine hills called the Velabrum, and part of the area that later would become the Roman Forum, an enormous project was undertaken. The valley, which at some points was only about 23 feet above sea level, was filled in with earth and raised by about 6 feet. We now know that the terrain, although dry most of the time, was subject to periodic floods from the Tiber. By raising the level, the Romans were able to reclaim this centrally located area for the growth of the town. Here, in fact, the first forum was later built.

Ammerman, with his excavations, proposes also a series of specific observations. The surrounding area must have already had a fairly high density of population. A project so massive shows a remarkable level of cohesion of the inhabitants even as early as the seventh

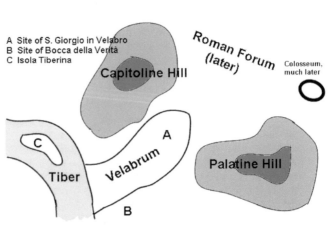

A Site of S. Giorgio in Velabro
B Site of Bocca della Verità
C Isola Tiberina

Capitoline Hill

Roman Forum (later)

Colosseum, much later

A

C

Tiber

Velabrum

B

Palatine Hill

century BC. Since slavery was not yet practiced, the work must have been performed by the citizens themselves, required to participate in public service. That also implies long-term planning. In fact, it required years to complete, the availability of ample manpower and a substantial organization directed toward the public good.

WALK THREE - Imperial Rome
From the Colosseum to the Forum

In this area, between the Capitoline and the Palatine hills, later the site of the **Forum**, the first inhabitants, shepherds and peasants, met to exchange goods and ideas. The growth of the military and political power of Rome gradually transformed the area into an important commercial, administrative and religious center. The basilicas, temples and houses, early on of wood and brick, were during the centuries enlarged and rebuilt mostly in marble. Crossing the Forum, the **Via Sacra** was the route taken during triumphal ceremonies by victorious generals and emperors. The **Miglio Aureo** (golden milestone), a gilded column, showed the distances from Rome to major cities; the **Senate**, reconstructed by Julius Caesar, was later transformed into a church. The Vestal Virgins kept Rome's eternal flame in the **Tempio di Vesta**. During the walk through the Forum we can appreciate how, in the fields of politics and architecture, Rome left an exceptional contribution to the development of the West.

The **Palatine Hill**, the best location in town and site of the imperial palaces, was the center of power and from here for centuries the destinies of tens of millions of people were decided. Two dissimilar and enormous buildings were erected by two emperors, Nero and Vespasian, for substantially the same motives: legitimization of power and self promotion. On the ashes of the apartments destroyed by the tremendous fire of 64 AD, Nero built the **Domus Aurea**, a sumptuous complex which occupied many acres in the center of the city. Vespasian, only a few years later, conceived the construction of the **Colosseo** (the Colosseum), the largest amphitheater of the ancient world, where the Roman populace was entertained by violent spectacles of executions of criminals, killing of wild beasts and gladiatorial contests. The **Basilica of San Clemente**, a fascinating example of a medieval church, has, in its mysterious lower reaches, constructions from various periods on several levels, including an ancient temple to Mithras. The basilica is a symbol of Rome itself, with a continuous architectural presence during the centuries, from the ancient structures to the medieval period, the Renaissance, the Baroque, and the modern. **61**

In this walk:
1 The patchwork surface of the **Arch of Constantine**
2 The **Colosseo** (Colosseum), the largest amphitheater of the ancient world
3 The **Basilica of San Clemente**, with architectonic layers spanning 2000+ years
4 **Domus Aurea**, the apex of opulence and extravagance of the emperor Nero
5 The **Roman Forum**, the economic, political and religious heart of the city. The structure of the Roman republic, centered on the **Senate**, inspired the American founding fathers.
6 The **Palatine hill,** site of sumptuous imperial palaces

At the exit for the Colosseo metro stop you will see the Colosseum in front of you, the Arch of Constantine to the right and some ruins connected to the Roman Forum more to the right. Head toward the Arch.

Map for Walk Three

1 Arco di Costantino (Arch of Constantine). (M Colosseo)

In this area the Via Sacra (Sacred Road) began, extending to the Campidoglio (Capitoline hill). The arch was built in honor of Constantine after his victory over Maxentius in 312 AD. Believing that his success was due to the Christian God, Constantine stopped the persecution against the Christians and the following year, with his Edict of Milan legalizing Christianity, he allowed them to practice their religion openly. He also had the first church of Saint Peter's built, moved the capital to Byzantium, now Turkey, and called it Constantinople, today Istanbul. Together with the Arch of Titus and the Arch of Septimius Severus, both in the Forum, this is one of the few remaining triumphal arches. It has survived in part because it had been incorporated into the fortress that the Frangipane family built here in the Middle Ages. These arches were part of a long tradition with which the Senate honored victorious generals and emperors. To lighten the weight on the arches, the upper part of the monument is hollow, divided into four rooms, but it is closed to the public. While at first glance it seems to be dedicated entirely to the emperor, a more careful examination reveals otherwise.

The eight round sections were taken from an arch dedicated to Hadrian. The eight statues at the top represent Dacian prisoners and were in Trajan's Forum, as were the panels on the interior of the central arch. The eight rectangular panels high up came from an arch in honor of Marcus Aurelius, and depict in bas-relief the emperor in various scenes from his life. In this architectonic patchwork, however, there is a unifying triumphal theme, and, had these pieces not been used on the Arch of Constantine, they would have been lost to us.

Artistic Recycling
In addition to the problem of imperial succession, the continuous civil wars and the pressure of the barbarians at the borders, in this period the new Christian values shook the Roman society to the core. These stresses in political and moral fields, which led later to the fall of the empire, were felt also in the field of art. To genuine inspiration of the preceding centuries, the expedient was substituted, and the ideal gradually gave way to the superficial and ritualistic. So we see the phenomenon that in the fourth century will become the norm: the removal of parts of old monuments to make new ones.

Figure of one of the Dacian prisoners

To visit the Colosseum, buy a combo ticket online or at one of the less crowded sites such as the Forum or the Palatine. Ordering tickets ahead will allow you to bypass the lines. Check online for "Colosseum tickets" and the opening times.

2   The Colosseo (Colosseum) (M Colosseo).

While you go around, you will notice that the façade on the north side is in better condition than the more deteriorated south. The largest of all the hundreds of similar stadiums built all over the empire, it is also called the Flavian amphitheater after the Emperor Vespasian of the Flavian family, who began the construction. A capable general, he was catapulted into power after the misgovernance of Nero during a period of instability that produced several emperors, all quickly replaced. Even though Vespasian tried to speed up the construction, he was not able to see it finished. His son Emperor Titus inaugurated it on the 21st of April in the year 80 AD.

The Colosseum
In the eighth century, the English monk, the Venerable Bede, wrote:

As long as the Colosseum stands, Rome shall stand. When the Colosseum falls, Rome shall fall. When Rome falls, the world shall end.

63

On the upper level there is a museum with scenes of Rome before and during the construction of Via dei Fori Imperiali. They are supplemented by statues, photographs and a bookshop.

Exterior structure

Called "the Magic Circle" by Lord Byron, it could hold up to 70,000 spectators who, by means of 80 wide exits and a series of well planned corridors and stairways, could empty out in 12 minutes. It has represented the standard for sports arenas constructed all over the world.

The elliptical façade is decorated with the three orders of Greek capitals. The columns on the first level are Doric, on the second, Ionic and on the third, Corinthian. Each of the arches on the façade contained a bronze statue representing a hero or god.

The original exterior and ornamental parts, mostly marble, are nearly completely gone; however, you can easily see the base structure of the complex. Eighty bearing walls, built on pilasters of travertine, extended and rose gradually from the arena, like the spokes of a hub, to the façade anchoring the external oval structure. These **radial walls** permitted the existence of vaulted corridors on the lower levels. At the same time they supported the **benches** where the spectators sat and vaults and corridors on the upper levels. Constructed with differing materials, they were gradually lighter the higher they went. On the outside part, you can still see the crossed vaults, between the massive pillars, which support the structure above.

Vital statistics

The axes of the ellipse are 512 and 608 feet; the circumference is 1730 feet and it is 159 feet high. For its construction were used more than 100,000 cubic yards of material, among which half a million tons of travertine and 150,000 tons of the best marble. Extensively used were tuff, a type of more porous travertine, brick and concrete. The travertine blocks were held together with iron bars and lead poured to seal them. 300 tons of metals were used to join these blocks. The many holes on the walls visible today (see picture) are due to their later plundering for these metals.

In these corridors you see the holes where the iron bars which joined the blocks of travertine were removed ages ago. Today the entire structure, apparently solid, is instead extremely delicate. Gravity and the good original design are what keep it standing. The vibrations of the nearby subway, the traffic and pollution are continuous assaults on its stability.

The Invention of Concrete

One of the major inventions in construction was concrete, which used cement, rock fragments and sand. The addition of pozzolana, a reddish volcanic powder increased its strength and durability. Concrete literally revolutionized architecture, making possible the construction of ample vaults abundantly used in the large Roman buildings such as palaces, amphitheaters, baths and most notably in the dome of the Pantheon. The formula for concrete was lost with the fall of the empire and was rediscovered only with the advent of the Renaissance, about a thousand years later. The pinkish cast that you sometimes see in the ruins is attributable to the pozzolana. The combination of bricks and concrete is a method that has defied time. The bricks were placed on the outside and the rock and concrete on the inside. This technique was used in the Colosseo and in many other monuments.

Entrance number 53. Do you have your ticket?

Travertine

Travertine, a type of marble capable of withstanding enormous pressure, is still prevalent in the quarries of Tivoli, a town about 20 miles from the city. Each day, during the construction, 200 carts of material pulled by oxen arrived at the site.

Homegrown sacking?

It was commonly thought that the disappearance of monuments of the city was due to barbarian invasions and then to the sack by the Saracens, Normans and Lanzichenecchi mercenaries. Instead, the Romans were the main culprits. Prized construction materials, unused, at the foot of the ruined monument, gave rise to the systematic plundering of the Colosseo, which lasted for centuries. With these materials the palaces, churches and bridges of Rome were built.

An original **retractable roof** called the *velarium*, could protect spectators from the sun. Coordinated by hundreds of sailors, the roof extended from the outside walls toward the center, covering the spectators like a giant donut and leaving the arena open to the sky.

Today we only see about a third of the volume of the monument. It has resisted the weather, earthquakes and being denuded and sacked for two thousand years. Especially earthquakes, at least one every hundred years, have repeatedly shaken it and made parts to fall.

Substructure

In the early years, after flooding the arena, mock naval battles were also held. They were fought to the last, and to add to the suspense, crocodiles were released into this temporary artificial lake. The eruption of Vesuvius in 79 AD that destroyed Pompeii and Herculaneum was recreated, with a reproduction of the volcano with fire and ash emerging from the center of the arena, astonishing the spectators. While the games grew ever more sophisticated, it was decided to dig below the arena to increase the space for services. They reached three **underground levels** and several tunnels connected the underground rooms with surrounding auxiliary buildings. Underneath, numerous stalls for animals were created and a myriad of corridors and "elevators" to move them. Winches, operated by hand, raised and lowered lifts where **beasts** were enclosed. Important people, then as today, enjoyed special treatment. By means of underground passages, they could reach the tribunes, undisturbed by the crowds.

65

The original wood floor has been destroyed, so part of the extensive labyrinth of rooms and passages that constituted the service areas are easily visible. The Colosseo represented a masterpiece of engineering for its functionality, solidity of construction, the rapidity with which it was built and the complexity of the operations necessary for its functioning.

The games

Seats were assigned on the basis of social class. The closest tribunes were in marble and reserved for the emperor, magistrates and senators. All the other seats were made of brick to accommodate the rich classes and the military, next the upper classes, the common people and finally in the seats farthest back, the slaves and women. The spectacles were free and open to all, but required a ticket. The number on the ticket indicated which of 76 entrances to use. (The other four were reserved for the upper classes.)

A typical day began with the **killing of beasts** in the morning and executions of criminals during lunchtime. The **gladiators**, fighting each other or wild beasts, constituted the main event in the afternoon. As soon as they entered the arena they approached the imperial tribunes announcing, "Hail Caesar, we who are about to die salute you." What fascinated the crowd were differently armed gladiators with different skills but evenly matched. So you could see the *retiarii,* wearing only a loincloth and armed with a net (later a lasso) and a trident, facing a heavily armored opponent. They were normally chosen from prisoners of war, slaves and condemned criminals, but anyone could join in and we know that even some emperors participated. Commodus, (180-193 AD), son of the great Marcus Aurelius, took part in hundreds of staged fights. Four schools existed to prepare gladiators, situated between the Colosseo and the current church of San Clemente, guaranteeing a continuous supply of combatants.

By means of **tunnels**, the gladiators appeared directly in the center of the arena and therefore had no opportunity to escape. Those who won repeatedly were normally given freedom; however, incredibly, some chose to return to fight.

An ancient mosaic, now in the Colosseum

The first games

The inauguration of the games, April 21, in the year 80 lasted 100 days during which 9000 animals and two thousand men were killed. The animals included not only lions and tigers but also rhinoceros, bears, hippopotamus, elephants, hyenas and crocodiles, that is, every kind of exotic beast. This led to the creation of an enormous commerce in these animals to the point of the extinction of some species.

Thumbs up ... or not

The position of the thumb was used by the emperor and the crowd to spare the life of the victors or condemn them to die. We do not have documentation on the exact position; however, the "thumbs up" gesture, reenacted by Hollywood, is still used today all over the world as a sign of approval.

Action

Up to 28 lifts, operated by more than 200 men, could raise the beasts directly into the center of the ring. Trap doors let the animals leap into the action, rendering the crowd speechless. Recently a team producing a documentary recreated one of the lifts using ancient texts as guides. After carrying it into the Colosseum, they tested it, releasing a wolf into the ring, where he was presented with a treat instead of a battle.

Scholars have calculated that about 700,000 people were killed in the Colosseo. Often they were crucified, burned alive or fed to the wild beasts. To incite the sometimes-timid animals, blood was painted onto the bodies of the condemned. Sometimes people were forced to take part in a tragedy and, unlike actors who are only reciting a part in a theater, in the Colosseo were actually killed.

The 80 radiating walls that rise from the arena and support the outer ellipse

New Vegetation
During the centuries of abandonment of the Colosseo, numerous exotic plants and flowers, not native to the Mediterranean climate, were noticed. The most plausible explanation is that seeds were introduced to the area by spectators who came from various corners of the empire. Another possibility is that the seeds were hidden in the fur of the animals and then blown by the wind.

Remains of the ancient tribunes

Origin and evolution of the games
Gladiatorial combat is thought to have derived from the population that, before the Romans, inhabited the region of northern Latium and Tuscany, the Etruscans. There is actual documentation for this practice in the Campania region south of Rome. The Etruscans, to honor the dead, sometimes held a fight to the death during a funeral. This practice was copied by the Romans and used initially on occasions when a famous person had died. The first gladiatorial combat was offered in Rome in 264 BC. Here these staged fights to the death assumed political motivations. During the republican period, famous and rich people who wanted to run for high political offices began to sponsor gladiatorial spectacles, in order to increase their popularity. Until the time of Augustus (27 BC – 14 AD), gladiatorial games were held in the Roman Forum near the Comitium, with people sitting on temporary bleachers.

With the political progression from the republic to the empire, an unspoken agreement arose between the people of Rome and the emperor. The people gave up the right to vote, given that they had concluded that politicians were pretty much all the same, and the emperor for his part gave the people free entertainments and food for the needy: "**bread and circuses**."

Symbolically the Colosseo represented the dominion of Rome over the world in all its strength and brutality. However, the games also meant a continual exercise in public relations for the emperor and the ruling class who sat in the tribunes, the best seats. Everyone knew that the free games were due to the munificence of the emperor; they reminded the people who held the real power of life and death. For an emperor, however, to second the desires of the crowd when deciding the fate of the combatants was considered good public relations.

During the centuries, the Colosseo was claimed by important Roman families such as the Frangipane or Annibaldi and periodically abandoned. By walling up the arches, a practically impenetrable fort could be created. You can still see some arches left in this condition.

For a long time it was a hideout for thieves and prostitutes. Pope Sixtus V (1585-90) seriously thought of knocking it down; however, the period of reconstruction began with Pius IX. In 1870 the vegetation that had covered it for more than a thousand years was removed. A large cross was erected in the arena by Clement X to remember the martyr of the early Christians. Pope John XXIII brought back the ceremony of the Way of the Cross (Via Crucis) undertaken each Good Friday, which is transmitted all over the world. During the past few years the Colosseum has become the symbol against the death penalty for some Roman organizations. Italy, together with the other countries in the European Union, abolished the death penalty many years ago. Try to walk by in the evening also, because of the striking effects of the lighting.

End of the games
The Romans were so conditioned to the staged violence of the Colosseum that they continued to expect it. Only the lack of funds, which accompanied the disintegration of the empire and the opposition of the invading "barbarians" who had occupied Rome in the meantime, finally stopped them.

After the Roman elite was converted to Christianity, gladiatorial combat, prohibited by emperor Honorius in 404. Spectacles in the Colosseum, reduced to contests among beasts, continued until 523.

When exiting, go uphill to the upper part of Piazza del Colosseo. Cross the street and take Via di San Giovanni in Laterano as far as Via dei Querceti. The Basilica of San Clemente is on the left.

Gutenberg al Colosseo, *Via San Giovanni in Laterano 110 is an* **antiquarian bookshop.** *This street begins from the eastern part of Piazza del Colosseo.* Arte Colosseo *offers* **prints**, **old paintings and contemporary fine art** *at Via San Giovanni in Laterano 88, after Via Ostilia. For a* **pizza**, Trattoria Pizzeria Luzzi *is at Via di San Giovanni 88 at Via Normanni. From the tables outside the restaurant* Pasqualino *at Via dei Santissimi Quattro 66, you can see the Colosseo.* **Lunch and dinner** *at moderate prices.* Naumachia **trattoria** *is at Via Celimontana 7.*

3 The Basilica of San Clemente,

http://basilicasanclemente.com/eng, is named for the fourth pope, who died around the year 100 during the reign of Trajan. Clement was exiled to Crimea where he continued to convert people to Christianity, and for this, according to legend, was weighed down with an anchor and thrown into the sea.

This church is a time machine of the city **across the centuries**. Constructions from the first, third, fourth centuries, Middle Ages and then additions in the eighteenth century are overlaid on four levels. **Three churches** were successively built on this spot. After the fourth century church was sacked by the Normans in 1084, it was reconstructed at the beginning of the twelfth century. The main structure that we see today of the Basilica is from this period, but the atrium, the portico and the façade were added in the eighteenth century. The unusual mosaic in the apse with circular motifs is also from the twelfth century. The **Schola Cantorum** (choir) in the center of the Basilica was brought here from the old church underneath. On the columns you can see fish, doves and grape vines, which in the early years of Christianity symbolized Christ, peace and the Eucharist. On the left wall looking toward the altar there are writings that are believed to be among the first in Italian.

The apse with the gilded mosaic. Traditional sheep figures represent the apostles.

As in many medieval basilicas, including Santa Maria in Trastevere, the ceiling is decorated with deep gilded coffers and the **floor** is of the cosmatesque type, a patch-work of colored marble. Toward the middle of the nineteenth century excavations were begun that brought to light the remains of the fourth century church below

The Schola Cantorum (choir)

After getting a ticket, go down and prepare to go back in time, in the labyrinth of a sacred and profane world. San Clemente is an incredibly suggestive place and the underground exploration culminates in a visit to a space in the form of a grotto dedicated to the mysterious god Mithras. As you descend, there are well-situated lights and appropriate restorations, which allow you to see old frescoes and part of the ruins incorporated into the walls.

Continuing the descent, observe how the arches of the old church have been filled in to better support the newer church above. The fourth century basilica is also formed by a nave and two aisles, and is directly under the new. The numerous **frescoes** from the eighth to the eleventh centuries are rather faded, but an interesting fragment of a ninth century Last Judgment stands out. Frescoes of the lives of Sant'Alessio and San Clemente are also painted here (see Walk 2 - Ancient Origins, Sant'Alessio). Proceeding still lower, we find structures from the first and third centuries. On this third level there are the ruins of an enormous rectangular building with walls of tuff and travertine about two feet thick, which was the ancient **Roman mint**. Part of this massive edifice supports the current architectonic complex.

69

In the courtyard of a first century apartment block a **mithraeum** was erected, which included a *pronaos* (vestibule) and *triclinium* (dining room). In the latter we see the altar and the benches where the participants of this mysterious religion sat. The god **Mithras** was born from a rock and ascended into heaven. The vault of the grotto represented the heavens, that is, the universe. On the ceiling were stars and constellations known at that time. This religion put emphasis on loyalty and faith and, for this, held particular sway on the military. The Roman legions introduced it in all parts of the empire and remains of mithraeums have been found in many countries.

The muscular god Mithras is represented while killing a bull, whose blood makes the earth fertile. Even though the cult originated in Persia, a bearded and reclining Roman god, possibly Oceanus or Neptune, often assists in the foreground of the scene. A dog instrumental in finding the bull is sometimes depicted while the tail of the bull terminates in a large stalk of grain that symbolizes the cycle of life made possible by the blood of the animal.

Altar of the Mithraeum

An ancient cult

Mithras was a Persian god introduced to Rome by the soldiers stationed in the east. Like Jesus, Mithras was a savior god, come to earth to show the way and oppose evil; he died and rose again. His followers were baptized in bull's blood. The legionnaires built temples to the god Mithras all over the empire. This religion was very popular with the Roman aristocracy and was in direct competition with Christianity until it was outlawed in 395.

It has been estimated that during the third century about 2000 mithraeums flourished in the city. For another example, see the description of the Mithraeum in Walk 2, Santa Prisca.

The fourth and last layer consists, in part, of houses that were destroyed by the famous fire in 64 AD during emperor Nero's reign. One area, not yet brought to light, contains a structure from the republican period. The excavations continue and each year new rooms and floors are discovered. The sound made by rushing water under a grate in the floor is the final surprise.

The Boston connection

Excavations were begun on the third level in 1867, but gradually ground water seeped in to make it inaccessible. It rose until it reached the door of the triclinium in 1912, indicated by a sign posted. That same year Cardinal O'Connor of Boston had a canal built 700 yards long to drain away the water that pressed on the foundations. The water pours into the Cloaca Massima, a drainage system, built in the sixth century BC and still functioning, which empties into the Tiber. This channel crosses the fourth level under the church, six yards under the level of the mithraeum, and passes under the nearby Via Labicana.

*Go back on Via di San Giovanni in Laterano and as soon as you get to Piazza del Colosseo go right uphill into the park and take Viale della Domus Aurea. The entrance is on the left. The park of Colle Oppio offers a pleasant walk and views of the ruins of the Baths of Trajan. It can be necessary to make a **reservation weeks ahead** to see the Domus Aurea.*

4 Domus Aurea (Golden House). (Reservations required, guided tours only). https://www.tickitaly.com/tickets/domus-aurea-tickets.php. Nero had this enormous complex constructed after the famous fire of 64 AD. Begun in densely packed wooden apartments near the southern part of the Circo

Massimo, it spread over the hills and narrow streets, its fury lasting 9 days.

The destruction of a large part of the city center permitted the emperor to expropriate the land and build an enormous royal estate, right over the ashes of the many destroyed apartments. It didn't take long for the Roman people to doubt the official version that the Christians, who were persecuted by Nero, were responsible for the tremendous fire.

The royal estate extended from the Palatine hill to the top of the Colle Oppio (Oppio hill), on the Esquiline hill and the Caelian hill. The excavated area of the Domus Aurea is on the Colle Oppio. In the area where the Colosseum is now he had a large lake built. Numerous multilevel buildings were inserted in the bulwark that contained the hilly terrain with porticoed paths connecting them. Aesthetically the Domus Aurea is similar to the maritime villas of the early empire, characterized by scattered buildings, numerous panoramic views, gardens, terraces and porticoes. The originality of Nero's

Entrance to Domus Aurea

estate thus is not in its architecture but in the enormity of the complex and also in that it was built in the center of the city. Both factors were strongly resented by the people of Rome.

Several writers of the period described the estate. According to Tacitus, "it included a statue of Nero more than 100 feet high, a colonnade one mile long, a lake and a rural area populated with various domestic and wild animals…a large part of the palace was covered in gold and gems … one of the dining rooms was round, turning continually and the ivory ceiling had a mechanism that could emanate perfumes and rain flower petals on command.

An example of "grotesque" decoration

According to Suetonius, when the emperor inaugurated the house he declared himself satisfied and said that "finally I live in a house worthy of a man." However, to finance it he raised taxes and reduced the amount of precious metal contained in coins. The Roman elite, often invited to banquets in the estate, could not fail to notice his insecurities and gratuitous cruelty that culminated in the killing of his mother and his old tutor and counselor, Seneca. Nero, rather than be emperor, would have preferred to be an actor or musician, a taboo for a politician at the time, and was never able to master the subtleties of the exercise of power.

The grotesque style
Domus Aurea, buried under Trajan's Baths, was forgotten. With the dissolution of the empire and the consequent reduction in the population of the city, the Colle Oppio, in the center of the city, was used for agriculture. The ruins of Nero's house were rediscovered toward the end of the fifteenth century. The explorers, mostly artists and the curious, penetrated from above into the house and passing through the openings made in the upper part of the walls admired mainly the ceilings and vaults, which resembled grottoes. The type of art they found was then defined "grotesque." It consisted of people and animals, often fantastic, embellished with plants and scrolls. It was used by Ghirlandaio, Pinturicchio, Filippo Lippi, Raphael, Giovanni da Udine and others in sculpture, ceramics, in facades and interiors of palaces.

People admired leaders who, conscious of their power, used restraint, not those who used it wildly and capriciously. After he was declared a public enemy by the Senate, with the consensus of the legions, he committed suicide in 68 AD.

In recent times, there has been a re-evaluation of the emperor. What we know of Nero comes mainly from the description of his personality and actions by the historian Tacitus, who was a member of the senatorial class. Nero's admiration for the Hellenistic culture as opposed to the

Roman, his passion for acting, and especially the concentration of legislative power in his hands put him squarely against the Roman Senate. His devaluation of the currency gave more purchasing power to the silver coins used in commerce by the "common people." Finally, being the first emperor to persecute Christians has not helped his image.

The emperors after him tried to eliminate every trace of their predecessor. Vespasian had the Colosseum built on the artificial lake that Nero had created between the Colle Oppio and the Caelian hill. Later, Trajan had part of the Domus Aurea complex buried after conveniently removing all the marbles and precious sculptures, and used it as a foundation for the baths that bear his name. Ironically the idea to make every vestige of the Domus Aurea disappear produced the opposite effect. Only a few ruins of the Baths of Trajan have resisted the passing of the centuries, but a substantial part of the buried house of Nero has been preserved.

In his colossal nude **statue** positioned between the Palatine and Caelian hills, Nero was depicted as a sun god with rays of sun emanating from his head. This cult of light was expressed also in the Domus Aurea. Archeological excavations confirm that the frescoes and stuccoes were abundantly covered in gold leaf. Pliny recounted that special stones were imported from Cappadocia and that, "thanks to the stone, even when the doors were closed there was a glow like it was day." The entire layout of the Domus Aurea, with southern exposition, confirms this obsession with light, which entered by means of ample windows, numerous porticoes and terraces, reflection off water and other technical touches. During your visit, however, it is not easy to visualize the role that light played, since what remains of the ancient splendor is buried underground. Archeologists have excavated about 150 rooms, of which only a part are open to the public.

The visit will take you through a number of rooms and give you an idea of the size of the complex. Although most of the walls and vaults are covered with frescoes, 500 years (since rediscovery) of heat, cold, humidity and algae have taken their toll and the results appear as only a glimmer of their former polychromatic beauty. When you can identify a figure, such as the eagles in the "Hall of the Eagles" six or seven rooms in, or an occasional human figure, you feel you have struck gold. Most of the frescoes show architectural forms, arches, rectangles and circles, adorned with plant forms. What was not frescoed was originally covered in marble.

The **Room of Achilles** contains some better preserved frescoes of scenes from Homer's epics. Nero's artistic temperament no doubt decreed that much of the fresco decoration in the complex be inspired by scenes from Homer.

Finally, the visit reaches the **Sala Ottagonale** (Octagonal Room), which was the focal point of the east wing. This room faced forests, gardens and water displays. The construction of an octagonal space was revolutionary at that time. Abundant light comes from the large oculus in the vault.

The temperature is only 52 degrees F. (about 12 degrees C) and it is humid so dress accordingly.

Retrace your steps back to the Piazza del Colosseo. Pass the metro station and take Via dei Fori Imperiali, heading toward the Forum which will be on your left.

Walking along **Via dei Fori Imperiali,** just outside the huge Basilica di Maxentius are **large stone maps** on the wall, which document the parabolic expansion of Rome from a small city to a vast empire. Via dei Fori Imperiali was constructed by Mussolini to provide a grandiose showplace for Fascism. Many older buildings were torn down to make way. Although it allowed excavation to be done on the underlying forums, the road itself is an impediment to future archeological work in that it has become a vital part of the traffic pattern.

Along the street, right after Via del Tempio della Pace, there is a tourist kiosk and a **Visitor Center** which complements the Roman Forum. Here, find information about all of the other imperial Forums (see Walk 6), and most of the major ancient monuments of the city. This informative facility also has restrooms and a book/souvenir shop.

The entrance to the Forum is almost opposite the end of Via Cavour on Via dei Fori Imperiali

Before entering the Roman Forum, some small streets will take you quickly to Via Cavour where there are various stores. Take Via Tempio della Pace to your right, the only street on Via dei Fori Imperiali before Via Cavour. Continue on Via Frangipane and the left on Via Cardello to Via Cavour.

*Shamrock Irish Pub is at the corner of Via del Buon Consiglio and Via del Colosseo and another at Via Capo d'Africa 26. Or stop at the **wine bar** Cavour 313 (the name is the address). You can rent a **bicycle** or a **motorbike** at Via Cavour 302. The restaurant Valentino at Via Cavour 293 has good meals at moderate prices. Ristorante Enoteca (**wine bar**) Barrique is at Via Cavour 300. For a **chocolate** break, at Via Leonina 82 is La Bottega del Cioccolato.*

The streets parallel to Via Cavour, like Via Leonina, and the cross-street Via dei Serpenti are good choices for a snack or lunch. Some tourists and locals buy a sandwich or a piece of pizza in the bakeries and shops in the area.

In the Forum there are not enough indications and explanations. We find the audio guide that you can rent somewhat difficult to follow and partial. So to find the monuments keep our maps at hand, use the corresponding information and be ready to use your imagination.

A view of the Forum by Giovanni Battista Piranesi in the 1700's. Before 1800 there were 30 feet of debris and rubble covering the Forum. Livestock grazed among the ruins, and the Arch of Septimius Severus was partially covered.

5 The Foro Romano (Roman Forum)

is situated between the Palatine and Capitoline hills and is close to the Tiber. Another entrance to the Forum is located near the Arch of Constantine.

To be able to use this area for building, the Romans had to undertake major works to raise the level of the ground and drain the water from the overflowing river. To see how they filled the space, see the archeological excavations of the Velabrum described at the end of Walk 2 - Ancient Origins. Recent excavations bear out that the space was initially used as a necropolis. Channeling of the water was done during the reign of Tarquinius Priscus, of the Etruscan dynasty, at the beginning of the sixth century BC, with the creation of the Cloaca Massima. This underground drain canal still functions.

The first paving of a large piazza dates from around 600 BC. At the two extremes were built, at around the same time, the **Regia**, the residence of the king, and, on the opposite side, the first **Comitium**. This was one of the first expressions of political activity, used for popular assemblies that, with the years, evolved into the Senate. Many temples and public places, ever larger and more functional, adorned with numerous statues, were gradually erected in the Forum, reaching its apex in the late imperial period. During the regal period (VIII-VI centuries BC) and part of the republican period (VI – I centuries BC), the buildings were often made of wood and bricks. Later they were enlarged, made more spectacular and composed mostly of marble, a material capable of defying the ravages of time.

For more than 1200 years structures were continually built, added to, and dismantled. The **Via Sacra** (Sacred Way) began near where the Arch of Constantine is now, and traversed the whole Forum. Religious or triumphal processions paraded west, through to the Temple of Jupiter Capitoline, on the Campidoglio (Capitoline hill). With the growth of the city it became necessary to expand the area used for the Forum. Several emperors gave their names to these additional areas, such as **Augustus' Forum** and **Trajan's Forum** situated on the other side of Via dei Fori Imperiali. What we see now is the result of weathering, earthquakes and plundering for the precious construction materials.

In describing the Forum, we have minimized the description of the ruins that are visible now, but of little importance. We have instead put the emphasis on those monuments considered exceptional that may be not very visible. Ample information and historical background is provided in the following paragraphs, so, enter without hesitation and be ready to use your imagination.

> *From the entrance on Via dei Fori Imperiali, after the ramp, you reach the Via Sacra. We will travel through the Forum in counterclockwise order going west (right) toward the Campidoglio.*

A. Right after the entrance on your left is the **Tempio di Antonino e Faustina**, from 141 AD. On the façade there are six white marble Corinthian columns. The inscription on the architrave states that it was dedicated by the Senate to the imperial couple. In actuality, Antonio Pio had it built in memory of his wife. It was later transformed into a church and this fact has

guaranteed its conservation.

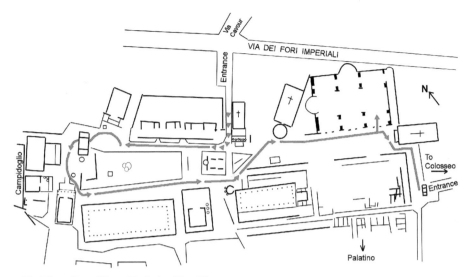

B. The Basilica Fulvia-Emilia. Right after the entrance on the right

was a basilica. Now it is delineated by numerous ruins not easily discernible. Its construction began in 179 BC and it takes its name from two of the ancient Roman families, the "Fulvia" and the "Aemilia." It was one of four buildings in the Forum used for conducting business and legal affairs. It was sacked by Alaric's Goths in 410 and restored a few years later. Green and blue marks, visible for a long time on the pavement, were a result of fires set by Alaric's followers who smelted bronze coins on this spot.

A Temp. Antonio e Faustina
B Basilica Fulvia-Emilia
C Curia
D Lapis Niger
E Base dei Decennali
F Arch Septimius Severus
G Umbilicus Urbis
H Miglio Aureo
I Temple of Vespasian
J Tabularium
K Temple of Saturn
L Basilica Julia
M Rostri Imperiali
N Colonna di Foca
O Tempio dei Castori
P Regia
Q Temple of Vesta

The western half of the Forum

Along the south wall of the basilica, closer to your path, are ruins of tuff walls that defined square rooms. These were a series of **shops**, all lined up, many times rebuilt since the republican period, where the moneychangers plied their trade. Still closer to the path there are remains of columns, parallel to the Basilica Emilia, that were part of a portico which dates from the first century BC and which extended in front of the shops.

Basilicas became churches

Starting with the Renaissance a systematic plundering of material began that brought about the almost complete destruction of inestimable monuments. Protests from artists such as Michelangelo and Raphael were for naught. Rome of the popes devoured pagan Rome. As you can see, frequently the only buildings to survive were those transformed into churches.

The Curia

C. Curia (Senate). The building we see today in the Roman Forum is the seat of the Senate rebuilt here by Julius Caesar and finished by Augustus in 29 BC. Its good state of preservation is due to the fact that it was transformed into a church in the seventh century and restored several times. The floor is made up of sheets of marble alternated with precious and multicolored marbles like porphyry and serpentine. Of course the walls were originally covered in marble. You can still see 3 low marble platforms on the left and right of the hall, where the seats of the 300 senators were positioned. The symbol "SPQR" frequently seen around the city translates as "Senatus et Populusque Romanus" or "The Senate and People of Rome." The **Senate's bronze doors** were moved to the Basilica of San Giovanni in Laterano and used for its main entrance, by Borromini. What are here now are replicas.

The government in the republican period

After 200 years of being governed by kings, the Romans started looking for alternatives. As they examined historically the various forms of government, it became evident that the different organizational schemes, the government of the one, the few or the many, in their pure forms, too often degenerated respectively into dictatorship, oligarchy and mob rule. The inspired Greek ideals were short-lived. For this reason they decided to set up a practical and mixed political system, combining the different elements and defining and balancing power among the separate branches of government. They did not know how to call it so they came up with "*res publica*" or "public thing." They therefore created a republic that, even though subject to a process of evolution, functioned for over five centuries, from the sixth to the first century BC.

All political offices were elected with terms of one year, or a year and a half, with the exception of the senators. Two **consuls** held executive power and each had veto power over the actions of the other. At the end of their terms, they became senators for life. In order to become consul, one had to have served in all of the main political and administrative positions. This helped to assure that the persons who went on to form the senate were truly competent and had vast experience. Finally, there were the military, patrician and popular assemblies where all citizens could participate. They debated, approved or rejected laws and decided questions of war and peace.

From a constitutional point of view, the consuls had the "royal" or presidential power, the senate represented the patricians and the various assemblies guaranteed the democratic aspect. The basic idea was to avoid having one person or one institution assuming absolute power as was true in the early days of Rome with the kings.

In the hall of the Senate are two marble bas-reliefs found nearby that describe two episodes during the reign of emperor Trajan. The one on the left depicts the destruction of the registers where citizens' tax debts were recorded. The right relief shows Trajan instituting economic aid for the children of needy families.

The Roman experience has been of fundamental importance in the development of western democracies. The American founding fathers, when they wrote the Constitution, looked to historical experience of the various forms of government including naturally that of Great Britain, but also in particular the experience and the ideals of the Roman republican period. The founding fathers were well versed in the classics. The actual expression "founding fathers" comes from the Latin and was widely used by the Romans to indicate those men that made the Roman republic possible. In a 2002 speech, the historian David McCullough was quoted as saying, "They were steeped in, soaked in, marinated in the classics: Greek and Roman history, Greek and Roman ideas, Greek and Roman ideals. It was their model, their example."

Washington, the first American president, voluntarily leaving his office after only two terms, established a precedent in the history of the young republic, acting as a new Cincinnatus and the comparison pleased him. Cincinnatus (519 – 430 BC) was elected "dictator" for a limited period, in order to save the Roman legions from certain annihilation by the Aequi. In just a few days he defeated the enemy, refused all honors and left office. Several years later he was called again to save the republic, did his duty, voluntarily gave up power and retired to his farm.

Institutionally the **Senate** had a consulting function, guiding the actions of the legislative assemblies and the magistrates. Its prestige was enhanced by the leadership, demonstrated during the 3 Punic Wars against the Carthaginians between 264 and 146 BC, which menaced the very existence of the republic. Controlling the state financing from public projects to wars, the Senate had enormous political power and thus was often in conflict with the executive power, especially toward the end of the republican period. To have an idea, just think of the political contrast between the President and Congress of the U.S.

The senators were endowed with gravitas, that is, they had vast experience in the political, administrative and military apparatus, and for this they gradually accumulated much of the real power to the detriment of the other institutions. In fact for long periods they assumed direction over the state. Voting was done in this way: the senators in favor of the proposal went to sit on the right and those opposed went to the left. Toward the end of the republic, during Cicero's time, in 50 BC, they had absorbed part of the executive and legislative power, but with the advent of the empire it was relegated to mere formal functions. Perhaps one of the most difficult periods for the pride of these men, doubtless intelligent and capable, was when the emperor Caligula made his horse a senator, brought it to the Senate building and considered it their equal. The new Senate building, the Curia Giulia, by initiative of Julius Caesar, replaced the older Curia Ostilia.

At the exit of the Curia, the area directly in front was the ancient Comitium, a circular shape with steps. During the five centuries of the republic, the senators met on the northern part while the magistrates met on the southern. In this area there was also a platform where foreign ambassadors spoke.

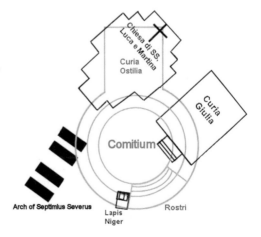

D. On the plaza near the Senate is the **Lapis Niger** or **Black Stone**. This area, even in ancient times, was covered by a black stone and fenced. It is believed that Romulus, the founder of Rome and first king, was killed in this spot by senators for his despotic use of power. In the lower reaches, a monument with the earliest known writing in Latin was found. The Romans venerated their founder even 1000 years after his death.

E. On the other side of the Via Sacra, on the left, the **Base dei Decennali**, a marble column base with bas-reliefs, celebrated the tenth anniversary of the Tetrarch, that is, the government of four princes. With this new institution Diocletian (emperor from 284 - 305) tried to resolve the difficult problem of the succession. To the emperors of the East and the West he added two junior partners (caesars) who were to succeed them. On the side toward the Via Sacra are depicted female figures called Winged Victories. The west side of the base shows a bull, a sheep and a pig, who are to be sacrificed, animal handlers and a person in a toga.

F. The Arch of Septimius Severus is in the western part of the Forum, at the foot of the Campidoglio. It was erected in 203 AD to celebrate the victories of the emperor over the Parthians, a people from the area that is now in the northern part of Iran, and over the Arabs. It is one of the few arches, built to honor victorious generals and emperors, still standing and in good condition.

Four panels in bas-relief depict events in the two campaigns against the Parthians. We can also observe the war machines used by the Romans in that period. The monument is highly decorated and influenced numerous architects both ancient and modern. In particular, the figures reclining above the central arch inspired portals of renaissance palaces and country houses all over Europe. The female figures lying on the arch are called "winged victories." Mars, the god of war, is represented in the keystone of the central arch.

Written in stone?
In the writing on the upper part, in the fourth line from the top, the name and title of the second son of Septimius Severus, Geta, have been chiseled away. After his brother Caracalla ordered his assassination, the writing was changed to "*optimus fortissimisque principibus*" (great and strong princes).

G. Just to the left of the arch, continuing in a counterclockwise direction is positioned a circular base, the **umbilicus urbis** (umbilical of the city). It was considered the symbolic center of Rome and the point from which the world of the living (mundus) was in contact, by means of a deep fissure in the ground, with the mysterious underground world. According to legend, Romulus made a hole here and buried symbolic items. The first inhabitants of the city brought dirt from their town of origin and threw it in the hole where it was mixed in. They called this the "mundus" and with this as the center, the perimeter of the city was traced.

The umbilicus urbis

The Miglio Aureo

Daily News
Julius Caesar had the first daily newspaper published in 59 BC, the *acta diurna*. Produced on papyrus, it was displayed in the Forum and supplied news of public interest for all to read. Since the publication was official, it naturally included important government affairs. Sensationalism, however, as in our time, was not ignored. There were notices about important people, divorces, gossip, results of gladiatorial combat and the weather. Without pause, the newspaper was published for 280 years. It could be received by mail, together with letters, in the various parts of the empire. The words journal and journalism derive from *diurna*.

H. Further up is the **Miglio Aureo** (Golden Milepost), built by Augustus in 20 BC. This was a column, covered in gilded bronze, from which all distance measurements were made for the vast road system, which spread out all over the empire for more than 60,000 miles. On the column were indicated the distances to major cities. From here we can appreciate the source of the expression "all roads lead to Rome."

I. The three elegant Corinthian columns which form a right angle belong to the **Temple of Vespasian**. These were the only columns continually standing and visible during the centuries. They marked the existence of the Forum that was buried under the accumulation of debris and the ravages of time. Looking at the columns, on the right, is the **Temple of Concordia.** According to tradition, it was erected by Camillus in 367 BC to celebrate the peace between the patricians and the plebeians after the passage of specific laws that assured the equality of the two classes. On the left the **Portico dei Consenti** from the first century, with the attractive Corinthian columns, was rebuilt in 367 as the inscription states. In the rooms behind the columns there were statues of the "*dei consentes*" or gods of counsel. (Photo next page)

J. Beyond, on the Campiodoglio, you can see the large arched openings of the **Tabularium** under the Palazzo dei Senatori (see Walk 7, the Campidoglio). From here, as well as from the terraces on the sides of the Campidoglio, there is a good view of the Forum. The Tabularium, erected in 78 BC was the state archive.

The arched openings of the Tabularium are visible behind the 3 columns of the Temple of Vespasian. On the left is the low Portico dei Consenti.

K. The group of 8 granite columns, of which two are red, belongs to the **Temple of Saturn** (below), one of the oldest temples, whose original construction dates from 479 BC. It was erected not long after the nearby Temple of Jupiter Maximus Capitolino on the Campidoglio, which held the state treasure in the republican period.

L. Continuing counterclockwise we start going east, toward the Colosseum. On the right are the remains of the **Basilica Julia**, begun in 54 BC by Julius Caesar and completed by Augustus. It was 330 feet long by 160 feet wide, and had five aisles separated by brick pilasters covered in marble. The seat of several civil tribunals, according to circumstances the open space could be utilized fully by lowering

large curtains from above to create rooms of various sizes. The central nave was three stories high with large windows opening up at the top. As with many other buildings in the Forum, it was severely damaged during the fire of 283 AD and promptly restored. Here is where the two bas-reliefs now in the Senate were located. Numerous incisions on the steps, especially on the east side, are the remains of games used by youths and others who crowded the area of the Forum at all hours of day and night. As with the Basilica Fulvia Emilia, the building materials were systematically removed so that not much is left.

M. Rostri Imperiali. (Imperial rostrums) Between the Arch of Septimius Severus and the Basilica Julia, around the middle of the first century BC, Caesar had erected a platform where orators could pronounce their speeches.

Incisions on the steps for ancient games

Here, Shakespeare's Mark Antony gave his famous speech, after the assassination of Caesar on the ides of March in 44 BC, "Friends, Romans, countrymen..." The famous orator Cicero, representing the Senatorial class, had pronounced 14 orations against him and in defense of the republic, declaring him public enemy of Rome. One year later, in 43 BC, the same Mark Antony had Cicero's head and hands hung on the Rostra. Later Augustus built another platform that is the one more visible today which has been partially reconstructed. Only a wall remains (right), it is straight and still has the holes where the rostra (prows) from captured enemy ships at the decisive battle of Actium, between Mark Antony and Augustus in 31 BC, were inserted.

Official record
The *acta Senatus* contained the records of the Senate. During the imperial period, Augustus continued to keep them but prohibited the publication. They were conserved in the archives and in the libraries but one needed permission to consult them.

N. The **Colonna di Foca**, the tall column on the left with part of a Corinthian capital still on it, had a golden statue on top. It was dedicated to emperor Phocas (Foca) on the first of August 608 and it is important in that it is the last monument to be constructed in the Forum. From the first paving of the Forum in 600 BC until 608 AD, for 1200 years numerous important structures were successively erected, first in wood, then in brick and later in marble, and demolished in the area. After 608 began the progressive abandonment of the monumental center of the city. During the Middle Ages the population of Rome decreased even further, the area of the Forum was deserted, and, left to itself, was buried in debris. The Forum was used as a pasture for a long time and during the last few centuries was covered with numerous dwellings. Excavation began in the early 1800's and at a faster pace after the unification of Italy in 1870.

Nearby, the **vine,** the **olive** and the **fig**, sacred trees, grew in this area since antiquity. The zone was left purposely unpaved for many centuries by the ancient Romans. The trees have recently been replanted in the same spot.

Right after, still on the left, is an area called the "**pozzetti,**" or shafts, now covered with a grate. These holes in the ground connected to numerous rooms and underground passages which served as services for the early gladiatorial games. Until about the era of Augustus (27 BC – 14 AD), gladiators fought in the center of the Forum. Excavations in this area during the last century brought to light the remains of a wooden elevator, possibly used to bring up heavy and awkward objects necessary for the spectacle. Continuing on the path to the left are several **honorary columns**.

O. The **Tempio dei Castori**, (Temple of Castor and Pollux) on the right as you continue east toward the Colosseum, has three large Corinthian columns in a row, which support part of the architrave (photo right). The cult of Castor and Pollux or the "Dioscuri" has a Greek origin, based on the sons of Zeus and it was assimilated by the Romans in ancient times. An archaic Latin inscription from the sixth century BC dedicated to the twin gods Castor and Pollux was found at Lavinio, a town near Rome.

The strict Roman religious rules prohibited foreign cults in the *pomerium*, the sacred confines of the city, but the Dioscuri soon came to be considered a native religion. Statues of the Dioscuri are found at the top of the steps that go up to Piazza del Campidoglio from Piazza Venezia (see Walk 7), and in the Fountain of Montecavallo on the Piazza del Quirinale (Walk 6).

P. Just beyond is the **Regia**, or king's palace, a roughly triangular space that once extended as far as the Temple of Romulus. This was the king's residence for the first two centuries of the existence of the city. Originally symbolic of the king's hearth, with the advent of the republic, the eternal flame kept by the Vestals became the symbol of Rome. All that remains is a small platform opposite the Tempio di Faustina near the entrance.

Q. Continuing, you can see part of the circular **Temple of Vesta** where the Vestal Virgins maintained the sacred flame of Rome as a symbol of the continuity of the state. The fire was extinguished on the first of March, the start of the new year, and relit with tapers from the temple flame. The girls were chosen at a young age, from 6 to 10, and stayed for 30 years. After the women of the imperial family, they were the most important in Roman society. Their main duty was to make sure that the flame never died and to maintain the vow of chastity. However if it was discovered that they were no longer virgins, they were walled alive and their partner was condemned to die by flogging in the Comitium. After their period of service, however, if they wished, a Vestal Virgin could marry.

A little further on, on the right was the **Casa delle Vestali (the House of the Vestals)**, their residence. The enormity of the complex that contained 50 rooms, a large open courtyard with statues of the Vestals, a four-sided portico and 3 pools with fountains shows how well they were treated. The ground floor consisted of numerous rooms, among which were a small windmill, an oven and a kitchen. Two stairways from the portico led to the upper floor where the Vestals lived. These rooms contained many heated baths. During the excavations, numerous female statues were found, positioned on marble bases in the southern part of the portico. They are thought to depict the *Vestali Massime*, that is the head priestesses of the Temple. These statues show women completely clothed and in modest poses, conforming to their position

Privileges of the chosen

The Vestals enjoyed many privileges, among which the most important was the emancipation from paternal authority. They had reserved seats at the spectacles. After the building of the Colosseum, they had their own reserved tribunes close to the arena, while all other women had to sit in the farthest seats. They went around Rome wearing special white clothing and a braided hairpiece, so they were immediately recognizable. If a person condemned to die met a Vestal the day he was to die, he was pardoned.

Proceed past the Regia and follow the path on the map of the eastern part of the Forum.

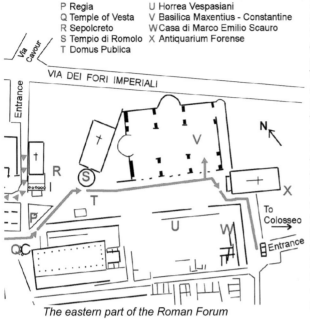

P Regia
Q Temple of Vesta
R Sepolcreto
S Tempio di Romolo
T Domus Publica

U Horrea Vespasiani
V Basilica Maxentius - Constantine
W Casa di Marco Emilio Scauro
X Antiquarium Forense

Via Cavour

VIA DEI FORI IMPERIALI

Entrance

N

To Colosseo →

Entrance

The eastern part of the Roman Forum

R. The **sepolcreto** (tomb complex) is on the left, next to the Tempio di Faustina where the path comes back to the Via Sacra. Here ashes of the dead in the pre-Roman period, from the tenth to the seventh centuries BC, were buried. During the seventh the place was used only to bury children. This finding corresponds with what we know about the law passed after the founding of the city, which prohibited burial inside the limits. Excavations have uncovered various burial sites of different types and sizes.

A view of the western portion of the Forum seen from the Palatine Hill, with people walking on the path. In the foreground is the Casa delle Vestali, in the center the small Temple of Vesta, on the left are the three tall columns of the Tempio dei Castori, at the top are the Arch of Septimius Severus and the Curia.

S. Soon after on the left are ruins of a private house and then the **Tempio di Romolo (Temple of Romulus)**. This round building was erected by emperor Maxentius (306 – 312 AD) in memory of his son Romulus, who died very young. (Photo next page)

Its good state of preservation is due to the fact that it was incorporated into the Church of Saints Cosmas and Damian. The bronze door, between two porphyry columns, is the original. The entrance is decidedly raised compared to the road, such that you can see part of the foundation. During the excavations, toward the end of the nineteenth century, the road was dug down to the level of the ground during Augustus' reign (27 BC – 14 AD), about three centuries earlier and clearly lower.

T. Opposite the Temple of Romulus, a small roof is visible that covers the remains of the **Domus Publica,** the house of the Pontifex Maximus, the highest religious authority. This post was held by many important Romans including Julius Caesar from 62 BC until his assassination. During that time he lived here.

U. Right after, about 20 yards to the left is a medieval brick portico. Further ahead, on the path to the right, is the **Horrea Vespasiani** (Vespasian's warehouses) built after the famous fire that burned Rome during the reign of Nero in 64 AD. These buildings were initially used for a fish market, as demonstrated by the finding of many shells, and later it was used also as imperial administration offices.

V. The path to the left leads to the **Basilica of Maxentius and Constantine**, begun by the emperor Maxentius in 306 and completed by Constantine. The basilica was of enormous proportions: 80 yards by 60 with three huge coffered barrel vaults supported by 8 gigantic columns. The remaining one covered the north aisle and contains a large apse where a colossal statue of Constantine was installed. Remains of some of the enormous capitals can be seen above.

It was used as a civil court. Many of the famous Renaissance architects such as Brunelleschi, Bramante and Michelangelo, and others up to modern times, were inspired by it. For centuries afterward it provided construction materials for newer projects. The last column was transferred in the seventeenth century, by Pope Paul V, to the front of Santa Maria Maggiore.

The coffered ceiling of the Basilica of Maxentius was decorated with gilded stucco.

Come back to the path and continue uphill toward the arch.

Vision of victory

The two brothers-in-law (Constantine was married to Fausta, Maxentius' sister) had a decisive battle for the succession at the Milvian Bridge, still standing today. Constantine, even though at a disadvantage 4 to 1 in soldiers, was in the end victorious, resulting in Maxentius' death. Constantine, a pagan at the time, had a religious vision, which indicated that under the cross he would triumph. He put the sign of the cross on his soldiers' shields and defeated his rival. A year later he legalized Christianity all over the empire.

Location, location, location

Marco Emilio Scauro sold his house in the Forum in 53 BC for about 15 million sesterces. To put that in perspective, in the first century a legionary would earn about 1200 sesterces a year, a praetorian legionary about 3000. A cow would go for 400 to 800 sesterces and rent for a house varied from about 200 to 1000 per year. Olive oil went for 2 or 3 sesterces a quart.

W. On the right is the **Casa di Marco Emilio Scauro** (House of Marco Emilio Scauro), protected by a modern roof. The house was built in 74 BC, that is, in the late republican period, and was part of a densely populated residential quarter. Cicero, the famous lawyer, had a house nearby that bordered with the residence of the Pontifex Maximus, where Julius Caesar lived. Centuries earlier, Scipio the African, the general who defeated Hannibal, also had a house in the Forum, which was centrally located and of course very valuable.

X. Many archeological finds have been moved from the Forum and collected in the **Antiquarium Forense,** on the ground floor of Santa Francesca Romana, between the Arch of Titus and the Basilica of Maxentius, next to the cloister of the church of Santa Maria Nova. Here are remains from the Comitium, Lapis Niger, the sepolcreto and the Forum, including from wells near the Temple of Vesta, consisting of animal bones and household furnishings from the ninth-seventh century BC. A miniature reconstruction of the area's excavations can be viewed alongside photographs and drawings. Check at the entrance to see if access is available.

Y. The **Arco di Tito (Arch of Titus)** commemorated the victory of Vespasian over the Egyptians and of his son Titus over the Judeans who had rebelled. It is located in the eastern part near the Colosseo and visible also from outside the

Forum from the area near the Arch of Constantine. The underside of the arch is decorated with a coffered vault and at the center is depicted the emperor Titus being carried to heaven by an eagle. On the bas-relief on

the left are in evidence silver trumpets and a seven-armed candelabra, part of the booty from the conquest of Jerusalem (photo right).

The opposite panel shows the triumphal chariot with Titus and several symbolic personages. As with the Arch of Constantine, its good state of preservation is due to its having been incorporated during the Middle Ages into the fortifications of the Frangipane family.

85

Past the arch, follow the signs to the ticket booth at the entrance of the archeological area on the Palatine. Otherwise, if you do not wish to visit the Palatine, go back out where you entered, along Via dei Fori Imperiali, or walk downhill toward the Colosseum where there is a Metro station.

6 Palatine Hill. (Colle Palatino) According to legend, Romulus

founded Rome in 753 BC on this hill. In fact, it has been confirmed that there was a human presence from at least the tenth century BC. Already in the late republican period the Roman elite coveted a house on the Palatine, including such figures as Cicero, Marc Antony, Agrippa and Germanicus. But it was Augustus in 23 BC who established a precedent followed by the succeeding emperors who decided to maintain and expand their residences here. Emperors habitually tore down at least part of their predecessors' palaces and rebuilt sumptuous palaces to their own liking.

From here, the destiny of tens of millions of people was decided for centuries. Everything from Lucullian banquets and orgies to political intrigue all the way to war, peace and emperor's assassinations were carried out on this hill. After Constantine moved the capital to Constantinople the area declined in importance.

The octagonal fountain of Domus Flavia

During the Renaissance the hill was occupied by many of Rome's important families who used some of the existing buildings and planted gardens and vineyards. Some of these were the Barberini, Spada, Mattei, and Roncioni. The most extensive and impressive were those of the Farnese family and the name **Orti Farnesiani** is still sometimes used to indicate the area.

As you walk around this vast area keep in mind that, although much is now covered by grass, in the imperial era it would have been covered with splendid buildings.

On the slopes of the Palatine imperial tribunes were also built, which looked out over the Circus Maximus, allowing the emperors to watch the chariot races from their palaces. It is a very pleasant walk among the ruins, especially during the summer, leaving behind the crowded Forum and taking refuge under the shade of the pines and in the museum.

Domus Augustana

Going up, and continuing in a southerly direction you get to the **Palatine museum** where statues and frescoes help to recreate the ancient splendor of the place. Exhibits describe the huts found here that date to 770-730 BC (See the information in Walk 2 about the origins of

86 Rome). The most ancient ceramics have been dated to 900-830 BC.

Looking at the Palatine Museum with your back to the Forum the main emperor's palace occupied the top of the hill. It was divided into 3 parts. The **Domus Flavia** on the right was the official area where the emperor held meetings, audiences and received ambassadors. Included is the octagonal fountain (the octagon shaped brick structure is clearly visible) in the middle of an open courtyard with gardens (the peristyle). The next (on the right of the Museum) and most sumptuous room was the *triclinium* (banquet room) where the emperor's table was one step up to separate him from the crowd. The oval shaped ruins delineate the nymphaeum or fountain with many niches from where water spewed.

The second part (on the left) and adjacent was the **Domus Augustana**, (House of Augustus) his private residence, on 2 levels. It contained a pool with a temple in the middle, reachable by a bridge, and a colonnade and many rooms that terminate with gardens and fountains. The lower level was built 36 feet below and is the most fascinating of the entire complex for its design and its cozy atmosphere.

The third part, the **stadium** or hip-podrome, (still further on your left) is a space 160 by 48 meters clearly delin-eated. The building was surrounded by a two-story brick portico. The best place to see it is from the top of the Domus Augustana. It was an art gallery with sculptures and flowerbeds, fountains and pathways. Many of the sculptures on display in the Palatine Museum come from this area. The oval track was added at a much later date.

Frescoes in the House of Augustus

Three buildings lay under the Domus Flavia. The **House of the Griffins** gives us an idea of the type of residence and decoration of the really rich. The **Aula Isiaca**, the remains of a very large home of the republican period, contains artistic decorations relating to the Egyptian cult of the goddess Isis, in fashion

after the battle of Actium. The third complex buried under the Domus Flavia is **Livia's Bath**, from the time of Nero, which demonstrates the richness of design and decoration of Nero's Domus Aurea. See number 4 of this walk.

Check to see which of these areas and others are open to the public.

Further south is a terrace with a good **view** of the Circo Massimo, the Aven-tine hill and the Terme di Caracalla (Walk 2). From here you have a good view over the Forum. In the western

section, excavations have found holes in the earth that indicate remains of huts from the ninth century BC (photo above).

Go back to the Arch of Titus, where you can exit in the direction of the Colosseum.

Go back to the Arch of Titus, where you can exit in the direction of the Colosseum.

The entire walk marked on the map is only about 1 ½ miles not including the walking you may do in the Forum, which would add about half mile. The walk in the Palatino could add another mile (3 miles total). If time is short, do not miss the Colosseum, San Clemente and the Roman Forum.

Looking west down the Via Sacra toward the Arch of Septimius Severus

Walk Three - Imperial Rome
Additional Restaurants

Pasqualino, Via dei Santissimi Quattro 66, Tel. 06.700 45 76.   Good value. View of the Colosseum from the outside tables. €€

Hostaria Da Nerone, Via delle Terme di Tito 96, Tel. 06.481 79 52. Small, with a lively atmosphere, and near the Colosseum. €€

Trattoria Valentino, Via Cavour 293, Tel. 06.488 13 03. Good prices. €€

Angelino ai Fori, Largo Corrado Ricci 40, www.AngelinoaiFori.com. Classic and Roman cooking. Good view of the Forum. €€€

Massenzio ai Fori, Largo Corrado Ricci 5, Tel. 06.6679 07 06. Specialty is seafood and pizza. Tables outside. €

Naumachia, Via Celimontana 7, www.NaumachiaRoma.com. Roman and Tuscan cooking. Also pizza. €

Tree Folk's Celio, Via Capo d'Africa 29. Facebook. British style pub. €

Julius Caesar

During most of the first century BC, Rome was involved in wars of conquest and civil wars. For years a furious struggle for power engulfed the Roman world between the populists headed by Marius and the aristocratic senatorial class headed by Sulla. Finally, in 82 BC Sulla prevailed, proclaimed himself dictator and installed a reign of terror where thousands of upper class Romans were tortured and murdered including dozens of opposition senators and 2600 knights.

The heads of his enemies were mounted on spears in the Forum. It was payback time for what the followers of Marius had done just a few years before, when the corpses of nobles and senators littered the streets of Rome and their heads, dripping in blood, were hung on the rostra in the Forum.

Gaius Julius Caesar had **two strikes against him**: he was the nephew of Marius and married Cornelia, the daughter of Cinna, the other populist boss. Caesar refused to repudiate Cornelia as the dictator ordered, so Sulla confiscated his wife's dowry, his father's inheritance and condemned him to death. Sulla wanted Caesar dead, and to those who suggested his young life be spared Sulla replied, "You do not understand, there are many Mariuses in him." Followed by assassins and feeling in constant danger, Caesar was able to survive by sleeping in different places every night.

Back in Rome, years after the death of Sulla, in a safer political climate, he threw himself into politics, his vast ambition bound for obtaining power. Two other political and military figures were preeminent at that time in Rome: Gnaeus Pompey (Magnus), the conqueror of the east, and (Marcus Licinius) Crassus, who had stopped the insurrection of the slaves guided by Spartacus. Caesar conceived the idea of the **triumvirate**, allying with Crassus and Pompey to support each other's interests in the struggle against the aristocratic senators. Caesar had his daughter married to Pompey. To get the votes of Pompey's allies he borrowed money from the super-rich Crassus and lent it to them at no interest. As **consul** in 59 BC, he was able to obtain legislation favorable to all three through political maneuvers and intimidation, finally landing the governorship of Transalpine Gaul, together with 3 legions.

> **Caesar and the pirates**
> During a trip by sea, the young Caesar was kidnapped by pirates off the coast of Turkey. According to the laws of the period the ransom of a Roman nobleman must be paid by the cities of the coast where the kidnapping happened, for failing to provide adequate "coast guard" protection. Once free, he raised money, ships and men, attacked the pirates, killed several, got rich booty and took many prisoners that he asked to be put to death. Since the local authority did not agree completely with his requests, he took it upon himself to crucify them.

In order to be a successful politician, you needed military victories. From 58 to 51 BC, Julius Caesar conquered France (Gaul) and Belgium. He landed in England but, realizing he did not have enough forces to conquer it, he left. More than half the population of what is now France was killed, deported or enslaved. The last pocket of resistance was the town of Uxellodunum where both hands of the captives were cut off, condemning them to beg for food for the rest of their lives.

Near Bonn, he had a **bridge** built on the river Rhine in 10 days, working days and nights. He passed over the bridge with 25,000 men, engaged the German tribes, defeating them, then crossed back over the bridge and burned it.

In the intense political climate heightened by the deaths of Crassus, and of Pompey's wife (Caesar's daughter), the conflict between Caesar and Pompey was now inevitable. Caesar moved from Northern Italy toward Rome in the winter of 50 BC with only one legion, crossing the Rubicon. Because a general was not allowed to bring his army beyond that limit, this act thrust civil war closer. Tradition says that he spoke the famous **"The die is cast."** Resistance was limited. Many people genuinely liked him, for his approach favored the common man, as opposed to the aristocracy. Those who feared him most were remembering the vengeful behavior of Sulla of the previous generation's

Caesar's bridge model

civil war when he did not hesitate to murder the opposing faction after conquering a city. When it became clear that Caesar was inclined to reconciliation and to pardon his enemy, his advance toward Rome was without much opposition.

From 49 to 45 BC the civil war was fought on many fronts, across Italy, Spain, Greece and North Africa. Pharsalus in Greece was a decisive battle, forcing Pompey to flee to Egypt, where he was killed. Finally, in 45 BC Caesar returned to Rome where one of his first enlightened actions was the recall of the people exiled by Pompey and the restoration of civic rights of those put on the list of proscription of Sulla. He then set about integrating the provinces and reducing the extreme power of Rome. In only one year before his assassination, he planned an extraordinary number of initiatives and reforms.

Some things never change
Crassus became very rich in a modern way: investing in business such as land improvement, mines and business loans, activities not strictly proper for an aristocratic Roman. He was also the first temp help agency since he had a large number of highly trained slaves that he was renting out.

He ordered the publication of a **daily paper** that included the activity of the Senate for all the citizens to read that could be sent throughout Italy and the provinces. He gave Roman citizenship to the inhabitants of northern Italy, increased the number of senators from 600 to 900, allowing also the inhabitants of the provinces to participate. He provided public work for the population of Rome that was already around 700,000. For at least 100,000 people, his veterans and overflowing Roman citizens, he **founded more than 20 colonies** in the provinces. Among the most important today are: in France Arles, Lyon, Nimes, and Orange; in Greece Corinth; in Spain Tarragona and Seville; in Switzerland Geneva. In the rich East he reduced the taxes and removed the right of collection from the often rapacious Romans to the local government. He **reformed the calendar** that, except for some corrections made by Pope Gregory XIII in 1582, is the same that we use today. He planned an artificial port near Ostia and the draining of the Pontine Marshes just south of Rome, a feat finally accomplished only in the 1930's.

With his reforms in place to assure stability just before his assassination March 15, 44 BC, Caesar was directing his attention to Dacia (Romania) later conquered by the emperor Trajan and planning the conquest of Parthia (currently Iran) where the legions of Crassus had been defeated. Although admired by many for his triumphs and policies, he changed inexorably the institution from a
90 republic to a dictatorship, ushering in Rome's imperial period.

WALK FOUR - Rome Opens to the World

This walk starts at the unforgettable **Trevi Fountain**, a necessary stop for every tourist in Rome. Piazza di Spagna with the **Barcaccia** fountain, the **Spanish Steps** and **Trinità dei Monti** church is the most famous piazza in Rome. For three centuries this area has attracted foreigners residing in the capital, and has been a gathering point for Italian and foreign artists. Although there are many painters' and sculptors' studios, art galleries and antique stores, the bohemian atmosphere of years past is fairly reduced. Many artists, writers, composers and famous persons have resided in this area. Among them: Goethe, Rubens, Liszt, Stendhal, d'Annunzio, Berlioz, Bizet, De Chirico, Henry James, Hawthorne, the scientist Guglielmo Marconi, the director Federico Fellini and naturally the poets Keats and Shelley for whom the **Casina Rossa** in Piazza di Spagna is dedicated. You can also visit the artist **De Chirico**'s studio and a permanent exhibit in the house of the writer **Goethe**. **Via Condotti** and the nearby streets are the mecca for brand name clothes shopping. Stores like Gucci, Armani, Bulgari, Ferragamo, Fendi, Valentino, Prada and many others are a few steps from each other.

Today, people from all countries are attracted by the many charms of the area. The walk goes through Campo Marzio, where the Roman legions trained, leads over to **Ara Pacis**, constructed by the emperor Augustus to celebrate the "pax romana" (Roman peace) after a period of interminable conflict, and the **Mausoleum** of the emperor. Finally we reach the vast **Piazza del Popolo**, **Via Margutta** and the **Belvedere** of the **Pincio** (Pincian Hill).

In this walk:

1 **Fontana di Trevi**, the most beautiful tribute to water
2 The **Campo Marzio** area, where the Roman legions trained
3 **Ara Pacis**, the symbol of the "pax romana" and Augustus' Mausoleum
4 **Via Condotti,** the most elegant street and the center of international fashion. A curiosity is the SMOM, the smallest state in the world.
5 **Piazza di Spagna**, over the years a magnet for artists, Italian and foreign
6 **Via del Babuino**, with one of the "talking statues"
7 **Piazza del Popolo**, the doorway to Rome, with Santa Maria del Popolo, containing artistic connections to the book and film "Angels and Demons"
8 **Goethe's House**, a continuous exhibit of the works of the German poet, dramatist, writer and scientist
9 **Via Margutta**, the street of the artists

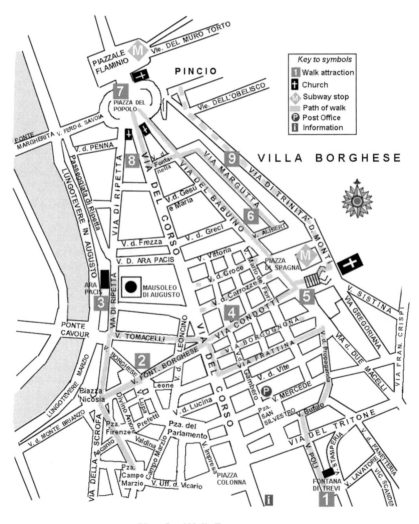

Map for Walk Four

Many famous visitors to Rome have been inspired to write of their impressions. Here are a few:

"Yes, I have finally arrived to this Capital of the World! I now see all the dreams of my youth coming to life… Only in Rome is it possible to understand Rome."

*Johann Wolfgang von Goethe
(German writer 1749-1832)*

"When thou art at Rome, do as they do at Rome."
    Miguel de Cervantes, Spanish writer (1547 - 1616)

"Every one soon or late comes round by Rome."
    Robert Browning (English Poet 1812-1889)

Restaurants with outdoor tables on a typical street

1 Fontana di Trevi (Trevi Fountain) appears suddenly in all its splendor, as you emerge from the narrow streets that surround it. Its name comes from the "tre vie" (three streets) that intersect here. The films *Three Coins in the Fountain* and *La Dolce Vita* have popularized it on an international scale. In 1644 Pope Urban VIII asked Bernini to design a new fountain. But it took many years, the will of many popes, and the genius of several artists, and finally in 1762 the work was finished on a design in the late Baroque style of the Roman architect Nicola Salvi. A tribute to water, the composition is dominated by an imposing Neptune on a cart formed by an enormous shell, pulled by two horses. The triton on the left tries to control his agitated horse which symbolizes the **stormy ocean**, while the one on the right blows through a shell while guiding his horse easily, representing **calm waters**. The sense of movement and enormity is amplified by the small square that the structure occupies. It is a spectacular and incomparable effect. From whatever part of the world the tourist comes, even from distant cultures, he cannot fail to be enchanted, faced with this spectacle. Be prepared to share the pleasure with a lot of people, especially during the summer.

The "calm" horse

The custom of throwing a coin over your shoulder into the fountain, to assure your return to Rome, is celebrated and photographed at all hours of the day and night by people from all over the world

Most of the ancient Roman fountains have been destroyed. However, from descriptions by some writers it seems that the Fountain of Trevi is the type of terminal fountain that the representatives of the ruling Roman elite would have built in their continual courting of public opinion: grandiose, in marble and capable of making a big impression.

The fountain is fed by water from the still-working Acqua Vergine aqueduct, constructed by the son-in-law of the emperor Augustus, Marcus Agrippa, in 19 BC. The bas-relief on the upper left shows the inauguration of the aqueduct. The flow of water was interrupted with the breakup of the empire and later was restored by Pope Nicholas V in 1453. The other bas-relief panel shows how, according to legend, a young girl indicated to some thirsty soldiers where

the spring was, which then gave the waters the name Acqua Vergine. The two statues in the niches represent Abundance on the left and Health on the right. Note also the four **statues** on top of Palazzo Poli on which the entire fountain rests. They do not represent the four seasons, as was thought for some time, but the benefits of water.

When the fountain is clean and the sun shines on it, the reflection on the stone can be almost blinding. If you look in the area under the rocky edge just above the level of the water you can see delicate plants sculpted in relief in the travertine. Between the complexity of the work and the sound of the water, plus the crowd of tourists, you will want to stay a while. It is also wonderful to see at night for the play of light on the water and stone.

The Aqueducts. For the first five centuries, the Romans used local springs, wells and the Tiber. The development of the city and the increase in population necessitated the search for other water sources. Appius Claudius (the same who began the construction of the Appian Way) is responsible for the first aqueduct, finished in 312 BC, bringing the water called Acqua Appia. The last aqueduct, Acqua Alessandrina, was built in 226 AD by emperor Alexander Severus. During the late empire, Rome boasted 11 aqueducts running a total of more than 300 miles, 1212 public fountains, 11 imperial baths, and 926 public baths. Naturally, the construction of the aqueducts required gigantic engineering works, like the perforation of hills and filling of valleys, moving enormous quantities of soil to maintain the slope and the construction of dozens of miles of arches. The water flowed by means of gravity in underground stone channels for most of the way and, once it reached the city, the aqueduct passed over miles of the famous arches whose ruins we can see today. Channels were sealed with hydraulic cement.

The fountains of Rome
The source for Acqua Vergine is at about the fifth mile on Via Tiburtina, the road to Tivoli. Today there is a modern aqueduct Acqua Vergine Nuova (new) that forces the water through prefabricated pipes. The old aqueduct for Acqua Vergine Antica starts from the same place and is still operational, working on gravity. It takes about a day for the water to reach the Trevi fountain.

This enormous quantity of water was distributed to homes in the city by means of a system of pipes, made of lead imported from England.

The aqueducts also fed the public baths, which were open to all for a nominal fee, the imperial baths, the public fountains and troughs, villas and the gardens in the suburbs. In the central office of the water department about 700 people worked: architects, plumbers, inspectors, stonemasons, bricklayers and others. Hundreds of slaves in charge of maintenance walked along the aqueducts to report leaks and to remove vegetation.

The vast knowledge of hydraulic engineering that the Romans had accumulated went lost with the fall of the empire and the arrival of the Middle Ages. In 1429, in the monastery of Monte Cassino, a book describing the distribution of water was found. De Aquis Urbis was written about the year 100 by Sextus Julius Frontinus, responsible for the water department during the reigns of Nerva and Trajan.

Departmental corruption
Frontinus was the head of the water department around the year 100 AD and was known as a man of integrity. Soon after taking office, he measured the volume of water entering the aqueducts and again when it entered the city and found a significant difference. A deeper investigation pointed to the role of the "aquari," the slaves who worked on the maintenance of the aqueducts. Taking illegal payments, they were ready to "forget" to stop a leak or even to create a new one. Everyone who lived near an aqueduct could benefit, as well as the aquari who could save up money to buy their freedom.

The discovery of the book with its incredible historical and engineering content rendered it easier to restore the aqueducts. The popes from the Renaissance on worked to reconstruct the city; they repaired some of the old aqueducts and erected the numerous fountains that we admire today.

Take Via Poli toward Piazza Poli, cross Via del Tritone, continue on Via Poli, turn right on Via del Bufalo and continue on Via di S. Andrea di Fratte which then becomes Via di Propaganda.

At Via della Mercede 12, near Via Capo le Case, an **inscription** on the wall indicates that Gian Lorenzo Bernini lived and died in this building. The major exponent of the Baroque style and creator of many statues, fountains and much interior decoration in Rome, his genius influenced many artists all over Europe.

Turn left on Via Frattina which is one of the most elegant streets, then right on Via del Corso and then, at Largo Goldoni, left onto Via Fontanella Borghese.

Pizza Ciro, *Via della Mercede 43 offers* **pizza** *and other Neapolitan dishes.* Anglo-American Bookstore, *(Tel. 06.679 52 22),Via della Vite 102 near Via Mario de' Fiori, has* **books in English** *on the classical period and tourism, among others.*

2 Campo Marzio in ancient times was an empty plain northwest of the

city center. Here, in the plain delimited by the curve of the Tiber, the Capitoline and the Pincian hills, the Roman army trained and occupied military quarters until the fourth century BC. Later, numerous temples, stadiums and baths were erected there. The name comes from Mars, the god of war (*campo* means field). After the barbarians cut the aqueducts, in the Middle Ages, the reduced population concentrated along the Tiber river, where they could get water and receive merchandise by river. So this area, which in ancient times had never been inhabited, became the center of the city for many centuries. The fulcrum of this medieval neighborhood was in Piazza di Campo Marzio and Piazza Firenze. The nearby streets are interesting and picturesque, such as Vicolo Valdina, Via Ascanio, Via dei Prefetti, Via del Divino Amore and Vicolo della Palla Corda. Continuing south from here you reach the Pantheon and can connect to Walk 1 - The Heart of Rome

Palazzo Borghese. The Borgheses were one of the most famous Roman families and had vast properties in the area. Palazzo Borghese was begun by Vignola in 1560 and then finished by Carlo Maderno. Called the "harpsichord" because the plan of the building suggested the shape of that musical instrument, with the "keyboard" formed by the nearby stairway of the port of Ripetta (now gone). The façade has two balconies with a hanging garden on the highest one. Inside is a beautiful courtyard adorned with 96 paired columns alternated with numerous antique statues.

Continuing down Via Fontanella Borghese to Largo di Fontanella Borghese, you will find an **open-air antique market** that sells books, etchings and lithographs. It is only a few yards after the Palazzo Borghese.

Continue on Via di Clementino to Piazza Nicosia

The elegant **Fountain of Piazza Nicosia** by Giacomo della Porta has water falling on several progressively larger basins. Originally placed in Piazza del Popolo in 1572, it was moved a few yards to make way for the obelisk, and remained there until 1823. Valadier had it moved again to make way for the four lions around the obelisk. After the next move it was taken apart and packed away in the city's warehouse. It was reconstructed here in Piazza Nicosia in 1950.

From Piazza Nicosia go back to Piazza Cardelli and continue south on Via Metastasio to Piazza Firenze and Piazza Campo Marzio.

Giolitti, *a wonderful **ice cream** store thought by many to be the **best in Rome**, is at Via Uffici del Vicario 40.*

Retrace your steps to Piazza Cardelli and continue north on Via di Ripetta up to Piazza Porto di Ripetta.

Between the two churches San Rocco and San Girolamo degli Schiavoni right after Piazza Porto di Ripetta, you will see the **Fontana della Botticella** (Fountain of the Little Keg) (right). The water falls on a basin that sits on a barrel. It reminds us of the merchandise, and in particular the casks of wine, unloaded from the nearby Ripetta river port that opened in 1704.

Near the two churches of San Rocco and San Girolamo degli Schiavoni, along the Tiber, was the Porto di Ripetta. Here boats brought goods from the hinterland, such as wine, coal and grain. The beautiful steps of this river port, that gradually descended the banks, were the inspiration of de Sanctis for the construction of the magnificent steps in Piazza di Spagna.

A refuge
The church of San Rocco hosted the Ospizio delle Celate (the hospice of the hidden), for unwed pregnant girls. The obstetric hospital was next to the church and the girls could stay for free. During their stay, if they wanted, they could keep their faces hidden for the entire time. No one asked for identification and their identities remained anonymous. The institution lasted for about three centuries when it was unexpectedly eliminated by the new Italian government at the end of the nineteenth century, right when other countries began to adopt this social service.

Continuing north on Via di Ripetta you will soon visit two ancient monuments.

3 Ara Pacis. www.arapacis.it. Ara Pacis means altar of peace, and it was constructed by Caesar Octavian Augustus between 13 and 9 BC to celebrate the *"pax romana,"* the Roman Peace, a period of peace and prosperity after the military victories in Spain and Gaul (as France was called in ancient times). The bas-reliefs are sculpted in Carrara marble and constitute a splendid example of classical sculpture. The procession depicted on the south and north sides of this rectangular structure took place on the 4th of July, 13 BC and represents the passage from the republic to the empire and the advent of Rome as the only superpower.

On the side of the monument opposite the river the characteristic lictors holding the fasces, the bundle of sticks that symbolized the authority of the law, appear. Right after is the emperor Octavian Augustus with the future emperor Tiberius touching his arm. Then, hooded, the carriers of the ceremonial flame, followed by an old man carrying the sacred imperial axe. Afterwards is the face of Marcus Agrippa, best friend and son-in-law to the emperor, Augustus' wife Livia, and Julia, the only daughter, who was later disowned by her father. Note the child pulling on the toga to get attention.

Facing the river, the Roman elite passes in review on the side of the monument. This includes priests, senators and magistrates.

The highest priest, the Pontifex Maximus, uses part of his toga to cover his head. His religious functions and the title in following centuries were appropriated by the emperor and then passed to the Pope, who is also known, in fact, as the Pontiff.

This modern building protects the ancient Ara Pacis from the elements.

The Ara Pacis was found in the area where Via Lucina is now, and was brought to light in pieces at several times after 1568. Finally it was entirely recovered using more modern techniques of excavation, among which was the freezing of the soil. The reconstruction work was done in the 1930's using also, as a guide, a relief in the Vatican Museums, which was then transferred near the Mausoleo di Augusto.

Augustus' daughter Julia

The emperor Augustus found himself faced with a society in which couples tended not to marry, there was a high rate of divorce and people were less attracted to religion. He decided to improve the situation by trying to restore and revive the ancient moral values. To do this, among other things, he had laws passed which outlawed adultery. Julia, his only daughter, even though married to his best friend Marcus Agrippa, was a woman of easy virtue and continued to shock Roman society. In 2 BC she was finally tried for scandalous behavior and exiled to the island of Ventotene in the Gulf of Gaeta in a fantastic villa on a high promontory overlooking the sea. She often dove off the cliffs of the island to swim naked. A moat was dug around the house. Each visitor had to be searched and registered and by explicit orders of the emperor, no wine could be served.

In front of Ara Pacis is the **Mausoleo d'Augusto** or Augustus' Mausoleum, circular in shape, which the same emperor had constructed for himself and his descendents from the family Julius-Claudius. He had it begun in 28 BC after the famous victory of Actium against Marc Anthony and Cleopatra. Octavian Augustus, according to historians, had visited the tomb of Alexander the Great and it is probable that Alexander's tomb inspired his mausoleum (below).

The structure, with a diameter of 300 Roman feet (a little less than 300 feet), is larger than that of Hadrian (Castel Sant'Angelo), which measures 64 meters (210 feet). The building included the ashes of the emperor, with his autobiography engraved onto bronze tablets.

Near the door were two granite obelisks, which were later reused; one was transferred to Piazza dell'Esquilino behind the church of Santa Maria Maggiore, and the other went to complete the fountain of Monte Cavallo at Piazza del Quirinale.

Emperors, relatives and pretenders to the throne were buried there, several prematurely deceased. Some, it is thought, were poisoned by the second wife of Augustus, Livia, who, after innumerable manipulations, was finally able to have her son Tiberius become emperor. Nero and Julia, the disowned daughter of Augustus, were notable exceptions of members not accepted in the family mausoleum.

'Gusto, *(€€€€) under the northern part of the colonnade, at Piazza Augusto Imperatore 9, is a* **restaurant, pizzeria, wine bar and buffet** *with an area dedicated to an international bookstore for wines and cooking.* Gusto al 28 *is a more casual option with tables outside under the colonnade. A third locale is in the nearby Via della Frezza 16.*

From Piazza Augusto Imperatore take Largo Schiavoni and turn left on Via Tomacelli to Largo Goldoni. Continue straight and cross Via del Corso. Take Via Condotti toward Piazza di Spagna.

4 Via Condotti. The triangle between Via del Corso, Via del Babuino and Via Due Macelli and Via della Mercede has been traditionally defined the "foreigners' ghetto." It was concentrated mainly in the area between Piazza di Spagna and Via del Corso and now contains many sixteenth and seventeenth century palazzos.

The so-called "artists' ghetto" had its center in Via Sistina and Via degli Artisti. The two worlds came in contact especially in the streets and places around Piazza di Spagna. Most of the streets are oriented east-west, that is from Via del Corso to this unforgettable piazza. Going from north to south are: Via Vittoria, Via della Croce, Via delle Carrozze, Via Condotti, Via Borgognona, Via Frattina, Via della Vite and Via Mercede.

Via Condotti is the most elegant street in Rome for its luxury stores and surrounding old palaces. The name is derived from the word *condotti* or water conduits that carried the Acqua Vergine waters. Dating from ancient times, they were put out of service during the Middle Ages, but were restored in the 1400's

by Pope Nicolas V.

On this street several famous personages resided, among them **Guglielmo Marconi** (the inventor of the radio), who lived in the home at number 11 until his death in 1937. Other famous residents include **Carlo Goldoni**, the famous playwright, who lived here from 1758 until 1759, and one of the most famous Italian poets, **Giacomo Leopardi,** at number 81.

Typical store hours:
Most of the stores in this area are open from 9:30 or 10 AM to 7:30 or 8 PM. Some stores can be closed during the early afternoon, from 1:30 - 3:30, especially outside the center.

The area between Piazza di Spagna and Via del Corso is also the center for international high fashion. Famous brand name stores sell elegant clothing for men and women, jewelry, shoes, housewares and artistic objects. The products are good quality at naturally high prices.

In the area of **Piazza di Spagna** there are the boutiques of Valentino, Dolce e Gabbana, Missoni, Sergio Rossi, and Rocco Barocco. On the surrounding streets are Armani, Bulgari, Cartier, Prada, Ferragamo, Gucci, Hermes, Alberta Ferretti, Vuitton, Max Mara, Elisabetta Franchi, Pandora, Versace, Moschino, Givenchy, Fendi, Laura Biagiotti, Fratelli Rossetti, Chanel, Emporio Armani, Etro and Gente.

The portal of SMOM

At Via dei Condotti 68, near Via Bocca di Leone, is the **Sovereign Military Order of Malta, (SMOM)**. It is considered by some to be the smallest country in the world, even though it does not meet all the criteria that define a state. It is so small that it has no educational or transportation system, public services or its own police. You can easily recognize it by the red flag with a white cross outside the door or in the courtyard.

The Vatican and some other Catholic states recognize it as an independent country, and it enjoys extraterritoriality. It maintains embassies in several countries such as Hungary, Austria, Spain and Poland, but not in the U.S.

Here we see another of the sophisticated contrasts that shows Rome at its best. Within a few steps, we go from the enormous attraction and modern transience of shops that represent international fashion to an institution that has consistently applied over the centuries one of the highest Christian ideals: aid to the sick and needy. SMOM, which counts only a few hundred citizens, among other things prints its own **stamps** and decides its own car **license plates**. The letters SMOM on a car render it immediately identifiable. This discontinuous state consists of the palazzo in Via Condotti, the villa on the Aventine hill (see Walk 2), and the Casa dei Cavalieri di Rodi (House of the Knights of Rhodes) at Piazza del Grillo in front of Trajan's Forum (See Walk 7). Originally a religious order, for a long time, however, it had a military purpose to defend or reoccupy the Holy Land. Today its charitable mission is conducted throughout the world, mainly through its 100 hospitals and 40 assistance groups with more than 80,000 volunteers permanently active in areas of crisis. Their members are also particularly active in the fight against leprosy and in assistance to the terminally ill.

Knights of Malta

The original name was Cavalieri di Rodi (Knights of Rhodes) a religious confraternity founded by the monk Gerard in the twelfth century with the purpose of assisting pilgrims during their stay in the Holy Land. They were forced to flee Jerusalem after it was retaken by the Turks in 1308. With the expansion of the Ottoman Empire in the following centuries, they transferred to Rhodes and then to Malta where they built the capital city of Valletta. In fact, they are now known as the Knights of Malta (Cavalieri di Malta). After the Napoleonic occupation of the island, they moved to Ferrara, Catania and finally to Rome.

The Order has diplomatic relations with more than 84 states, is a permanent observer at the United Nations and it is present in more than 100 countries with its national and international organizations, foundations and coordination centers.

Birreria Viennese Blanko *at Via della Croce 21, besides* **beer***, offers pizza and Austrian dishes.* Antica Enoteca di Via della Croce, *(€€€) Via della Croce 76b, is a* **wine bar** *and restaurant.*

Antico Caffe Greco at Via Condotti 86 was founded in 1760 as is inscribed at the entrance and it is the oldest in Rome. A Greek, Nicola della Maddalena, established Rome's most famous coffee house here 15 years before the American Revolution. It was considered the café of intellectuals, since many **literary figures, artists and famous personages** visited here. Among its customers it boasted sovereigns like Ludwig of Bavaria, various popes, Dickens, Mark Twain, Wagner, Goethe, Stendhal, Schopenauer, Franz Liszt, De Chirico, Carlo Levi, Orson Welles, and even Casanova and Buffalo Bill, among others. Signatures from many of its patrons can be observed. (Remember that service at a table costs more than being served at the bar in most places.)

Italy, and Rome in particular, have attracted and inspired **writers** for centuries. In the first half of the nineteenth century, it was a magnet for the Romantic writers who found their muse among the ruins and monuments of Rome. Schooled in the Greek and Roman classics, they came to absorb the atmosphere of the forums, baths, basilicas and hills. After all, what could be more romantic than the rich ruins of a great civilization, now lost, covered with "ivy, lichens and wallflowers," as Hawthorne put it?

Some visited; others took up residence for years, writing parts of their famous works here or on their return home. Some of the more memorable are those filled with classical symbolism, such as the poem *Rome* by Lord Byron, and Shelley's *Prometheus Unbound*. Shelley's *The Cenci* relates a famous scandal and dramatic trial ending with the execution in 1599 of several of the protagonists. Others are more contemporary travel books, relating the writers' impressions, such as Dickens' *Pictures from Italy*, and Stendahl's guidebook *Rome, Naples and Florence* from 1817 In an intriguing combination, Hawthorne's psychological novel, *The Marble Faun,* contains detailed descriptions of monuments, streets and museums in Rome, starting from the title sculpture, which is found on the second floor of the Palazzo Nuovo in the Capitoline Museums.

What did they say about Rome?
Lord Byron: "O Rome! my country! city of the soul!"
Charles Dickens: "Every inch of ground, in every direction, is rich in associations and natural beauties."
Nathaniel Hawthorne: "Our heartstrings have mysteriously attached themselves to the Eternal City." (Hawthorne and his wife spent several years in Rome).
Henry James: "There are days when the beauty and climate of Rome alone suffice for happiness."
Goethe: "In Rome I have found myself for the first time."

5 Piazza di Spagna (M Spagna) is the
most famous piazza of Rome, an irregular space
among the most spectacular in the world. The
Spanish Steps, the Barcaccia fountain at the base
and the Trinità dei Monti church at the top constitute almost a theatrical set. It takes its name from
the palazzo of the Spanish ambassador to the
Holy See situated in front of American Express.
This area attracted the first influx of secular tourists in the eighteenth century, especially German
and English poets and artists and gentlemen visiting Europe. It has maintained a worldly, artistic
and international atmosphere for centuries.

At the bottom of the steps is the **Barcaccia
Fountain**, (photo below) now in a narrow part of
the irregular piazza, but built in 1629, one hundred
years before the steps themselves. The boat is
the basin of the fountain. It is symmetrical, the
stern and the prow are identical and it is partly
submerged in the water, situated below the level
of the street. According to legend the fountain
recalls an event during the flooding of the Tiber in

*The Barcaccia, the Spanish Steps and
the Trinita dei Monti church*

1598. The swollen river flooded part of the city, inside the Pantheon the water
was 18 feet high, and when at last it retreated, a boat was found abandoned

on this hill. The design of the
Barcaccia is by Pietro Bernini,
father of the more famous Gian
Lorenzo Bernini, and the position
of the fountain, below the level of
the street, is due to the low water
pressure of the Acqua Vergine that
fed it. The artist surely would have
preferred to design a taller, more
elegant fountain with more jets of
water. Considering the limitations,
the work is amazing, as well as the
harmony of the whole combination.

The **Spanish Steps** were designed by Francesco de Sanctis in 1720 and
consist of a series of ramps with 12 steps each. Between each section there are
numerous places to stop and rest. The distance from the piazza to the top of the
steps is only about 72 feet; however, the complexity of the work gives a different
impression. If you ask people how high they think it is, they would say between
100 and 150 feet. This was the only work of De Sanctis, and it is believed he
was inspired by the beautiful drawings of the Port of Ripetta by Alessandro
Specchi, which handled commerce on the river, but is now destroyed

The Spanish Steps were financed initially by a bequest of a French diplomat and
later by a contribution of the French King Louis XV himself. At the base of the
steps you can see the fleur de lis, symbol of the French royal family, together
with the eagle, symbol of the family Conti of Pope Innocent III. The steps are
particularly beautiful in spring when they are covered by vases of azaleas. Here,
artists from many parts of the world sell their works.

The church of **Trinità dei Monti** is characterized by its double towers with bells
and a double entrance ramp. It was begun in 1502 on instructions of King Louis **101**

XII of France and it is the reason for the French involvement in the architectonic complex over succeeding years. Consecrated in 1585 by Pope Sixtus V, King Louis XVIII had it restored after the damage due to the invasion of Rome by Napoleonic forces. The author of the façade is not known with certainty, but it is commonly attributed to Carlo Maderno or Giacomo della Porta.

The **Casina Rossa (Red House)** www.keats-shelley-house.org is situated to the

right of the steps at Piazza di Spagna 26. Here the English poet John Keats and his friend Joseph Severn lived. To the poet, sick with tuberculosis, his doctor advised the mild climate of Rome, but he died a year later in 1821 at only 25. His tragic end was the inspiration for the poet Percy Bysshe Shelley to write *Adonais*, but he also died only two years later, drowned near La Spezia. All three are buried in the Protestant Cemetery (see Walk 2, number 3). The house of these Romantic English poets was transformed into a museum in 1906. By means of donations and research, numerous books, letters, prints and pictures have been assembled. More than 8000 volumes, among which many first editions of Keats and Shelley, enhance the library.

The **Giorgio de Chirico Museum** at Piazza di Spagna 31 (http://www.fondazi-onedechirico.org/?lang=en) is the house where the artist lived with his wife from 1948 until his death in 1978. Advance reservations are required. His studio has been preserved and exhibits numerous models and paintings. He was distinguished as a surrealist painter and sculptor. His style consisted often in faceless mannequins alongside unrelated objects, characteristic of the technique used by the surrealists. During his stay in Paris, he was known also for painting deserted city scenes. De Chirico had a profound effect on the surrealist movement and especially on the painters Yves Tanguy and Salvador Dali'.

*A **subway** station is on the left side of the piazza, near Vicolo del Bottino.*

At number 23, left of the Steps, is **Babington's**, founded in 1896 by two Englishmen to satisfy the tastes of their countrymen. It still offers, besides tea, a variety of typical English dishes such as meat pies, pancakes and eggs with bacon.

*Nino, (€€€) Via Borgognona 11, is considered one of the best **Tuscan restaurants**. A McDonald's is at Piazza di Spagna 46, on the right of the Steps, near the large column (Colonna dell'Immacolata). Hostaria al 31, (€€€) Via delle Carrozze 31, also has outside tables. Most of the cafés in the area are of good quality for a **coffee, sandwich, or ice cream**. Alberto di Castro, Via del Babuino 71, is an interesting print shop.*

Take Via del Babuino toward Piazza del Popolo.

6 Via del Babuino.

The street is straight and lined mostly with palazzi from the seventeenth century, along with some from the sixteenth and eighteenth. On this street lived several famous **artists** such as the painters Salvatore Rosa and Poussin. The Roman poet Trilussa was born here. Together with Via Margutta it boasts numerous antique stores and art galleries.

Along the street is a **fountain** with an ancient statue of Silenus, a god of the forest, depicted as part man and part goat, reclining on a marble tub. The human part was often pictured as an old man with a beard in a jovial intoxicated state. Originally this statue held a bagpipe in its hand. Long ago his form must have been disfigured and frightening with the missing hands and corroded lines of his face. When the statue was moved here, in the sixteenth century, it was already so ugly that the Romans quickly baptized it "*babbuino*" or baboon. This epithet became so popular that it actually caused the name of the street to be changed from Via Paolina to Via del Babuino. This is another of the "talking statues" used by the populace to air their opinions about the Pope, the nobility and the authorities in general that, otherwise, would not have found expression. (See Pasquino, Walk 1). At Via del Babuino 153b is the Anglican All Saints' Church from the end of the nineteenth century. Note the contrast between its austere neo-gothic style and the rest of the area.

> La Luna d'Oro, *Via dei Greci 23 is a pizzeria and restaurant. At* Discount Alta Moda, *Via del Gesù e Maria 16, you can find last season's high fashions, bags and shoes greatly reduced.*

7 Piazza del Popolo (M Flaminio) was the first impression that visitors had, from the Middle Ages on, of the eternal city since, given the fact that most

arrived from the north, they passed through Piazza del Popolo. It takes its name from one of the churches that delimit the square, **Santa Maria del Popolo,** (*popolo* is Italian for people), because it was built with money from the common people. Later, by extension, the piazza took the same name.

The church itself is far outshone by the collection of art within its walls. Originally built in 1099 by Pope Paschal II on the site of Nero's supposed grave, what we see now is basically the rebuilt Renaissance church from 1472-77 under Pope Sixtus IV. The simplicity of the façade with one circular window belies the incredible riches in the interior. Martin Luther stayed in the adjoining Augustinian monastery during his trip to Rome in 1511. It is now a gallery for art exhibits.

Although you will probably enter from the side, the chapels are **described from the front entrance**. The first chapel on the right entering the church from the front, the **Della Rovere Chapel**, built by Cardinal Domenico della Rovere, has frescoes by Pinturicchio: *The Adoration of the Child* above the altar and lunettes around the ceiling showing scenes from the life of Saint Jerome. The third chapel is that of Giovanni **Basso della Rovere**, nephew of Pope Sixtus IV who was from the Della Rovere family (as was later Pope Julius II) with frescoes from the school of Pinturicchio. Oak leaves entwined in the decorative touches in several chapels are the symbol of the Della Rovere family.

The **Cerasi Chapel** to the left of the main altar houses 2 magnificent paintings by **Caravaggio** (1600-01), master of chiaroscuro. The *Crucifixion of Saint Peter* (left) portrays the immense effort to raise the cross with Saint Peter's head pointing down. The *Conversion of Saint Paul* also shows the energy and unusual positions of the subjects. The *Assumption* is by Annibale Carracci.

Raphael designed the **Chigi Chapel** for the Sienese banker Agostino Chigi, second on the left from the main entrance (1513). This chapel figures prominently in Dan Brown's mystery *Angels and Demons*, although with some poetic license as to who did what. The unusual pyramid shaped marble tombs on both sides were designed by Raphael, although Bernini did modify them later with the addition of the medallions. The *Birth of the Virgin* above the altar is by Sebastiano del Piombo. On order of Pope Alexander VII (1655-67), the Baroque master Bernini completed the decoration with the addition of the marble floor, the hanging bronze lamp with cherubs, and the sculpture to the right of the

altar. The statue of *Habakkuk* shows Bernini's flair for portraying energy and movement. The distinctive **marble medallion** in the center of the floor shows a kneeling skeleton holding the Chigi coat of arms. A reference to the Holy Year of 1650 is indicated by the capital letters in the inscription. (MDCL in Roman numerals is 1650.). Bernini is also responsible for additional Baroque touches throughout the church, such as stucco angels and saints. Another macabre tomb with a marble skeleton is that of the architect **Gisleni** who designed it for himself. Located to the left of the main door, it also shows a butterfly to suggest death and rebirth in the next life.

Art exhibitions are frequently held in the Sala del Bramante in the Church of Santa Maria del Popolo at Via Gabriele d'Annunzio 1.

The current layout of **Piazza del Popolo** shows French influence. In fact, it was designed and carried out by Giuseppe Valadier between 1811 and 1824, combining a neoclassic style in the use of statues, grandeur and the semicircle, with the more characteristically Roman churches, obelisk and fountains. The result is a blend of classic and Baroque.

Three streets lead to the piazza in the form of a trident: Via di Ripetta, Via del Corso and Via del Babuino. Three churches also delimit it: Santa Maria di Montesanto and Santa Maria dei Miracoli which are considered twins, but not identical, and the already mentioned Santa Maria del Popolo on the opposite side The large **Egyptian obelisk** dedicated to Ramses II was moved to the center of the piazza in 1589, replacing the fountain that is now in Piazza Nicosia. At the four corners around it are **four marble lions**, which emit a stream of water that seems like a wide, thin sheet of glass.

Two fountains lie at the two extremities of the ellipse; the one on the west side, toward the Tiber, represents the sea god Neptune with tritons holding dolphins. The one opposite is the goddess Rome with the two rivers, the Tiber and the Aniene, represented by bearded men in a reclining position, and between them the wolf with Romulus and Remus (photo next page) In the background above it you can see the imposing arched "mostra" fountain with a large waterfall, which serves as the terminal fountain of the Acqua Vergine Nuova. Right above that is the **belvedere of the Pincio**, easily reached from the piazza, where you can see a wonderful panorama of the city, beautiful especially at sunset.

The **piazza** was once the location for capital executions; the last occurred in 1826. From here also the crowd viewed fireworks set off from the Pincio, and
until the end of the 1800's, the traditional horse races during carnival started,

going down Via del Corso toward Piazza Venezia. Since traffic was restricted, the area has been given back to the people who, as you can see, have rediscovered the pleasure of strolling.

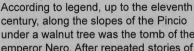

Nero's ghost
According to legend, up to the eleventh century, along the slopes of the Pincio under a walnut tree was the tomb of the emperor Nero. After repeated stories of witches, evil spirits and the ghost of Nero roaming the area, the Romans decided to put a stop to it. They cut down the tree and threw it and the surrounding dirt that contained the emperor's remains into the Tiber. After that, superstitious stories of the supernatural in this place decreased considerably.

The belvedere of the Pincio with the terminal fountain of the Acqua Vergine (above) and detail of the fountain (right).

One mile north of Piazza del Popolo, at Via Guido Reni 4A is **MAXXI**, a new museum dedicated to **contemporary art** and creativity.

*There are **two historic bars** with outside tables in the southern part of Piazza del Popolo (expect to pay more for the ambience). The **bar** Rosati in Piazza del Popolo 4 has as customers many artists and actors, visible mainly on summer evenings. For many years the author Alberto Moravia was a constant fixture as he lived nearby on Via dell'Oca. The **bar-restaurant** Canova, a short distance away at Piazza del Popolo 16 takes its name from the sculptor Antonio Canova who, in the nineteenth century, had his studio near here.*

*Buccone, Via di Ripetta 19, near Piazza del Popolo, has a vast selection of wines and beers and also **gastronomic specialties.** The Anglo-American Book Shop, Via ella Vite 102, specializes in **books** in English. Dell'Oca, Via dell'Oca 43, an extension of Via della Penna, also has **pizza** and outside tables, at good prices.*

From Piazza del Popolo, take Via del Corso.

8 Goethe's House, Via del Corso 18, http://www.casadigoethe.it/en/, offers an exhibition of the poems of the writer, accompanied by lithographs and objects that unite art and literature Here Johann Wolfgang von Goethe, German poet, dramatist, writer and scientist, resided. There is a permanent exhibit, which occupies about 5000 square feet, and special exhibits are periodically presented. In Rome he studied art, architecture and ancient Greek and Roman literature. The immersion in the classics suggested to the writer more detachment from emotional content and gave him new perspectives that put more emphasis on calm and the perfection of form. *Faust*, his greatest work, is an allegory of human life and one of the masterpieces of German and world literature. He was one of the first of the important writers to express the modern individualistic spirit. His stay in Rome was the fulfillment of a dream Goethe had had for a long time. In his words:

"I am finally here in this capital of the world … Now that I am here I have found peace and it seems I have found it for the rest of my life." **105**

As a "refuge from the north" he was fascinated by the sensuality of the south, of its more carefree way of living and of the calm and serenity of the Italians.

> *From Via del Corso, on the left take Via della Fontanella, cross Via del Babuino and go straight down Via Margutta.*

> Lowenhaus, *a Bavarian* **beer** *hall, at Via della Fontanella 16b offers dishes slightly modified for Italian tastes. Right after crossing Via del Babuino,* Il Margutta Vegetariano *(€€€) Via Margutta 118 has a variety of* **vegetarian dishes** *in a sophisticated environment. The atmospheric* Osteria Margutta, *(€€€) Via Margutta 82, has been a meeting place for famous and cultured personages.*

9 Via Margutta.

There is a hidden Rome known only by the fortunate few who live there and pretty much unknown by the rest. It is the Rome of Via Margutta or better what is hidden behind the façades of its palazzos. It is the special place of the artists whose studios face courtyards where stairways and paths climb among bushes of ivy and roses up toward the Pincio. Many artists

have lived and worked on this street since the sixteenth century, and even today it is the location of several studios and galleries.

In tone with the artistic atmosphere of the area, the **Fountain of Via Margutta** (left), or the Fountain of the Artists, was erected, which is composed of two easels, the tools of a painter and two masks, one smiling and one sad. Here also, at number 110, the late great director **Federico Fellini** and his wife the actress Giulietta Masina chose to live. Their names are cut into the stone on a plaque on the wall.

> *Where Via Margutta bends to the right, there is a small internal piazza with shops and* Babette, *(€€€) a* **restaurant** *with tables in the courtyard.*

> *At the end of Via Margutta take Via Alibert and go left on Via del Babuino to go back toward Piazza di Spagna. Climb the Spanish Steps to Piazza Trinità dei Monti and go left on Viale Trinità dei Monti.*

While exploring the street, from time to time you may discover the romantic beauty of the courtyards and views in the direction of the Pincio, with charming glimpses of terraces, stairways and picturesque houses.

Further down, near number 81, there is a **sign from the 1740**'s declaring punishment for those who leave trash. In perhaps a bit of exaggeration, it warns that corporal punishment for leaving trash, besides a fine of 10 scudi, could include the rack (rota), lashes, or "whatever the master of the street decides, according to the age and sex."

From the top of the Spanish Steps, you can take one of the most fascinating walks.

Before heading down Viale Trinità dei Monti, if you go briefly to the right on Via Gregoriana, there is a curious building, **Palazzo Zuccari**, also called the house of monsters. The main door is made in the form of a wide open mouth, ready to swallow anything, and the motif is repeated with open mouths on the windows.

Strolling along **Viale Trinità dei Monti** toward the Pincio, you have a great view of the characteristic and picturesque roofs, attics and domes of this area of the city. On the right at Viale Trinità dei Monti 2 you may visit the beautiful **Villa Medici,** built in 1540 on an area where in ancient times there were sumptuous villas.

Here the residence of Lucullo, (119 – 57 BC), a famous Roman general, was located. Underneath the villa a labyrinth of mysterious rooms was found, and an enormous cistern that fed Lucullo's pool and gardens. The villa contained Roman art, which was then transferred to the Uffizi Gallery in Florence, and it has been, since the beginning of the nineteenth century, the seat of the **French Academy**. It allows French artists, writers, and composers the opportunity to study the enormous classical heritage of Rome. Galileo Galilei was also a guest here in 1633, when it was the Tuscan embassy, during his difficult stay in Rome. Galileo's column was erected in his honor, in front of the villa. Guided tours of the villa and the magnificent gardens are available. The Academy of France in Villa Medici offers periodic art exhibitions. https://www.villamedici.it/en/.

The **Pincio** is a park connected to Villa Borghese, and from the belvedere above Piazza del Popolo the panorama extends to the dome of Saint Peter's and beyond. Viewing the sunset from here is a wonderful spectacle.

Instant messaging?
A special cannonball was used to decorate the fountain in front of Villa Medici. It is said that Queen Christina of Sweden, who lived in Rome from 1655 to 1689, had an appointment with the painter Charles Errard and, being late, she decided to have a cannonball shot from Castel Sant'Angelo to the entrance of the villa. It hit the bronze door and left a dent that is still visible. In the seventeenth century, since there were no telephones, a cannon shot was a quick way to send a message at a distance. This is the legend, considered to be fact by tourist guides of past centuries. However, some experts doubt that the cannons available in those days at Castel Sant'Angelo were capable of reaching the villa, about a mile away.

After Viale Trinità dei Monti, at the fork stay on the right and continue on Viale Adamo Mickiewicz up to the Pincio.

If you still have time you may visit Villa Borghese, a large park with three museums, fountains and novelties to discover. (See Walk 6 for the description).

From the Pincio, to get to the metro station Flaminio, you can come down on Viale Gabriele d'Annunzio to Piazza del Popolo and then go to the right along the church Santa Maria del Popolo, pass under the arches to reach Piazzale Flaminio. As an alternative, you can return to Piazza di Spagna where there is another metro station.

The whole walk is about 6 kilometers (3 ¾ miles). If time is short, do not miss the Trevi Fountain, Piazza di Spagna, Via Condotti and the surrounding streets and Piazza del Popolo.

Additional Restaurants

Il Chianti, Via del Lavatore 81, www.vineriailchianti.com. Tuscan cuisine and typical Tuscan wines. Tables outside. €€

Baccano, Via delle Muratte 23, www.BaccanoRoma.com. Restaurant and wine bar, near Trevi fountain. €€€

Il Piccolo Arancio, Vicolo Scanderberg 112, www.piccoloarancio.it. Traditional cuisine. Tables outside. Near Trevi Fountain, near Via del Lavatore. This is part of a chain that also includes Arancio d'Oro and the trattoria Settimio all'Arancio. €€

T-Bone Station, Via Francesco Crispi 29, www.t-bone.it. Large steaks and also American dishes such as fried chicken and hamburgers. €€

Al 34, Via Mario dei Fiori 34, www.ristoranteal34.it. Pleasant atmosphere. €€€

Nino, Via Borgognona 11, www.ristorantenino.it. Tuscan cooking. €€€

Il Leoncino, Via del Leoncino 28, Tel. 06.687 63 06. Simple place, serves thin crusty pizza. €€

Matricianella, Via del Leone 2, www.matricianella.it. Trattoria. €€

'Gusto, Piazza Augusto Imperatore 9, www.gusto.it. Near Via di Ripetta. €€€

La Buca di Ripetta, Via di Ripetta 36, www.labucadiripetta.com. €€

RistorArte Margutta (Margutta Vegetariano), Via Margutta 118, www.ilmargutta.bio. As the name suggests, vegetarian dishes are served. Between Vicolo del Babuino and Via del Babuino. €€€

Fountains of Rome

Rome and water are inseparable. The ancient Romans built aqueducts from distant pure water springs to bring an abundant supply to their citizens. These aqueducts continued to function until the invading barbarians interrupted the flow. During the Renaissance several of the aqueducts were restored, returning the abundant streams to the capital, allowing popes and administrators to construct fountains of many shapes and sizes, giving the best artists of the day free rein to produce their masterpieces. Traditionally, water passes directly from the several distant sources to the consumer, without being stored in reservoirs, thus each of these "waters" has its unique characteristics, and was debated as easily as different qualities of wine.

The water came originally from several springs and rivers outside Rome. The first was the Acqua Appia, brought to Rome via aqueduct in the third century BC. By 226 AD, when the last was built, eleven aqueducts poured water into Rome, providing water also for the public baths, which had proliferated. In 410 AD, when the Goths attacked Rome, there were 1212 public fountains, 11 imperial baths and 926 public baths.

Some of the waters came from as far as 50 miles from Rome, and passed underground for most of the distance, before being raised up to the familiar aqueducts for the last few miles in the city; sometimes more than one water traveled in distinct channels on one aqueduct.

The six aqueducts of modern Rome are, with their founding date, Acqua Vergine Antica (1453), Acqua Felice (1586), Acqua Paola (1611) which comes from Lake Bracciano, Acqua Pia Antica Marcia (1870), Acqua Vergine Nuova (1937) and Acqua Peschiera (1949). The first three are reconstructions of ancient aqueducts. Each water source had, as its entry into Rome, a monumental fountain, which carried the insignias of the emperor or pope who had built it. The Trevi fountain (this Walk) and the Fountain of Moses (at right) from 1587 (Walk 6) are two of these terminal fountains.

One of the most ancient fountains, of only a handful that are left from imperial Rome, is the fountain at the base of the steps of the Palazzo dei Senatori on the Campidoglio. (Walk 7) (photo right). The two large **river gods** represent the Tiber and the Nile. The Romans symbolized a great river as a fully mature,

bearded man, dressed in a flowing robe that indicated the flow of water, reclining upon some symbol of the river he represented. The Nile rests upon a sphinx and the Tiber upon Romulus, Remus and the wolf. The other hand of each holds a cornucopia, symbolizing the wealth and fertility derived from abundant fresh water. The Nile fountain was originally a statue in the ancient Constantine Baths.

The playful **Fontana delle Tartarughe** (Fountain of the Tortoises) (Walk 7) (left) was designed by Giacomo della Porta and executed by Taddeo Landini in 1584. Four graceful youths in bronze push tortoises over the edge of a marble bowl above them, while resting one foot on a dolphin that is happily spouting water. Walk around the fountain to see all the different angles displayed and the lightness and effortless energy.

Walk 1 provides some famous and some not-so famous fountains. In Piazza Navona, the most famous fountain in the piazza is the one in the center, the **Fountain of the Rivers** designed by Bernini (right). It took three years to complete, from 1648 - 51. It is considered his greatest triumph in fountain design. Four marble figures represent the major rivers in the four continents then known.

The other two fountains in the piazza are symmetrically placed at the ends of the piazza and are older than the central one.

The fountain at the southern end boasts a statue by Bernini, called il **Moro**, which is a Neptune-like figure grasping a large fish by the tail. The fountain at the northern end has nineteenth century statues of **Neptune** and tritons. Details about these fountains are in Walk 1.

Several modest but intriguing examples are the Fountain of the Water Vendor (il **Facchino**) (at right) on Via Lata just off Via del Corso and the recently restored **Fountain of the Books** near Piazza Navona.

Piazza Barberini sports two masterpieces by Bernini, the **Triton** and the **Fountain of the Bees**. Bernini's influence on fountains, buildings and sculpture was

enormous, especially since he lived to the age of 80. See Walk 6.

Also on Walk 6 are the four (Quattro) fountains inset on the four corners of the intersection of Via delle **Quattro Fontane** and Via del Quirinale and Via del XX Settembre. The four fountains are from 1588.

Fountain of the Bees

The Triton fountain

The **Fountain of the Naiads** in Piazza della Repubblica (left) created protest and indignation when it was unveiled in 1901 for the four bronze nymphs which seemed all too pagan at the time. (Walk 6).

The **Mascherone fountain** on Via Giulia (Walk 1) is one of the more inventive designs. The mask is of ancient origin and leans against the wall, spouting water into a trough.

In addition to the artistic and monumental fountains, there are numerous small black metal fountains called "*fontanelle*," which bring drinking water to many neighborhoods. They are sometimes popularly called "*nasoni*" (*naso* means nose), because of the downward curved faucet. The proper way to drink is to place a finger at the end to block the downward flow, thus causing the water to arch out of the small hole at the top of the spigot at a convenient level at which to drink. Since the water is always flowing, this provides a nice refreshing drink.

No matter where you are walking, take note of the many fountains (there are more than 2000 in Rome), ancient and modern, that you see. Fountains are classified in two types, waters that rise into the air, such as the Triton fountain in Piazza Barberini, or waters that fall, such as the very famous **Trevi fountain**, described at the beginning of this walk. In all, the playful splashing and cool

cascading of the water in the fountains continually refresh the city of Rome.

WALK FIVE - The Vatican

When you walk into **Saint Peter's Square** you find yourself embraced by the two splendid colonnades by Bernini. **Saint Peter's Basilica** is the center of world Catholicism, but non-Catholics will also find the experience incomparable. The **basilica** was built over the old Saint Peter's which had lasted almost 1200 years. Many artists of the Renaissance and Baroque periods, especially Michelangelo and Bernini, contributed to the magnificent effect that strikes the visitor. Entering the basilica, you understand immediately the enormous spiritual and physical importance that it represents. The **Vatican Museums** offer a collection of incomparable masterpieces from the classic Greek period to modern times. The genius of Michelangelo shines in the **Sistine Chapel**, the tender **Pietà** and in the design of the majestic dome. A unique experience is the climb to the top of the **dome**, to the lantern, which gives you a beautiful view of a large part of Rome. The last stop is **Castel Sant'Angelo**, built as a Mausoleum for the emperor Hadrian and used through the centuries as a fortress for the Pope, a prison, barracks and finally as a museum. The "**Passetto**" is a fortified passageway built inside the Vatican walls that allowed the Pope to take refuge in the stronghold of Castel Sant'Angelo in case of danger. At the end, we suggest an area for shopping and dining.

There is a lot to see, so, unless you have several days, it is necessary to establish some priorities and decide which things, for you, are the most important. Like our other walks, we tried to optimize the available time and to concentrate the walk into one day. For some ideas on how to personalize the route, see the section at the end entitled "**Plan your visit to the Vatican.**"

For up-to-date information see the Vatican information site:
http://stpetersbasilica.info/touristinfo.htm

111

In this walk..:

1 The **Vatican Museums** leading to the Sistine Chapel by Michelangelo
2 The **Raphael Rooms,** frescoes for the apartment of Pope Julius II
3 **Sistine Chapel** with Michelangelo's ceiling and wall frescoes
4 **Piazza San Pietro** with Bernini's imposing yet graceful **colonnade**
5 **Saint Peter's Basilica**, the greatest masterpiece of Christianity, which contains exceptional works by the masters of the Baroque and Renaissance. The lantern at the top of the **dome** offers a fantastic view of the Vatican and the city
6 The **Vatican Gardens** (reservations required)
7 **Necropolis** under Saint Peter's
8 **Castel Sant'Angelo** with its fascinating museum, containing 19 centuries of history
9 The **Passetto** which connected Castel Sant'Angelo to Saint Peter's
10 **Ponte Sant'Angelo** with Bernini's sculpted angels

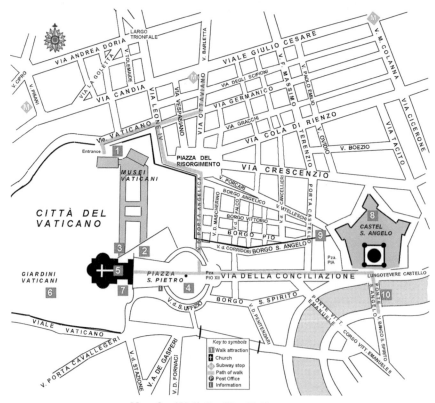

Map for Walk 5 - The Vatican

In this walk you will also find

The best area to eat: The Borgo for dinner and Viale Giulio Cesare and surrounds for lunch and shopping

Starting point: Metro station Ottaviano (or the station Cipro – Musei)

Vatican City extends for only 108 acres and is the smallest country in the world. It was created February 11, 1929 by means of agreements between the Italian state and the Church, and so it is only some decades old. It has, nevertheless, a history going back nearly two millennia since it is associated both with the introduction of Christianity in ancient Rome and, for more than a thousand years, the temporal power of the Pope. It includes Saint Peter's Square and Basilica, the Apostolic Palaces (including the Vatican Museums) and the Gardens. The Pope is the sovereign of the Stato Città del Vaticano (the **Vatican City State**) and is also the religious leader of the more than a billion Catholics spread out over the world. The situation has changed from that in the Middle Ages when emperors found it necessary to be crowned by the pontiff for their legitimization. It was believed then that the pope had a God-given power to crown an emperor. Today we can no longer speak of a papal supremacy; however, the Vatican and the Pope still have a large spiritual, political and social influence.

The Vatican has its own judicial system, prints its own postage stamps, has a post office, a pharmacy, a railroad station, a television station, a gas station and small supermarket (where the prices are substantially lower than in the rest of the city but only people who have a special card may shop there). It has its own special police called the **Swiss Guards**, which date from 1505, (the multicolored uniforms are said to have been designed by Michelangelo), it publishes its own newspaper l'Osservatore Romano and its radio station transmits every day in a dozen languages. The cars carry the designation SCV (Stato Città del Vaticano), called by critical and irreverent Romans "Se Cristo Vedesse!" or "If Christ could only see them…"

For many years the popes preferred to live in the Lateran Palace on the other side of Rome. The Vatican was the home of the popes since the fourteenth century when the Pope, on returning from exile in Avignon in France (1309 – 1377), decided to reside here permanently instead of the deteriorating Lateran Palace. The Church had for centuries governed the central part of the peninsula up until the political unification of Italy, which culminated in 1870 with the taking of Rome by the Piedmont army. The Pope took refuge in the Vatican and it was not until the Concordat of 1929 that there was a resolution of the affairs between the Vatican and the Italian State.

The Metro station Cipro is slightly closer to the entrance to the Museums but we consider the Ottaviano station to be more convenient. At the exit of the Ottaviano metro station, follow the indications for San Pietro and go south on Via Ottaviano. When you get to Via Germanico turn right and walk until you reach the Vatican walls. Walk along the wall on the right on Viale Vaticano until you get to the entrance to the museums.

International Politics
At the Potsdam Conference in 1945, when Stalin was advised to consider the position of the papacy he responded sarcastically, "How many divisions does the Pope have?" He thus showed an absolute lack of historical comprehension toward an institution that has endured two millennia. Only 50 years later, in fact, the Polish Pope John Paul II had an important role in the liberation of his nation and put in motion that process that finally contributed to the dismantling of the Soviet Union, without having even one soldier.

*Del Frate, Via degli Scipioni 118 is a **wine bar**. Castroni, at the intersection of Via Ottaviano 55 and Via Cola di Rienzo 196 is a **gourmet deli, café** and **pastry shop**. Saxophone Pub, Via Germanico 26 has beer, salads and a variety of **sandwiches** with tables outside. One of the small restaurants of the Insalata Ricca chain is at Piazza Risorgimento 5 near Via Vespasiano. Gelateria Old Bridge is at Via dei Bastioni di Michelangelo 5. As always, try to avoid places very close to the attractions and too full of tourists, where the quality has the tendency to go down. Instead, head for the places frequented by both locals and tourists, as for example the places along Viale Giulio Cesare.*

1 The Musei Vaticani (Vatican Museums), on Viale Vaticano, are open every day except Sunday and holidays. http://mv.vatican.va/. **Reserve online in advance to avoid the long lines.** The last Sunday of the month admission is free. There is a choice of several routes denoted by colored stripes; however, some people find them inefficient and not clear enough. Following our indications here, you can personalize your visit. NOTE: Your route may be different from that described here as doors and halls are opened and closed, changed to direct the flow of people.

Generally speaking, to visit all of the areas described will take about 2½ hours. If you skip the Raphael rooms, about 1½ hours will be sufficient. **You need to walk through the entire museum to get to the Sistine Chapel, which takes at least a half hour.** Signs at various points allow you to choose your itinerary. Book and souvenir shops are available at several points in the museums.

One of the many beautiful mosaics

The Vatican Museums are an assemblage of several distinct museums, which are all contained in the enormous building to the right of Saint Peter's Basilica. With miles of corridors and galleries it would be easy to spend days trying to see it all, but most people have limited time and will want to see the main attractions. The **Sistine Chapel** is of course the goal of most; it lies at the very end of the walk through the museum; therefore, you must decide how much to stop and see along the way. There are some important pieces to see and we have described them in the probable order that they will be encountered; however, sometimes the route is changed. So visit a few of the more important areas first along the way and save the *pièce de resistance* for the last.

Walk up the marble steps to the ticket office. An escalator will take you to the beginning of the museum. You may choose to rent an audio guide, which explains the most important masterpieces throughout the museum, including the Sistine Chapel.

You should not miss the most important pieces, which are, in our opinion, after the Sistine Chapel, the sculptures **Apollo Belvedere**, the **Apoxymenos**, the **Belvedere Torso** and the **Laocoön**, and the wall paintings in the **Raphael rooms**. According to your interest and the time you have, visit other important galleries which include the **Etruscan Museum**, the **Egyptian Museum,** and the **Biblioteca** (Library) which contains old handwritten manuscripts and scrolls. The **Pinacoteca** (picture gallery) contains works by Raphael, Giotto, Titian, Perugino and Caravaggio, among others. Other galleries along the way show classical statuary and Renaissance painting.

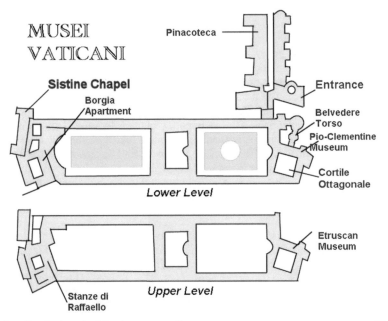

MUSEI VATICANI

Pinacoteca

Sistine Chapel

Borgia Apartment

Entrance

Belvedere Torso

Pio-Clementine Museum

Cortile Ottagonale

Lower Level

Etruscan Museum

Stanze di Raffaello

Upper Level

During the first part of the tour you will pass through the **Cortile della Pigna** (right), so-called for the large ancient bronze pinecone (pigna) set into an enormous semicircular niche. Fashioned in the first century, this fountain was for many years the centerpiece of the atrium of the old Saint Peter's.

Continue on toward the **Pius-Clementine (Pio-Clementino) Museum**, past a room of sculptures and

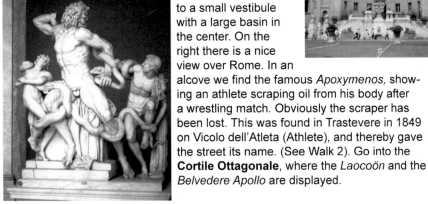

proceed up the stairs to a small vestibule with a large basin in the center. On the right there is a nice view over Rome. In an alcove we find the famous *Apoxymenos,* showing an athlete scraping oil from his body after a wrestling match. Obviously the scraper has been lost. This was found in Trastevere in 1849 on Vicolo dell'Atleta (Athlete), and thereby gave the street its name. (See Walk 2). Go into the **Cortile Ottagonale**, where the *Laocoön* and the *Belvedere Apollo* are displayed.

The Laocoon

The **Vatican collection** was begun in 1503 when the *Belvedere Apollo* was brought to the Vatican, by Pope Julius II, to be joined in 1506 by the *Laocoön.* Over the succeeding years hundreds of sculptures and paintings were added. Between these two sculptures there is a profound contrast: the Apollo has been considered an idealized body representing male beauty while the Laocoön represents pain and tragedy. The Apollo, which originally held a bow in the left hand and an arrow in the right, is a fine Roman copy from 130 AD of an original Greek bronze from 330 BC.

Many of the best sculptures in Rome were copies of Greek masterpieces, most of which have not survived. We must content ourselves with just an idea of their original grandeur. The Laocoön, whose date is uncertain, either the first century BC or first century AD, was carved by artists from Rhodes perhaps from an earlier bronze original, and is one of the most famous statues, certainly the most famous ancient grouping. It was found in 1506 near the Domus Aurea on the Esquiline Hill. The artists Sangallo and Michelangelo were sent by Pope Julius II to investigate the site. It is said that even before dismounting from their horses they recognized what it was because of the references Roman writers had made about the famous legend. The story is told in a dramatic scene in the *Aeneid* by Virgil. The Trojan priest, Laocoön, had doubts about the Trojan Horse and tried to warn his fellow citizens. This attempt to interfere with fate, the normal course of events that would have led to the conquest of the city of Troy by the Greeks, triggered the gods' anger. They sent monstrous sea serpents to destroy him and his two sons.

Continue through the rooms to the nearby **Room of the Muses (Sala delle Muse).** The *Belvedere Torso,* (left) a much-eroded statue from the first century

found in the Baths of Caracalla, was much admired by Michelangelo who sketched it frequently in his youth. As you follow the signs to go to the Raphael rooms (or the Sistine Chapel), you pass through a circular room with a

beautiful large octagonal mosaic covering part of the floor and an **enormous porphyry tub** (right), probably from Nero's Domus Aurea. This room is called the Sala Rotonda (Round Room).

Go upstairs and down the hall to the Raphael rooms

Walking down the long corridor you pass through the **Sala dei Candelabri** (Room of the Candelabras) and the **Sala degli Arazzi** (Room of the Tapestries) that contains many very large sixteenth century tapestries with elaborate scenes, some including exotic animals. The colors have faded but the works are still quite extraordinary.

The **Sala delle Carte Geografiche** (Room of the Maps) (photo above) has marvelous large maps of all the Italian regions on the walls. Large windows give views of the Cortile della Pigna and Cortile del Belvedere and on the other side a glimpse of the beautiful Vatican Gardens. Continue to follow the signs to the Raphael rooms. You will probably go through the rooms in the following order.

2 Stanze di Raffaello (Raphael Rooms). Pope Julius II would not use the apartments of his predecessor, the infamous Borgia pope, Alexander
VI, so he decided to lodge upstairs.

The four small connecting rooms, called the "stanze di Raffaello," became the new papal residence together with the Sala del Chiaroscuro, the Old Room of the Swiss, the Niccolina Chapel and the Loggia. Julius II decided to have Raphael, just twenty-five, decorate the walls, which took him ten years. You are facing some of Raphael's best masterpieces.

The **Sala di Costantino** (Hall of Constantine), the largest of the four main rooms, was painted by Raphael's assistants after his death, using his sketches, and shows the life of Constantine, including his baptism. The *Vision of the Cross* led him to victory by fighting under the banner of the cross in the *Battle of Constantine over Maxentius* at the Milvian Bridge. The *Donation of Constantine* commemorates the legend that Constantine granted dominion over Rome and the Western Empire to the pope. A forged document was held for many years to be the basis for this claim.

The *chiaroscuro* (contrast of dark and light) of the numerous wall paintings of statues gives the adjoining room its name, the **Sala del Chiaroscuro** (Room of Chiaroscuro).

The **Stanza di Eliodoro** (Room of Heliodorus) (1512-14) was originally a private room and is decorated with frescoes by Raphael and his assistants. One panel shows, with dramatic lighting, the *Liberation from Prison of Saint Peter*. In another we see *Pope Leo I Repelling Attila the Hun* (440-461) from Rome, where, above, Saints Peter and Paul are armed with swords. Another shows the *Miracle of Bolsena* where a skeptical priest is convinced of transubstantiation. *The Expulsion of Heliodorus from the Temple* fresco gives the room its name. These scenes are all related politically to Pope Julius II's desire to be free of the French occupation of Italy.

The **Stanza dell'Incendio nel Borgo** (Room of the Fire) (1514-17). This was the dining room, and it contains the episode *Fire in the Borgo*, the neighborhood near the Vatican, which occurred in 847 AD. In the background, part of the **façade of the old Saint Peter's**, which lasted almost 1200 years, can be seen. After it was taken down, in the sixteenth century the new Basilica of Saint Peter's that we see today was built in the same place. The other frescoes are by Raphael's helpers and the ceiling is by Perugino, Raphael's teacher. Above the door, a fresco shows the *Coronation of Charlemagne* by Pope Leo III at Saint Peter's in the year 800.

The Stanza della Segnatura (Room of the Signatures) (1508-1511) is the most famous and was completely done by Raphael. This was the library and the room where papal bulls were signed. The four walls depict Theology, Justice, Philosophy and Poetry. The greatest masterpiece is the *School of Athens*, which represents the triumph of scientific and intellectual pursuits. Plato, Aristotle and Socrates are accompanied by Euclid, Archimedes, Pythagoras, Heraclitus and other important philosophers and mathematicians in a beautifully composed classical building.

Using artistic license, he permitted himself to use faces of some of his contemporaries. While Bramante's appears on Euclid, the lone figure of Heraclitus in the foreground, added after the rest was painted, shows Michelangelo's face (detail at right). Leonardo da Vinci's face appears on Plato, who is shown discussing with Aristotle. Plato points up toward the spiritual world. Behind him are represented the philosophers who appeal to emotion and intuition.

On the right, Aristotle, exponent of good sense and earthly matters, appears as a mediating influence with his hand extended. Behind him are the representatives of reason who emphasized logic, geometry and grammar. Raphael signed this by placing the initials RVSM on Euclid's neckband. (Raphael Vrbinus Sua Mano, or Raphael of Urbino his hand.)

Over one of the windows is the *Parnassus*, showing the god Apollo who plays his lyre, in the center surrounded by nine muses, nine ancient poets and nine contemporary poets. Ancients such as Ovid, Virgil, Sappho and Homer to modern Petrarch, Ariosto and Boccaccio converse or write. The large figure in blue, head tilted skyward, is Homer, flanked by Dante on the left and Virgil on the right.

The art of fresco

During the Renaissance from the fourteenth to the sixteenth centuries, the most commonly used method was that of fresco, which used water-based pigments applied on wet plaster. After the plaster was applied to the surface, called the *intonaco*, the artist had about 10 to 12 hours to complete the painting. While the plaster dried, the pigments were integrated into the surface. The technique of painting on fresh plaster is called *buon fresco*. Sometimes additional color is added after the plaster has dried; this is called *a secco* and is less durable. Michelangelo's ceiling of the Sistine Chapel in the Vatican is the most famous fresco in the world and is almost entirely done *buon fresco*.

The *Dispute over the Sacrament* shows, in the lower part, popes, cardinals and believers to represent the earthly domain, while above are figures from the Old and New Testaments. Those from the New have halos. In addition to many saints, such as Thomas Aquinas, Saint Francis, and Saint Bonaventure, there is Dante Alighieri. Above the altar, 4 cherubs hold the Gospels. In addition to the outstanding frescoes, take note of the ceiling and beautiful cosmatesque mosaic marble floor.

> *After visiting the Raphael rooms, in order to get to the Sistine Chapel, follow the signs, which will have you descend and walk through the Borgia apartments, remarkable mainly for the decorated ceilings, and then long galleries containing modern religious art.*

3 The Sistine Chapel (Cappella Sistina). The name Sistina comes from the pope Sixtus IV for whom the chapel was built around 1475 – 80. When a pope dies, the Conclave of Cardinals meets here to elect his successor.

Originally the ceiling was a simple blue with gold stars and only the **walls** were covered with frescoes which date from 1481 – 83, by some of the greatest artists: Perugino, Botticelli, Ghirlandaio, and Pinturicchio, among others. The frescoes depict scenes from the lives of Christ and Moses. The **life of Jesus** includes *The Baptism of Jesus,* by Perugino, The *Temptation of Jesus*, The *Calling of the Disciples*, *The Sermon on the Mount*, *Christ Handing the Keys to Peter* (5th from the entrance, on the left), (detail below) and the *Last Supper.*

On the opposite wall are scenes from the **life of Moses**: *Moses in Egypt*, scenes from his life including *Crossing the Red Sea, Tables of the Law, The Punishment of Korah* and *Moses' Death*.

A reference to the papacy as the successor to the Roman Empire is brought home by the inclusion of the Arch of Constantine (not visible in this detail) in *Christ Handing the Keys to Peter* and *The Punishment of Korah*. We saw in the Stanza di Costantino, as the first Christian emperor, Constantine is considered instrumental in the creation of the church in Rome. Looking at the walls, four distinct bands can be discerned: the lowest area is painted *trompe l'oeil* to look like curtains, the large frescoes of Christ and Moses are next, above those a series of popes are painted between the windows and finally, above the windows are the semicircular lunettes by Michelangelo depicting the ancestors of Jesus

The Ceiling. In 1508, Julius II commissioned Michelangelo to fresco the ceiling of the chapel built by his uncle, Sixtus IV. Michelangelo at the time was working on a monumental tomb for Julius of which his statue of Moses was to be a part. (This imposing statue resides in Saint Peters in Chains (San Pietro in Vincoli,) see Walk 7). Michelangelo much preferred architecture and sculpture to painting, but the pope insisted and Michelangelo finally relented. He spent the next four years dozens of feet from the floor on wooden scaffolding, (but not on his back as popularly thought), working alone for the most part.

His technique evolves
Michelangelo was trained in fresco by the master Ghirlandaio, but subsequently spent his career doing sculpture and architecture. He did not think of himself as a painter and in fact, the early scenes on the ceiling took him quite a long time to complete. His technique improved as he went along as did also the expressiveness and boldness of his figures. Contrast those of Noah, painted first, with the later ones, where fewer, larger and more powerful figures dominate.

Evidence from the period, among which a letter from Michelangelo himself, stated that the Pope gave carte blanche to the artist. Michelangelo decided on the **theme of creation.** We see his genius not only in the execution of the frescoes, the artistic means with which he expresses himself, but also in his extraordinary capacity for conceptual synthesis in the choice of the scenes.

As you try to absorb the nine major panels down the center, you scarcely notice the figures flanking medallions to either side of alternate scenes. Working your eyes toward the windows are prophets and sibyls, other figures in the triangular spandrels, which are in turn topped by the dark "ignudi" figures. All the while, architectural elements, columns and cornices form the setting.

The nine episodes from the Old Testament book of **Genesis** can be divided into 3 groups: the origin of the universe, of man and of original sin. The first group contains the *Separation of Light from Darkness*, the *Creation of the Heavenly Bodies* and the *Division of the Land and Waters*. The central three contain the most famous figures that you will immediately recognize as *God Creating Adam* and giving him life by touching his outstretched hand, plus the *Creation of Eve* and the *Expulsion from Paradise*. The final three, which, however are the first ones painted by the artist, are the *Sacrifice of Noah, The Flood* and *The Drunkenness of Noah*.

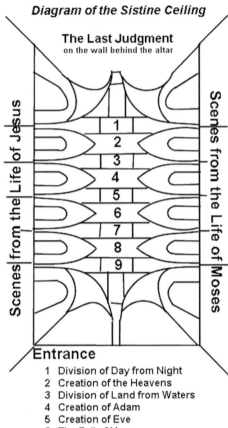

Diagram of the Sistine Ceiling

The Last Judgment
on the wall behind the altar

Scenes from the Life of Jesus

Scenes from the Life of Moses

Entrance

1 Division of Day from Night
2 Creation of the Heavens
3 Division of Land from Waters
4 Creation of Adam
5 Creation of Eve
6 The Fall of Man
7 Noah's Sacrifice
8 The Flood
9 Noah's Drunkenness

The panels are chronological starting at the far end near the altar. Beautiful triangles called spandrels and semicircular areas called lunettes fill in the areas above the windows. Here sibyls (oracles) and other prophets who predicted the coming of Jesus and forerunners of Jesus are painted. Nude youths fill in the smaller spaces between them.

The masterpiece can be appreciated on three levels that reflect the unity of body, mind and spirit. The **physical** aspect is the most evident from the many beautifully rendered bodies. The aspect of the **mind**, painted in the areas on the sides of the Creation, is shown by the presence of the prophets and sibyls who represent knowledge. The creation stories show the element of the **spiritual** and mysterious, notably, for example, in the indistinct and ethereal God in the first painting where He is separating the dark from the light.

In marked contrast, on the end wall, also by Michelangelo, is the dark **Last Judgment**. This replaced an earlier fresco by Perugino and was done many years after the ceiling, from 1536 to 1541. It shows Christ in the act of judging with Mary and other saints at his side. He leads the righteous to paradise on the left and sends the damned to hell down on the right, where Charon waits in his boat for the final trip. Below, the dead rising from their graves emphasize the terror and gloom.

The drama and pessimism reflected the changed mood of the city. A few years earlier, in 1527, Rome had been sacked, and the growing Protestant movement had brought increased uncertainty. The drooping shorn skin of Saint Bartholomew reveals Michelangelo's self-portrait.

Symbolism
Many of the saints around Jesus can be identified by the symbols of their martyrdom: Saint Andrew near the Virgin holds a cross, Saint Sebastian the bow and arrow, Saint Lawrence a burning grate, Saint Catherine of Alexandria a rack, and Saint Bartholomew with his shorn skin.

The nudity of many of the figures shocked Pope Pius V (1566 – 72), who ordered leaves and loincloths painted on. During the recent restoration, those that could be removed safely were cleaned off. The painstaking cleaning took about 20 years and has brought the frescoes to their original brilliance. **No photographs are permitted,** and you may find it easier on your neck to do some of the viewing with help from binoculars and a mirror. If you can take your eyes from the ceiling, gaze down at the multicolored cosmati-type geometric marble floor.

Just outside the northern section of the colonnade, at Via di Porta Angelica, is the interesting **Fountain of the Four Tiaras**. It is formed by 3 papal tiaras surmounted by a fourth. The three **crowns** that make up each tiara symbolize the three powers of the Pope: the religious, the judicial and the political. The 6 large **keys** represent the primacy of the Pope in matters of faith and the opening and closing of the doors to heaven.

*A good place for shopping, especially for moderate priced clothing, is along Via Cola di Rienzo, which begins at Piazza Risorgimento. Castroni at Via Cola di Rienzo 196 has a large selection of **deli products**. At 179 near Via Ovidio is Coin, a very well furnished **department store**. Franchi at number 200 at Via Terenzio is a **deli** and **tavola calda** with a variety of dishes. Benetton is at number 193-209.*

4 Piazza San Pietro (Saint Peter's Square) is delineated by two semi elliptical colonnades by Bernini. Built over 20 years and begun in 1656, the two welcoming arms symbolize the opening of the Catholic Church to the rest of the world. In line with the steps of the basilica, the ellipse extends to a granite marker in the road that delimits the border of the Vatican State with Italy. The piazza typically fills on Wednesdays when the Pope holds an audience and on Sundays when he speaks to the crowd.

The **colonnade** is made of four rows of Doric columns and is geometrically precise. The focal points of the ellipse are marked by easily recognizable special stones on the ground between the obelisk and each of the fountains. As you approach one of the 2 focal points the columns become perfectly aligned and the farthest three rows of columns disappear. It is an **incomparable effect**.

The colonnade is composed of 284 columns, 88 pilasters and around the top of the cornice are 140 statues of saints. The Piazza delineated by the two arms measures 340 by 240 meters (1114 by 789 feet). For many centuries the carriages of dignitaries visiting the Vatican passed inside the rightmost colonnade to arrive at the official entrance at the bronze door. The effect of the rapid succession of these numerous enormous columns, while the carriage was moving, together with the dimensions and the grandeur of the piazza must have been even more impressive than today.

The monolithic **obelisk** at the center of the piazza is of red granite and was brought to Rome during the reign of emperor Caligula. With the cross at the top it reaches 40 meters (131 feet). It was originally situated in the center of Nero's Circus (another hippodrome), built in the first century, which was erected on the left side of where the basilica is now. (See the diagram at number 5). In 1586 Pope Sixtus V had it moved to the center of the piazza where it now resides. It was necessary to use 40 winches to lift the more than 300 tons of the obelisk, a raised "road" was built to transport it laterally and at last a cage to anchor it in the final spot. Eight hundred workers and 140 horses were employed. The orders for the direction of the operation were given by the original system of the sound of a horn, which required complete silence. An edict proclaimed the death penalty for anyone who interfered with the work or who made any noise at all. A gallows was erected on the piazza to execute the sentence immediately. They say that the man responsible for the transfer, Domenico Fontana, had horses already saddled, ready to escape in case the monolith fell. Fortunately everything went well.

The two **fountains** are lined up with the obelisk and symmetric with respect to the colonnade. The one on the right is by Maderno and is older, built in 1613, while the other is by Bernini and was erected in 1677.

On the piazza on the left looking toward the façade is the **information office** for the Vatican. At this office you can get the last minute details for a visit to the Vatican Gardens (number 6) or the Necropolis (number 7). Both require advance reservations. A comprehensive Vatican information site is

http://www.vaticanstate.va/content/vaticanstate/en/informazioni-utili.html.

5 Basilica di San Pietro (Saint Peter's Basilica).

Be aware that no shorts, bare shoulders or miniskirts are allowed, for either men or women.

The basilica is open from 7 AM to 7 PM in summer, to 6 PM in winter.

Architecture from three distinct periods is superimposed in this area. The first refers to the ancient Roman period, and includes the Circo di Nerone (Nero's Circus). As you can see from the diagram, the north bleachers of the circus passed through the entire area where later both the old and the new church and the square were built. In the middle of the ancient hippodrome there was a division with at the center the Egyptian obelisk, which as we know, was later moved to Piazza San Pietro.

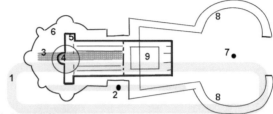

1 Circo di Nerone
2 Obelisk (original position)
3 Necropoli
4 Tomb of Saint Peter
5 Old St. Peter's
6 New St. Peter's
7 Obelisk (current position)
8 Colonnade
9 Atrium of old St. Peter's

While the imposing structure of the hippodrome deteriorated, the area was used as a burial ground for the earliest Christians. The second level consists of the construction of the first church of Saint Peter's. It was begun by emperor Constantine after his conversion, in 315 AD, and finished 50 years later. It was almost as large as the new church and it lasted almost 1200 years. Pope Silvester I consecrated it on November 18, 326 AD.

In 1506 Pope Julius II had the foundations begun for the new Saint Peter's Basilica but it took 120 years to bring it to completion. Most of the best contemporary artists contributed to its design: Bramante, Raphael, Sangallo, Michelangelo and Baldazzarre Peruzzi discussed at length whether to use the Greek cross or the Latin cross design. Later, still others planned or executed important parts of the basilica, as, Carlo Maderno the façade, Michelangelo the dome, while the colonnade and the general Baroque tone are due to Bernini.

Now the structure appears definitive, but during the 120 years necessary for its construction, powerful and contrasting views for its realization were vigorously debated. Both the popes and the artists were often people of passionate personalities. Without doubt, political exigencies had their role.

Bramante's original project called for a construction in the **Greek cross** form where the length and width of the two elements that form the cross are of the same size. His death sparked a fierce competition and Sangallo emerged the successor. He chose the **Latin cross**, where the two elements have different lengths, as the structural base for the project, and proceeded with the work.

Greek Cross   Latin Cross

While many artists took positions and passionately expounded their ideas, Michelangelo, by now in his seventies, finally intervened and promised to work on it for free on the condition that he be given carte blanche. He went back to Bramante's project of a Greek cross, demolished most of Sangallo's work and wanted to raise the dome higher, making it more similar to that of the Duomo in Florence. Later, Giacomo della Porta in 1590 decided to raise the dome even higher. In the meantime, the Counter Reformation led the Catholic Church to put more importance on the clergy, on processions and ceremony, which led to the preference for longer naves.

123

So, at last, in 1605, Pope Paul V had Maderno redesign the basilica in the form of a Latin cross. Maderno also designed the imposing façade, whose dimensions, together with the longer nave, hide much of the view of the dome for a spectator on the piazza below, contrary to the desires of Bramante and Michelangelo. In any event, the dome dominates the skyline of the capital and is easily recognizable from distant corners of the city. The two churches were consecrated exactly 1300 years apart. The old Saint Peter's November 18, 326 and the basilica we see today on November 18, 1626.

Come closer to the basilica.

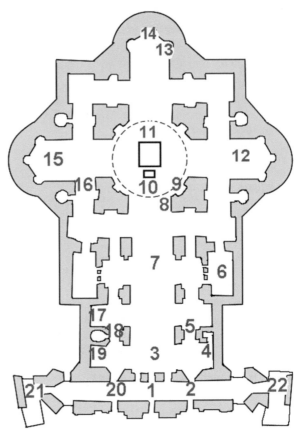

1 **Entrance**
2 **Porta Santa**
3 **Porphyry disk**
4 **Pietà**
5 **Monument to Queen Christina of Sweden**
6 **Chapel of the Blessed Sacrament**
7 **Central Nave**
8 **Statue of St. Peter**
9 **Entrance to the Grottoes**
10 **Confessio**
11 **Baldacchino**
12 **Right Transept**
13 **Tomb of Urban VIII**
14 **Gloria/Cattedra di Pietro**
15 **Left Transept**
16 **Treasury Entrance**
17 **John XXIII Monument**
18 **Last Stuarts' Monument**
19 **Baptistery**
20 **Manzù Door**
21 **Statue of Charlemagne**
22 **Statue of Constantine**

In the center of the façade is the balcony or "**loggia**" from which the Pope speaks and blesses the crowd in his "urbi et orbi" speeches to the city and the world on Christmas and Easter. While you go up the steps to the church, on the left and right are two statues, Saint Peter and Saint Paul. At the top of the façade rise 13 statues, which include Jesus, the 11 apostles except for Peter, and John the Baptist. Once inside the portico, at the two extreme ends you may notice two equestrian statues. The one on the right represents *Constantine* (#22), one of Bernini's best works, and the other depicts *Charlemagne* (#21).

(Numbers correspond to locations on the schematic above).

The entire length of the Basilica is 219 meters long (719 feet), the central nave is 26 meters wide (85 feet) and 46 high (151 feet), and the transept is 155 meters (510 feet) long. The diameter of the dome is 43 meters (141 feet) and the height up to the cross outside on top is 137 meters (450 feet). It can contain 60,000 people, there are 46 altars and natural light penetrates through 233 windows, including the smaller domes over the chapels. A few dozen Statues of Liberty could fit standing up in the nave. There are 147 popes buried in Saint Peter's.

Statue of Saint Peter

The central **bronze doors** (#1) are from the old church of Saint Peter's. High above the central main entrance, in the portico, there are the remains of a charming **mosaic by Giotto** (1266-1337), *La Navicella* (the little boat), also taken from the old church, which, unfortunately may be hard to make out because of the light opposite. The **Porta Santa** (Holy Door) (#2), opened only during Holy Years, usually every 25 years, is the door on the right.

When you enter, the immensity of the internal space cannot fail to astound you. But the sensation is not immediate since the harmonious proportions and the quantity of decoration are your first impression. **NOTE: access to some areas of the basilica may be blocked at various times.**

One of the marks on the floor showing the length of another major church.

Marks embedded in the floor straight down the center of the nave indicate the lengths of other major churches. Saint Peter's nave is 182 meters long, measured from the back of the apse (where the Cattedra of Saint Peter is) to the entrance. You may see how the others are all decidedly smaller. For example Santa Sofia is 109.57 m., Saint Paul's in London 158.10 m., The Immaculate Conception in Washington 139.14 m., Cologne Cathedral 134.94 m., Saint Francis of Assisi 114.76 m., and so on.

About 40 feet inside the central door, inserted into the floor is a reddish **porphyry disk**, (#3) transferred here from the old church, where emperors during the Middle Ages kneeled. The first was Charlemagne, crowned by Pope Leo III in 800. For a long time the sovereigns of the Holy Roman Empire, in order to govern, sought this kind of legitimization from the pope.

Walk to the right where in a chapel you can see Michelangelo's masterpiece, done when he was only in his twenties, the **Pietà** (#4). After an incident in which a deranged person attacked the figure of the Madonna with hammer blows, the statue has been protected by a transparent bulletproof panel. During the resulting restoration, on the hand of the Virgin, after careful examination, the letter M emerged in the lines of her hand on her palm. A detail that the master was able to keep secret for five centuries, even though this is the only statue that he ever signed, which you can see on a band across Mary's chest. Curiously, the Madonna appears to be quite young to have a grown son, and her proportions have been rendered with artistic license, especially as to the length of her legs. During World War II, casts of many of these treasures were made so that they would be able to do proper repairs in the event of damage.

Right after the chapel containing the Pieta, between the first and second chapels, rather high on the wall on the left side, a monument honors **Queen Christina of Sweden** (#5). She abdicated her throne in order to convert to Catholicism and spent her last years in Rome where she died in 1689. In the third chapel on the right, dedicated to the **Blessed Sacrament** (Santissimo Sacramento) (#6), there is a painting of the *Trinity* by Pietro da Cortona. Note also the bronze grille (grating) by Borromini. A small tabernacle by Bernini on the altar has columns placed in a circle similar to the small building known as the *Tempietto* by Bramante, which is in the church of San Pietro in Montorio on the Janiculum hill.

Continue down the nave toward the center where, on the inside part of one of the four enormous pilasters that hold up the dome, is the bronze statue of a **seated Saint Peter**, (#8) from the thirteenth century. Note how worn his right foot is, and how smooth from being touched by the faithful for centuries. Finally, note the absence of paintings, so common in other churches (there are only 2 in the whole basilica) since here the artists have expressed themselves by the use of mosaic.

The taxing pope

Pope Urban VIII sponsored the construction of the Barberini Library, which contained precious manuscripts, Palazzo Barberini and several churches. He tried to obtain the dukedom of Castro and Ronciglione but he was militarily defeated, even though he had excommunicated its owner, Edoardo Farnese. The painful realization of the defensive weakness of the Papal State led him to reinforce the defenses using more modern techniques. All of this brought expenses that the Jubilee indulgences of 1625 were not able to cover. He therefore felt compelled to repeatedly raise taxes and for this he was nicknamed "the taxing pope."

In front of the papal altar, the **confessio** (#10) by Maderno has 99 perennially lit lamps. The entrance to the **Treasury** (#16), a small museum of the gifts made to the Church over the centuries is at the end of the left aisle. The Vatican Museums contain the most important pieces. There is an admission charge for this area.

Looking down St. Peter's nave

Under the dome is the **baldacchino**, or canopy (#11) (left). It is set above the pontifical altar and we know that, for its construction, bronze from the Pantheon's portico was used. Pope Urban VIII in 1625 had no scruples about removing the bronze coffers from the porch of the ancient temple and having them melted down. This gave rise to the saying "What the barbarians didn't do, the Barberini did." Notice also the numerous bees on the columns, the symbol of the Barberini family of which Urban VIII was a member.

The very original spiral columns that support it were inspired by columns from the old basilica. The position of the main altar and the baldacchino, according to tradition, was directly above the **tomb of Saint Peter**, with the dome directly above it.

In the pilaster, near the main altar is also the entrance to the **Grottoes**, (#9) (distinct from the Necropolis) where there are the tombs of many popes, including the only English pope, Nicholas Breakspear, who took the name Hadrian IV in 1154. You can easily see which of the popes is the most popular. In the apse, behind the altar, Bernini's **Gloria** (#14) with a dove centered among rays of light is the symbol of the Holy Spirit. Beneath it, the bronze altar incorporates the **Cattedra di Pietro** (also #14) or the papal throne, once thought to have been Saint Peter's, but since dated to the ninth century. Bernini incorporated the old wood and ivory chair into his bronze Baroque creation.

Bernini's Contributions

Works by Bernini in Saint Peter's go from the small tabernacle in the Chapel of the Blessed Sacrament to the enormous bronze baldacchino over the papal altar. His art includes: Urban VIII's tomb, the Gloria and the Cattedra di Pietro in the apse, the niches in the supporting piers, the tomb of Alexander VII in a corridor off the left transept, the statue of Saint Longinus near the altar, and much of the floor and internal decoration. Outside, the equestrian statue of Constantine, the beautiful colonnade, and the fountain on the left.

On the right the **Tomb of Urban VIII** (#13) (below), also by Bernini, became the model for Baroque tombs all over Europe. In the left transept a particularly elaborate tomb with a grisly skeleton is by Bernini for Alexander Chislis (Pope Alexander VII). The left aisle contains, along with many papal tombs, a white marble monument by Canova to the **Last Stuarts**, (#18) Catholic pretenders to the English throne, who lived in exile in Rome. In the next to last chapel (going

out) on the right is a bas relief by Emilio Greco of Pope John XXIII welcoming delegates to the Ecumenical Council of 1962. This pope promised a profound renewal of the Church and he is remembered in the **Chapel of the Presentation** (#17). The remains of Pope Pius X lie under the altar of this chapel. Nearest the exit is the **baptistery** (#19). Of the five entrance doors, the one furthest to the left contains a bronze panel by the modern sculptor **Giacomo Manzù** (#20). The figure of Pope John XXIII is depicted on the lower right panel (next page).

Manzu's bronze door

You can get to the **dome** from just inside the entrance. Look for the word "cupola," and proceed to the ticket office. There is an elevator that will take you up inside to the base of the dome. The immensity strikes you when you look down from a height of about 150 feet and you see people walking around in the church. When you look straight out and up you see the letters around the inside of the dome, which seemed small from below but are actually about 6 feet high. Take note also of the large size of the tiles that make up the mosaics. The four circular mosaics at the base of the dome contain enormous figures of the four evangelists: Matthew, Mark, Luke and John. The pen in Mark's hand is five feet long.

Proceed up to the **lantern** at the top of the dome. There are 332 steps that take you inside a passage between the outside and the inside of the dome, to the summit where the view of the city and the rest of the Vatican, with its famous gardens, is fantastic. During the ascent, several small windows provide light.

On your way back, interrupt your descent to walk around

on the **roof** of the basilica. The immediate impression is of a small village with the minor domes, which seem like houses. In the open, going toward the piazza, you can see the backs of the 13 statues we mentioned, on top of the façade, and observe the smaller domes more closely. On the roof are also **bathrooms** and a **souvenir shop**.

Continue to go down, following the signs to the exit.

With prior reservations, often months ahead, you may visit the Vatican Gardens, the Necropolis or attend a papal audience. See below.

Papal audiences are held at various times and in various places (on the piazza, in the Vatican auditorium or in the basilica) when the Pope is in town. It is best to ask at the information office (see the end of number 4). For the ticket, plan ahead. Ask your bishop or write directly to the Prefecture of the Papal Household, 00120 Vatican City State. If you are already in Rome, contact the American Catholic Church, Saint Patrick's, https://stpatricksamericanrome.org/, tel. 06.8881.8727, or go in person to the office of the "Prefettura" through the bronze doors under the right colonnade the day before the audience, usually Tuesday before the Wednesday audience. Naturally, at the last moment tickets are not always available. In any case, the Pope appears on the balcony of his library (on the right looking toward the basilica) every Sunday at noon for the benediction of the crowd on the piazza.

6 Giardini Vaticani. The Vatican Gardens contain beautiful fountains, sculptures and exotic plants collected over the centuries, as well as lovely formal garden areas. To visit, you must take a bus tour, which makes several stops. Tours start at various times and take about 2 hours. It is best to reserve months ahead. http://mv.vatican.va/3_EN/pages/z-Info/MV_Info_Servizi_Visite.html.

7 Necropolis. To visit the excavations of the Necropolis, (*scavi* means excavations) which are at the lowest level under the church, you need to make a reservation a couple of months in advance. http://www.scavi.va/content/scavi/en/ufficio-scavi.html. The Necropolis was the area where many of the first Christians were buried and where it is thought that the tomb of Saint Peter was situated. According to tradition, the tomb of the first bishop of Rome is in a vertical alignment with the main altar, the baldacchino and the dome. The only way to visit is with a guide taking a tour that lasts 90 minutes, in various languages, including English.

There is no conclusive proof that the tomb is actually that of Saint Peter. The evidence suggests it strongly, however, since we know that this sepulcher has been venerated since the first century, that it contains the bones of an old and robust man and writing in Greek saying "Peter is here" has been found during the excavations. If you want to know more, take the tour of the Vatican Necropolis. Be aware that it is about 40 feet under ground with no windows and narrow passages.

*From Saint Peter's Square, to get to Castel Sant'Angelo, go down Via della Conciliazione. Most of the **Borgo** neighborhood is on your left.*

At Via della Conciliazione 63, at Via Padre Pancrazio Pfeiffer, is Ancora, *a **bookshop** that also carries DVDs, audio cassettes and religious articles.*

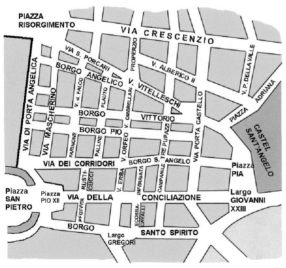

Borgo. This term describes the area between the basilica and the river, and is of medieval origin. The word comes from the German "burg" which means town or village. The area started as a group of buildings near Saint Peter's Basilica, to which, beginning in the eighth century, were added houses, inns and hospices often run by groups of foreigners who tried to facilitate the stay of pilgrims of their respective nationalities. Among the first were the Saxons, then the Longobards, the Franks, and so on. The area grew larger, with the addition of new roads, thanks also to economic incentives at the beginning of the sixteenth century. **129**

The neighborhood, mainly medieval, remained relatively intact over the centuries, even though buildings were added in the Renaissance and Baroque periods. In 1936 when the impersonal Via della Conciliazione was laid out, which celebrated the Concordat between Mussolini's government and the Holy See, the quarter was divided in two and many old buildings were torn down. Recently the relentless passage of time and modern economic needs have almost eliminated the local traditional artisans' shops. But it is still possible to see oases of a time gone by in the picturesque constructions and in some of the remaining shops.

> *Walk freely around on the side streets on both sides of Via della Conciliazione, especially around Borgo Pio, which is a pedestrian zone. Restaurants and trattorie, many reasonable priced, flood the street with tables.*

> *In the area between Via dei Corridori and Piazza Risorgimento there are numerous **shops**, places for a quick meal and restaurants. Part of Borgo Pio has been made into a pedestrian zone.* <u>Paoline Multimedia</u> *at Via Mascherino 94 offers **books, CDs and DVDs**, also in English. On Via Mascherino parallel to Via di Porta Angelica, at numbers 48 and 29 are two **souvenir** shops selling **religious articles**. They are usually less crowded and less expensive than those on the main streets.*

Rodrigo Borgia

Since the ninth century, several Roman families such as the Colonna, the Orsini, the Pamphili and the Frangipane fought to assure themselves of the papacy and supremacy over the city. Rodrigo Borgia, originally from Spain, was the most shameless in acting like a Machiavellian prince to obtain his ends. He was elected Pope in 1492 after having bought the votes of the electors and he took the name Alexander VI. He had several lovers and produced 4 children with the Roman Vannozza Cattanei. He governed with the idea of enriching himself and the nepotistic intention of favoring his children, never hesitating to use abuses, confiscations and assassinations. His scandalous conduct attracted the accusations of the austere monk, Girolamo Savonarola, whom Alexander VI condemned to burn at the stake. He celebrated the Jubilee in 1500 by personally appropriating the offerings of the faithful.

8 Castel Sant'Angelo is one of the most interesting museums and it is advisable to take a guided tour or use an audio guide which takes you through 19 centuries of history (photo previous page). (Closed Monday) http://www. castelsantangelo.com/.

At the entrance there are models that show the structure as it looked in the ancient period, after the changes made in the Middle Ages and finally in the Renaissance. However, when you explore it you will need to use your imagination a little to distinguish the original ancient Roman structure from the additions in successive periods. It was completed in 139 AD as a mausoleum for the emperor Hadrian and his family. Originally there was a bronze chariot with an enormous statue of the emperor on top. After being fortified, it assumed the function of a castle and it was able to withstand the barbarian invasions of the Visigoths in 410, and the Vandals who sacked Rome in 453. In 590, during a plague, the Pope organized a penitential procession. The current name comes from the fact that, when the procession passed near the Mausoleum of Hadrian, the archangel Michael was seen sheathing a flaming sword as if to suggest the end of the pestilence.

Many architects contributed to make it more habitable and difficult to conquer, and the church "treasure" was transferred there. In 1527 the Pope with several thousand people resisted for seven months the assault by German mercenary mutineers. In later centuries it became a prison, a barracks and finally, today a museum.

After observing the models, take the ramp where you can see some remains of ancient mosaics on the floor. The museum is on three levels, with a mixture of decoration from several different periods, plus the terrace at the top. This first level contains the funereal chamber of Hadrian. Going up to the second level, you find the **Cortile delle Palle**, the Courtyard of the Cannonballs, where the signs on the wall indicate the sizes of the balls shot by the cannons. In the

rooms off the courtyard are collections of arms from the Bronze Age to the present day. Above, on the third level are various rooms and apartments of the popes, with frescoes, some done by the school of Raphael, and the strongboxes, which held the papal treasure. If you take the stairway that has been carved into the ancient wall, you get to the terrace on top, at the base of the bronze angel, where there is a marvelous view of the city.

The **prison** had a terrible reputation since, besides the considerable humidity because of the nearness to the Tiber, the common prisoners were lowered into their cells from above, and they did not have enough room to lie down. However, there was an area where the more important prisoners were held. The sculptor and goldsmith **Benvenuto Cellini** was imprisoned there in 1538 and was left fairly free to do his work, in fact, too free. Incredibly he was able to escape in a daring flight that he described in his autobiography, but he was recaptured and completed his sentence. Beatrice Cenci was locked up and then executed (see Walk 1, number 16). The condemned were executed in a courtyard on the other side of the river. Frequently, however, victims of the abuse of power, even if innocent, were imprisoned and, too often, assassinated within these walls. Five popes were confined and assassinated here, as well as many of the victims of Pope Alexander VI, including 2 cardinals.

During 19 centuries, six different **angels** have graced the top of the castle, since they were continually consumed by exposure to the elements. The first was made of wood and did not last long. In 1497 the angel was destroyed by lightning, which also blew up the arsenal and a large part of the tower. At the beginning of the twentieth century the Italian composer Puccini chose it as the setting for the climax of the opera Tosca. During the Second World War it was used as a bomb shelter. Along the way is a pleasant terrace café with outside tables

The angel at the top of Castel Sant'Angelo

9 The Passetto.

For the whole Middle Ages, the castle was often at the center of confrontations between the Pope and the other Roman families who vied for supremacy over the city. In 847 a Saracen armada of 75 ships blocked the mouth of the Tiber and nearly ten thousand soldiers advanced on the city. The left bank of the river, with the seven hills, was protected by the Aurelian walls, and the attack was repelled. The pirates then headed for the right bank and sacked the Borgo quarter and the Basilicas of Saint Peter and Saint Paul. (Although Saint Paul's is on the left bank, it is outside the Aurelian walls.)

Pope Leo IV thought it best to protect the Vatican and the Borgo quarter, having them encircled by the Leonine Walls. Later, in 1277 Pope Nicolas III had a secret passageway built inside the Leonine Walls that connected the Vatican to Castel Sant'Angelo. It was called the "Passetto" and it allowed the Pope to escape quickly and well protected into the castle in case of attack.

You can visit the Passetto from inside Castel Sant'Angelo with group tours. Check at the entrance. In summer, there are frequently special events at Castel Sant'Angelo, allowing evening visits.

10 Ponte Sant'Angelo bridge was built in 134 AD to facilitate access to Hadrian's Mausoleum from the left bank, where most people lived. Naturally today it is open only to pedestrians. The ten graceful angels which adorn the bridge were designed by Bernini. Mostly created by his assistants, two were actually completed by Bernini, the Angel with the Crown of Thorns and the Angel with the Scroll. The originals reside in Sant'Andrea delle Fratte and those here on the bridge on your left looking toward Castel Sant'Angelo are faithful copies. The sculptures were commissioned to replace numerous gallows that had been erected on the bridge in 1500 and left in permanent exposition.

One of Bernini's angels on Ponte Sant'Angelo

Plan your visit to the Vatican

Remember that there is a dress code for Saint Peter's Basilica: no shorts, bare shoulders or miniskirts.

If you are interested in the Vatican Gardens or the Necropolis, you should reserve at least 2 or 3 months ahead. It is also best to reserve tickets for other attractions as well, to avoid long lines.

For the Vatican Gardens, see http://mv.vatican.va/3_EN/pages/z-Info/MV_Info_Servizi_Visite.html.

For the Necropolis, http://www.scavi.va/content/scavi/en/ufficio-scavi.html.

In order to avoid the line for the Vatican Museums, which in summer may be long, reserve tickets in advance, http://www.museivaticani.va/content/museivaticani/en.html.

If you want to see the museums, the Sistine Chapel, the basilica, the lantern on top of the dome and Castel Sant'Angelo in one day, you need to make some choices. The distance is considerable and especially in the summer months and during the holidays the crowd and the heat may slow down your plans. The best periods to visit are spring and fall and naturally the rest of the year excluding summer. In summer if you want to visit the museums and the Sistine Chapel the best time is early morning or around lunchtime, so you can reduce the time spent in line for tickets, which can be as much as an hour. You need to remember that the basilica is open later, until 6 or 7 according to the season, and the museums close earlier, although in summer sometimes they are open in the evening. Check the website. In the summer, if you are coming from Corso Vittorio Emanuele II, we advise you to visit Castel Sant'Angelo in the morning, eat a fairly early lunch in the Borgo and then visit the Musei Vaticani (or take the bus directly from Saint Peter's Square if possible). This allows you several hours for the museums, after which you have enough time for the Piazza, the basilica and the dome.

On Mondays most of the museums in the city are closed, while the Vatican Museums are open. If it rains on a Monday, you can expect many people will go toward the Vatican Museums, especially during the summer or during holiday periods.

Castel Sant'Angelo and Ponte Sant'Angelo

For this walk, it did not seem appropriate to specify the length. Much will depend on what you are interested in seeing, your priorities, and keep in mind that only considering the Vatican Museums, it is possible to walk for about 4 miles, although you will probably only walk about one mile there using our suggestions. It is best to dedicate at least a full day, but, if lack of time is a consideration, do not miss the Piazza, Saint Peter's Basilica and the Sistine Chapel.

Walk Five - The Vatican

Additional Restaurants

Hosteria dei Bastioni, Via Leone IV 29, Roman cuisine. Close to the entrance to the Vatican Museums. Tel. 06 3972 3034. €€

Benito e Gilberto, Via del Falco 19, Tel. 06.683 08 086. Nautical décor and atmosphere. Fish and seafood specialties. Borgo €€€

Taverna Angelica, Piazza Amerigo Capponi 6. Cuisine from various regions of Italy. https://www.tavernaangelica.com/ Borgo €€€

Les Etoiles, Via Vitelleschi 34, Excellent Mediterranean cooking with picturesque 360 degree views of the terraces, roofs and nearby dome of Saint Peter's. In the Hotel Atlante Star. https://www.atlantehotels.com/it/roof-garden-bar/bar.html €€€€

Da Romolo alla Mole Adriana, Via di Porta Castello 19, http://daromoloalla-moleadriana.it Traditional Roman cuisine. Good value. Near Borgo Vittorio. €

Velavevodetto ai Quiriti, 4/5, Trattoria, classic Roman cuisine. http://www.ristorantevelavevodetto.it €€

Passaguai, Via Pomponio Leto, 1, Wine bar. Near Piazza Risorgimento. http://www.ristorantecesare.com €

Da Toscano, Via Germanico 56, Tuscan and Roman cuisine. http://www.ristorantedaltoscano.it €€

Michelangelo in Rome

Michelangelo Buonarroti, a native of the Florentine area, spent nearly half his life in Rome. Briefly apprenticed to the master Domenico Ghirlandaio, he learned the art of fresco painting. But at 15 he began to study at the prestigious sculpture school at the Garden of San Marco. His precocious talent soon attracted the attention of Lorenzo de' Medici who brought him into the Medici household.

Michelangelo would flourish there in the stimulating atmosphere where he would also come to know two of the younger Medici who would later become popes, Leo X and Clement VII. After Lorenzo died, Florence was no longer so hospitable to him. He spent time in Bologna continuing to do impressive sculptural work, before being summoned to Rome in 1496.

At that time Rome was experiencing an awakening to classical art that had recently been unearthed after centuries below ground. Michelangelo was greatly influenced especially by the classical muscular nudes such as the Belvedere Torso and the Laocoon (at right), to which he was able to assist at its 1506 discovery. In Rome, after producing a large classical sculpture of Bacchus, he was given the commission to create the **Pietà**, which he finished in 1500 at the age of 25. Compared favorably to the standards of beauty of classical Greece and Rome, it was the only work Michelangelo ever signed, in this case in Latin on the band across Mary's chest.

Returning to Florence, he enjoyed new opportunities and produced the monumental and expressive **David** from 1501-04. But in 1505 Pope Julius II, impressed by the Pietà, called him to Rome. This pope, elected in 1503, had aspirations to a grandiose **tomb**, surpassing his predecessors'. This gave Michelangelo the opportunity to create a monumental design with 40 statues, and he dove into the project enthusiastically, procuring marble and making plans.

But while the marble piled up near Saint Peter's, the pope had other ideas. He demanded that Michelangelo decorate the ceiling of the **Sistine Chapel**, so named because it had been built by Pope Sixtus IV, Julius' uncle. Angered at the Pope's refusal to go forward on the tomb, the temperamental artist stormed off from Rome.

Seven months later, in the more neutral territory of Bologna, they reconciled and the pope had Michelangelo create an enormous bronze statue of Julius, a project that would take another 14 months away from his much-loved tomb. Resigned, he returned to Rome to begin the Sistine Chapel ceiling in 1508. For the next four years, high on wooden scaffolds, he created the magnificent vault, increasingly competent with the process of fresco, but always reiterating that he was a sculptor, not a painter.

Michelangelo's Moses, in Saint Peter in Vincoli in Rome

After Julius II died in 1513, the design for his tomb was much reduced in scale, other popes preferring to have Michelangelo work on their pet projects instead. However, work on the tomb proceeded, slowly, and included the imposing statue of **Moses**, which is now its centerpiece, in the church of San Pietro in Vincoli. (See Walk 7).

Back in Florence, Michelangelo worked on important architectural and sculptural projects such as the Medici tombs and library in San Lorenzo. But in 1534 he again left Florence for Rome, never to return.

Rome had been sacked and pillaged in 1527 by the mutinous troops of Charles V, the Holy Roman Emperor, and the mood in the city, influenced also by the rise of Protestantism, was dark. When Pope Clement VII commissioned Michelangelo to decorate the soaring altar wall in the **Sistine Chapel**, this atmosphere was reflected in his depiction of souls in torment in the **Last Judgment.**

After finishing the fresco in 1541 he turned his energies toward architecture. His design for the remodeling of the **Campidoglio** (above photo), (see Walk 7) included the gentle **cordonata** stairway, the addition of the Palazzo Nuovo to balance the palazzo on the opposite side and the beautiful piazza with its inlaid geometric star design.

Palazzo Farnese (Walk 1) sports his classic three-tiered façade. In succeeding years he designed the Sforza Chapel in Santa Maria Maggiore, and the church of **Santa Maria degli Angeli** that he carved out of the tepidarium of the ancient baths of Diocletian (both Walk 6).

Yet the most important contribution in Rome was his design for the **dome of Saint Peter's**. Chosen as chief architect in 1546, he was involved in many aspects of the continuing reconstruction of the church, although most of his designs, including the dome, were completed after his death in 1564.

WALK SIX - Baroque Rome
In the Footsteps of Bernini

This walk starts from the **Villa Borghese** park, where museums highlight the Baroque genius of Bernini and other artists, snakes down **Via Veneto**, passes impressive fountains and churches and finishes with ancient baths and antiquities near Termini station. The walk explores 26 centuries of the city, from the 7th century BC Etruscans in the Villa Giulia Museum to the Fountain of the Naiads created in 1914. Two main themes are in evidence. The **Baroque** period, epitomized by Gian Lorenzo Bernini, gave an indelible imprint to the city, clearly visible even today. One of the best examples is **Santa Maria della Vittoria**, while his personal vision of a church is clearest in the smaller Sant'Andrea al Quirinale. His rival **Borromini** displayed a different but equally masterful Baroque style. The other theme is articulated in the remains of the ancient Roman Diocletian Baths, the largest ever built, on which two churches were later built and the nearby **Palazzo Massimo** museum, which contains centuries' worth of artifacts from ancient Rome.

Porta Pinciana

In this walk:

Rome's "Central Park," Villa Borghese

The contrasting styles of Baroque artists Bernini and Borromini

A good shopping area, Via Nazionale

The starting point: Largo Federico Fellini (Porta Pinciana)

1 Villa Borghese park, the prestigious **Galleria Borghese**, containing masterpieces by Bernini and the Etruscan museum **Villa Giulia**

2. Via Veneto, which winds from the ancient Aurelian walls through the seductive atmosphere popularized by Fellini's La Dolce Vita

3 The macabre **Capuchin Cemetery,** where the bones of 4000 monks contrast sharply with the elegant atmosphere outside

4 Piazza Barberini, site of two fountains that underscore the collaborations between Bernini and the important Barberini family

5 Quattro Fontane and **San Carlo**, masterpiece of Bernini's rival, Borromini, and the **Quirinale**, today residence of the Italian president

6 Santa Maria della Vittoria, great example of Bernini's Roman Baroque

7 Aula Ottagona, where ancient statues are displayed in a building which was a cooling pool of the baths

8 Piazza della Repubblica and Michelangelo's **Santa Maria degli Angeli,** a church built using the walls of the ancient bath's warm pool

9 Terme di Diocleziano, the largest baths in ancient Rome, and Michelangelo's Cloister

10 Palazzo Massimo museum, where significant archeological finds and antiquities are reunited and complete ancient frescoed rooms recreated

11 Santa Maria Maggiore, one of the four patriarchal basilicas

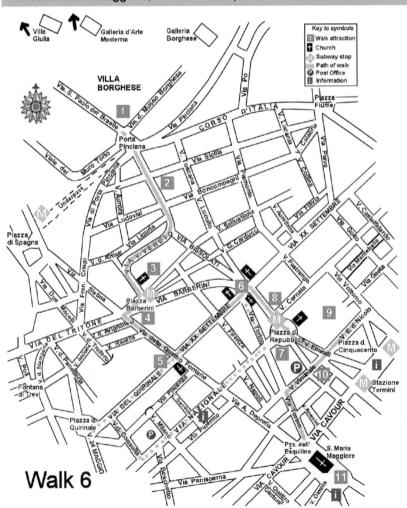

Walk 6

If you do not have reservations for Galleria Borghese and do not wish to visit the other museums, skip ahead to number 2, Via Veneto.

To visit the Etruscan Museum of Villa Giulia *and the* **Galleria Nazionale d'Arte Moderna** *it is most convenient to take the subway to Piazzale Flaminio, go up Viale Washington, Piazza del Fiocco and Viale Bernadotte until you are facing the Galleria Nazionale d'Arte Moderna. Then, to the left, proceeding on Viale delle Belle Arti, at number 131 you will find the Etruscan Museum of Villa Giulia.*

To visit the Galleria Borghese, *it is more convenient to start at Porta Pinciana at the top of Via Veneto. From the Piazza di Spagna subway station there is a tunnel with a moving walkway. Look for the signs that say "Via Veneto" and "shops." It will get you there in about 10 minutes. Porta Pinciana and Largo Federico Fellini are at the top of Via Veneto. Pass under the arches to get to Piazza Brasile, go into the park a little way and on the right take Viale del Museo Borghese which leads to the Galleria Borghese.*

1 The Villa Borghese park,

Rome's green treasure, has it all: **3 museums**, a little lake, a horse track and riding school, a zoo, foreign academies, archeological schools, an aviary, summer houses, fountains, sculptures, casual cafés, attractive secluded green areas, and unusual creations.

With a circumference of about 4 miles, the park is an oasis of green and peace in the heart of the city. The small lake is adorned with a **tiny classical temple** dedicated to Aesculapius, the god of medicine in Greek and Roman mythology. Although not ancient (it was built between 1785 and 1792), it triggers numerous photos.

Piazza di Siena, an open and grassy amphitheater lined with tall pines, inspired one of the movements of Ottorino Respighi's symphony *The Pines of Rome.* A relaxing walk in the park with a visit to one of the museums can easily take half a day.

To the southwest, across the dividing road Viale del Muro Torto, Villa Borghese connects to the **Pincio** gardens, named for the Pinci family who owned the area in the fourth century. The neoclassical Casina del Valadier, christened for the architect that designed it and the Piazza del Popolo below, occupies the highest point on the Pincian hill.

139

The park was created by Cardinal Scipione Borghese around 1610. The family opened it to the public during the nineteenth century, but as a result of some bad real estate speculations, Paolo Borghese was forced to sell the entire villa. In 1901, after long negotiations, the Italian state acquired the park, the buildings and all the works of art for only 3,600,000 lire or approximately $675,000.

Pleasant paths cross the park

Two hundred twenty-eight busts of famous Italians from various epochs line the paths, in addition to a water clock from 1870 and an obelisk of Antinous, emperor Hadrian's lover. (This area connects with Walk 4).

Galleria Borghese, on Piazzale del Museo Borghese, holds sculptural masterpieces by Bernini and paintings by Raphael, Titian, Caravaggio, Guercino and others as well as numerous ancient statues, mosaics and sarcophagi. The works on display are only a part of the vast collection that Cardinal Scipione Borghese began amassing in 1608.

Galleria Borghese

http://galleriaborghese.beniculturali.it/en/visita/visit-the-galleria-borghese

A passionate art collector and patron, the cardinal did not hesitate on occasion to commit the most flagrant abuse of power in his pursuit. He had Raphael's *Descent from the Cross* spirited away from the Church of San Francesco in Perugia, which provoked a popular revolt.

To obtain *Diana the Huntress*, he had Domenichino imprisoned, and released him only after the artist relinquished the coveted painting, which had been commissioned by another cardinal.

An early supporter of Bernini, he avidly purchased works by many artists, in particular, Caravaggio at a time when his paintings were not enthusiastically received.

The Borghese family came to Rome in 1547 from Siena, where they had been one of the most prestigious families for more than 3 centuries. Over 250 years later, their descendent Prince Camillo Borghese married Pauline, the sister of Napoleon Bonaparte. Her provocative clothing and long series of lovers caused much gossip in the city. The sculptor Canova, in 1808, depicted her half nude as the goddess Venus. When she was asked, "How could you pose nude in front of Canova?" She replied, "Why not, the room was heated!"

Both Romans and foreigners were very eager to have access to the enticing sculpture. After all, not every day do people have the chance to see a naked image of a live princess. They were accommodated by tipping the house servants, but, to further avoid this indignity, Camillo finally felt compelled to place the statue under lock and key.

Camillo was forced to sell 344 of the works collected by his family during the centuries to Napoleon, who transferred them to the Louvre in Paris, where

they form the body of the Borghese Collection.

Those on exhibit here, that were part of the original collection, bear the Borghese coat of arms on their name tags.

Note that each room (sala) has a **theme** and therefore the sculptures should be viewed together with the walls and ceilings. Mythological scenes cover many of the ceilings, so look around and up.

The sculpture of *Pauline Bonaparte* is in <u>Room I</u>. (Sala I)

Family emblems
Noble Roman families had recognizable emblems that artists frequently incorporated into commissioned works. The Borghese family used both a dragon and an eagle. Look for these at the entrance to Villa Borghese from Porta Pinciana, at the end of this walk at Santa Maria Maggiore, and on the vault of the portico of Saint Peter's.

In <u>Room II</u> is the **David** by Bernini, who captures the action in the moment of maximum concentration, while recoiling, just before launching the sling. The body is in tension and ready to spring into action. In this, the artist breaks with traditions of the past as he is on his way to embody the Baroque. On the ground lay the oversized armor that King Saul provided him for the confrontation. It is thought that the artist wanted to depict himself and that Cardinal Scipione held the mirror for him. Contrast this statue with the more famous David of Michelangelo, which resides in the Accademia in Florence, and the earlier bronze David by Donatello in Florence, which both show David at rest. The wall in the background bears a painting by Battistella Carracciolo on the same theme: the severed head of Goliath lies near a triumphant David.

The major attraction in <u>Room III</u> is the sculpture *Apollo and Daphne* by Bernini. The girl, in the attempt to flee from the god, is saved by her father who transforms her into a laurel tree with her hands and feet fastened to the ground. The painting in the center of the ceiling repeats the theme of the sculpture and also shows Cupid (derided by Apollo for his small bow) shooting an arrow of love toward Apollo, but a contrary one toward Daphne. The theme of transformation is echoed in the ceiling paintings of the four seasons and in the painting by Dosso Dossi of the beautiful enchantress Circe, who transformed people into lemurs. Apollo appears again in another painting by Dossi, wearing a garland of laurel leaves to remind him of the lost Daphne.

In Room IV, **Pluto and Persephone**, also by Bernini: Persephone's parents, Jupiter and Ceres, would not allow Pluto to marry their daughter, so he kidnapped her and took her to his home in the underworld. Notice how realistic are the indentations made by Pluto's fingers pressed into the thigh of the victim. In the golden niches are nestled ancient sculptures, and elegant mosaics decorate the areas between the pilasters.

Room V contains an ancient **hermaphrodite** sculpture, which has both feminine and masculine characteristics.

Room VI is the **Room of the Gladiator**, and the theme is struggle. The gladiator statue for which the area takes its name was sold to Napoleon in 1807. The main painting in the vault represents the council of the gods for the Trojan War. On the left are represented the gods in favor of Troy and on the right those against.

There are two masterpieces by Bernini. **Aeneas, Anchises and Ascanius** captures the moment when Aeneas, hero of Troy, escapes from the burning city. He rescues his father Anchises, who carries the *penati*, the gods protecting the family, while his son Ascanius carries the sacred fire of the hearth. Many scholars saw in this group the strong influence of his father, Pietro Bernini, an architect in his own right, since here the young Gian Lorenzo is still tied to the classical and manneristic style.

Bernini created the sculpture **Truth Revealed by Time** for himself as a monument to the art of sculpture. (Detail at right) It remained in the Bernini family until it was transferred here in 1924. The figure of Truth was to be accompanied by another, never executed, representing Time. As is frequently the case with Michelangelo, Bernini used the contrast of smooth and rough surfaces.

Room VIII contains six of the 12 paintings by **Caravaggio** originally belonging to the cardinal: *Madonna dei Palafreneri, Saint Jerome Writing* (at right)*, Young John the Baptist, Boy with a Basket of Fruit, Self Portrait as Bacchus* (sometimes called the Sick Bacchus for the ashen cast to the face) and *David with the Head of Goliath*. This is also called the Faun room, after the god of the forest. Notice the bucolic themes depicted on the ceiling. (For more about Caravaggio see Walk 1.)

On the upper floor, (primo piano) is the **Pinacoteca**, or picture gallery. Here are some of the works of the greatest Italian artists from the 16th to the 18th centuries, displayed in Rooms IX though XX. Most notably:

Room IX contains several paintings by Raphael, including the *Descent from the Cross*, which was seized in 1608, (with the complicity of the clergy), from Perugia to be added to the Cardinal's collection.

Room XIV is graced by sculpture and paintings by Bernini, including two self-portraits. A few ancient sculptures from the second century BC are also located here.

Room XVIII contains the *Pietà* by Peter Paul Rubens, one of the only non-Italian offerings.

Room XIX features two paintings by Domenichino.

Room XX's main draw is the *Sacred and Profane Love*, an early work by Titian, as well as three others of his later works.

View the beautiful Italian **gardens** from the windows at the back of the palazzo.

Painted Petition

The cut head of Goliath, held by the hair, is Caravaggio's own self-portrait. He was forced to flee Rome for having murdered Ranuccio Tomassoni in 1606. This painting was sent in 1610 to the Papal court as a painted petition asking to be pardoned. The pardon was granted but the artist died before he was able to return to Rome.

*To go to the **Galleria Nazionale d'Arte Moderna** from Galleria Borghese, walk down Via dell'Uccelliera, go left onto Via del Giardino Zoologico and then bear right onto Viale delle Belle Arti. The Galleria is on the right.*

The **Galleria Nazionale d'Arte Moderna** is at Via delle Belle Arti 131. The largest collection on a national scale, in 35 rooms it contains works from the 1700's to today. Italian artists Manzù, Carrà, De Chirico, Modigliani, Morandi and Boccioni are well represented in addition to Monet, Cezanne, Degas, Van Gogh, Henry Moore, Kandinsky and Max Ernst. Of particular interest are the works by the **Macchiaioli**, a group of Tuscan painters who used a style similar to that made more famous later by the French impressionists.

*Continuing on Via delle Belle Arti, on the left is the **Etruscan Museum**.*

The **Etruscan Museum of Villa Giulia**, at Piazzale Villa Giulia 9, is situated in the grandiose Renaissance villa that Pope Julius III had built as a summer residence in 1553.

http://www.villagiulia.beniculturali.it/. The Etruscans occupied part of central and northern Italy, extending to the south as far as Rome, between the ninth and the fourth centuries BC. In fact, the first kings of Rome were Etruscan and the Romans assimilated much of their civilization. The *Apollo of Veio*, the Sarcophagus of the *Reclining Husband and Wife* (at right), and the bronze *Cista of Ficoroni* stand out.

This is the largest Etruscan museum in the world, even though many archeological finds of the cities of Cerveteri, Tarquinia, Veio and Palestrina have been moved to other museums. Although everything in view has been brought out from excavated tombs, it is anything but gloomy. The Etruscans, as the Egyptians earlier, believed that when people died they needed their possessions in the afterlife, which they considered a continuation of the life on earth. This belief accounts for the richness of the archeological treasures which have come to light.

143

While you explore the building, you may find some erotic scenes, but the famous "winged phalluses" are held in the Gregorian Etruscan Museum in the Vatican. We do not know enough about the mysterious Etruscan civilization, but from examining the many archeological finds it seems reasonable to deduce that, unlike the Romans, they must have achieved a certain parity between the sexes. The sculpted male and female figures celebrate life without the barriers of inferiority and superiority often expressed in other cultures. Also displayed are necklaces, earrings, plates, candelabra and numerous objects that show imagination and excellent workmanship.

From the park, to visit Via Veneto, go south toward Porta Pinciana, pass under the arches and continue through Largo Federico Fellini, previously called Piazza Porta Pinciana.

2 Via Veneto.

Porta Pinciana was built in 403 by the emperor Honorius, carving this opening in the Aurelian Walls and then fortifying it. These well-preserved walls surrounded and protected the city during the late empire period (fourth and fifth centuries). (See Walk 2, Rome's Defensive Walls.)

Coming from Villa Borghese, after passing through the arches, you find yourself in Piazza di Porta Pinciana, renamed Largo Federico Fellini. From here **Via Veneto** snakes down to Piazza Barberini, among refined cafés, stores and hotels. The atmosphere

of the area, once very seductive, was popularized worldwide by the film *La Dolce Vita* directed by Federico Fellini.

International film stars during the sixties frequented the elegant venues on this street: Elizabeth Taylor, Richard Burton, Sophia Loren, Marcello Mastroianni, Gina Lollobrigida, Ingrid Bergman and many others. The indiscreet "paparazzi" and fans were always anxious to grab an autograph or a glimpse of some private embarrassing moment. Today the atmosphere is calmer; however, the refinement of the locales and hotels remain.

Continuing downhill on Via Veneto, on the left at the corner of Via Boncompagni is Palazzo Margherita, home since 1931 of the **American Embassy**. (Tel. 06.46741) (Head to the consulate next door if you are American and need assistance.) It was built at the end of the nineteenth century and is so named because the queen of Italy, Margherita, went there to live in 1900 right after the assassination of her husband King Umberto I by an anarchist.

*Toward the end of the street, on the left, at Via Veneto 27, is the Church of Santa Maria della Concezione, containing the **Capuchin Cemetery.***

*Harry's Bar, Via Veneto 150, is an **American bar** and international restaurant. Palombi, Via Veneto 114, evokes pleasure to just look at the **pastries and cakes** in the window. Hard Rock Café, Via Veneto 62, part of an international chain with American cooking, has **hamburgers, salads, French fries**. Jackie O', (€€€€) Via Boncompagni 11, is an elegant **disco** and restaurant, a trip to the past glory of Via Veneto.*

3 Capuchin Cemetery

3 Capuchin Cemetery. From the luxurious atmosphere of Via Veneto, after a few steps, you come to the macabre and austere **Capuchin Cemetery**. The contrast could not be more marked. On the right of the entrance to Santa Maria della Concezione at Via Veneto 27 is the door to the Capuchin Cemetery. It was built in 1626 and occupies five underground chapels decorated with the bones and skulls of 4000 Capuchin monks, by then dead for centuries. The bones come from the convent of the monks of San Nicolò de' Porcis, once situated on the Quirinal hill. Three hundred trips by cart were necessary to transport the bones. A sign at the entrance states in Italian:

"YOU ARE WHAT WE WERE. YOU WILL BE WHAT WE ARE."

The ceilings decorated with vertebrae, lamps suspended with fibulae and entire skeletons dressed in the characteristic brown robes of the monks, with

some seeming to stand guard at the crypts, constitute a spectacle that strikes the visitor. Many people find it shocking and at the exit it is not always easy to collect your thoughts.

The visit to the Capuchin crypt includes a multimedia museum describing the history of the order and their humanitarian work throughout the world.

Old curses

In modern society we can easily avoid unpleasant subjects. Other cultures, especially older ones, have sought a greater connection with their ancestors. By necessity, they were also surrounded, much more than now in the 21st century, with suffering and death. The shorter life spans of the population, due mostly to the lack of modern medicine and poor nutrition, contributed to this.

In many ancient cultures, like that of the Romans, there was a cult of the ancestors, showing the recognition and respect that the contemporary generation had for that of the past. Even now occasionally an expression in Roman dialect is used, but with less effect, that refers to a curse on all of one's ancestors.

In the nearby **Galleria Comunale d'Arte Moderna e Contemporanea** (City Gallery of Modern and Contemporary Art), Via Francesco Crispi 24, are works dating from 1881 to 1945. Items of the collection from after this date are shown in the ex-building of the Peroni brewery at Via Reggio Emilia 54.

*Bottega Italia, Via Veneto 15-23, near the Capuchin Cemetery, is a restaurant that offers **pizza** and **gelato**. One of the several **optical** stores in the center, La Barbera, is in Piazza Barberini 13, and another at Via Barberini 74.*

Continue down Via Veneto to Piazza Barberini

4 Piazza Barberini. (M Barberini).

On the piazza, the **Fontana del Tritone** (Triton Fountain) is another masterpiece by Bernini, from 1643. Bernini produced numerous works and his style greatly influenced the appearance of fountains, palazzos and sculptures in the city. The artist was incredibly prolific, understandable since he lived past the age of 80. The Triton kneels on an enormous shell held up by four dolphins while he blows straight up into a spiral shell, from which a spout of water cascades into the basin. Under the shell, on the rocks that support it, you may see some bees, the emblem of the Barberini family.

A few steps from the church, between the end of Via Veneto and the piazza, is the **Fontana delle Api** (Fountain of the Bees) by Bernini, completed in 1644. Below an enormous shell, three bees posed on the edge of the basin preside over streams of water spraying into the fountain. The piazza and street are named for the influential Barberini family. The greatest architects of the period, Carlo Maderno, Borromini and Bernini, contributed to the **Palazzo Barberini**, (entrance at Via Barberini 18): http://www.barberinicorsini.org/en/.

The spiral staircase by Borromini gives access to the **Galleria Nazionale d'Arte Antica** (National Gallery of Ancient Art), (entrance on Via delle Quattro Fontane). Among the numerous masterpieces are *La Fornarina*, Raphael's lover and favorite model, and *Henry VIII* by Hans Holbein. There are also works by Caravaggio, Guido

Fontana delle Api

Reni, Titian, Tintoretto, El Greco and a grandiose fresco by Pietro da Cortona that celebrates this powerful family in allegorical terms. The Gallery boasts a total of more than 2000 decorative objects and 1500 paintings with works from the 12th to the 18th century.

A visit to the sixteenth century apartments in the palazzo requires a reservation. Special art exhibitions are also held here.

Like many other monuments, the **Fountain of the Bees** was restored for the year 2000. The head of the bee on the right was reconstructed. Can you tell? The fountain was also cleaned of microorganisms and unsuitable plastering was removed. The black crust was cleaned using atomization and every crack, fracture or microfracture was plastered with hydraulic paint mixed with travertine powder, sand with marble granules and acrylic resin in emulsion. The basin was carefully stuccoed to close all the cells. Finally the monument was treated with protective waterproof material and an anti-graffiti product.

*Easyeverything is a large **Internet café** at Via Barberini 2, part of an English chain. The Albert Pub, Via del Traforo 132, is an **English-style pub**. The décor is all imported and they also offer **hamburgers and salads.***

From Piazza Barberini continue uphill on Via delle Quattro Fontane.

*A typical **trattoria/pizzeria** is Gioia Mia Pisciapiano at Via Avignonesi 34. Il Faro, Via Arcione 78 is a **tavola calda** and pizzeria.*

5 Quattro Fontane (Four Fountains).

The Church of **San Carlo alle Quattro Fontane**, Via del Quirinale 23, is dedicated to Carlo Borromeo, the 16th century cardinal of Milan. It is also called San Carlino for its diminu-

tive size. Borromini worked on this jewel over a period of thirty years. Its small size was dictated by the tiny plot of land the Spanish Trinitarian monastic order had acquired. In fact the whole structure could fit inside just one of the dome pilasters of Saint Peter's.

The only church done entirely by Borromini, it expresses most clearly his artistic vision. The undulating façade (see left) was completed last (1667) and reveals columns and surfaces arranged in a convex and concave arrangement on two levels. It seems more a sculpture than a building.

The interior plan is a modified ellipse, similar to a Greek cross plan, but stretched out. In fact, the whole impression is one of elasticity. Lacking in the ornate gilded and colorful decorations of other churches, especially those characteristic of Bernini, nevertheless, it is Baroque to the core, with its complex shapes and curves.

The pale monochromatic interior undulates with convex and concave surfaces and columns. Your eye is then drawn up toward the light and beautiful **elliptical dome**, (below) which is enlarged to cover the entire church, not just the central crossing as in a more traditional scheme. It is decorated with beautifully incised coffers of octagons, crosses and lozenges. Diffused light from the concealed windows accentuates the airy feeling.

Interior curves

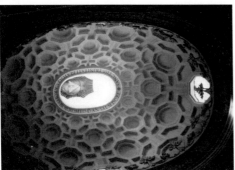

The chapel in the crypt made for him remains empty; Borromini committed suicide in 1667.

On the way out, pass through the small adjoining cloister, also bathed in light. Here too the surfaces are subtly complex and undulating. Its intimate size gives you a restful pause before you venture back out into the traffic.

147

Not far away, on the same side of the street at Via del Quirinale 29, is **Sant'Andrea al Quirinale**, another small church with a completely different atmosphere. It was designed by Borromini's contemporary, Bernini, and executed by his assistants. It has an elliptical plan; the main axis extends to the sides instead of to the altar. Known as "the pearl" for its rose colored marble, it was built for the Jesuits and numerous "IHS" (Jesus Savior of Mankind) emblems are visible on the walls.

Comparing the two churches, you can see how the two major exponents of Baroque expressed themselves. Bernini also took a long time to build this jewel and, by then elderly, passed many hours there in prayer and contemplation.

Rival Geniuses
Contemporary and rival of Bernini, Borromini was born in a small northern town and in Rome often felt himself an outsider. In contrast with Bernini's charm and outgoing personality, Borromini was an irritable solitary man. His style, though unmistakably Baroque, was at odds with the exuberance of Bernini's Baroque expression. Overshadowed by Bernini, the brightest artist star of the time, he became increasingly frustrated. But, in many ways, Borromini was more innovative. The façades and interiors of his buildings derived from geometric forms, such as ovals, curved planes, and complex volumes. See the discussion at the end of this walk, contrasting the two artists.

The goddess Juno, symbol of strength

The **Quattro Fontane** date from 1588 and are inserted slightly inside the four angles formed by Via delle Quattro Fontane and Via del Quirinale, which, at the intersection, becomes Via XX Settembre. Four gods are depicted in reclining poses. The male ones represent the Tiber (with the wolf) and the Aniene River; the female are Juno who symbolizes strength (at right), and Diana, loyalty, with a dog at her side.

If you could, for a few seconds, stand in the intersection, more easily done in August when the Romans are on vacation and the city is in the hands of the tourists, you could see 3 ancient obelisks in 3 directions: the ones at Santa Maria Maggiore and Trinità dei Monti at the two ends of Via delle Quattro Fontane and the third in Piazza del Quirinale, looking down Via del Quirinale.

The **Teatro dei Dioscuri**, Via Piacenza 1, above the tunnel of Via Milano, offers interesting art exhibitions.

> *You now have a **choice**. From the Quattro Fontane, to visit the Piazza del Quirinale, take Via del Quirinale to the Piazza. For shopping, you can go down Via della Consulta to Via Nazionale. Otherwise, walk down Via XX Settembre and skip ahead to number 6.*

Quirinale. See http://palazzo.quirinale.it/ for information on tours. The Palazzo Quirinale is on the Quirinal hill, the highest of the seven hills. In ancient times the Baths of Constantine occupied most of the area and contained the equestrian statues of the Dioscuri, now in the piazza. Because the Vatican, so close to the river, had a high incidence of malaria, in the sixteenth century the popes moved here to the Quirinal hill. Begun in 1574, several architects contributed to the palazzo, including Domenico Fontana, Gian Lorenzo Bernini and Carlo Maderno. Pietro da Cortona did the paintings, while Giovanni Fontana and Ferdinando Fuga worked on the gardens.

This sprawling palace of 1200 rooms was the official residence of the pope from 1592 until 1850. The four conclaves of the 1800's were held here, the cardinals staying within these walls. The election of Pius VIII lasted almost 3 months. During the proclamation of the Roman republic in 1848, Pope Pius IX fled, dressed as a simple priest, to the fortress at Gaeta just south of Rome, returning in 1850. After the unification of the country, which culminated in the taking of Rome in 1870 by Italian troops, the palazzo became the home of the kings of the united Italy and is now the official residence of the President of the Republic. A hidden jewel is the wonderful garden with numerous fountains, open to the public free on June 2, the anniversary of the republic. You can see the **Changing of the Guard** on Sundays on the piazza in the summer at 6 PM, and at 4 PM other times of the year. To be sure call 06.469 91.

The **Fountain of Monte Cavallo** in the piazza is a composite of 3 ancient monuments. In medieval tourist guides it was one of the main attractions and the favorite fountain of the English poet P. B. Shelley. The two marble statues, each depicting a man and a rearing horse, have been on the Quirinal hill since ancient times, and were never buried like so many other monuments. Roman copies of Greek originals, representing in Greek mythology the brothers **Castor and Pollux**, and known also as the **Dioscuri**, they stood at the entrance to the Baths of Constantine. The inscription incorrectly attributes them to the famous sculptors Phidias and Praxiteles.

The central **obelisk**, one of the two erected at Augustus' Mausoleum in the first century, was dug up and transported here to the center of the monument toward the end of the eighteenth century. Some years later the low **granite basin** was added to the composition. This was part of a fountain found in the Roman Forum, near the arch of Septimius Severus, which in the seventeenth and eighteenth centuries was used as a horse trough. The ancient Romans would easily recognize these three monuments, the Dioscuri, the obelisk and the basin fountain in the center, which, on this hill, have been given a new life.

The piazza and fountain in front of the Quirinal palace

The **Scuderie Papali al Quirinale** (the Papal Horse Stables), Via XXIV Maggio 16, offers interesting art exhibitions. Check for times and ongoing events. https://www.scuderiequirinale.it/

To go to Piazza San Bernardo, retrace your steps on Via del Quirinale and continue on Via XX Settembre. If instead you are interested in doing some shopping, take Via della Consulta and go left on Via Nazionale.

Via Nazionale. Besides Via Cola di Rienzo, described in Walk 5, Via Nazionale is another good shopping area with prices ranging from moderate to expensive. The street extends from Piazza della Repubblica to Largo Magnanapoli and has numerous clothing stores and leather shops. Shopper-friendly benches have been installed along the sidewalk. The surrounding buildings were built around the end of the nineteenth century for the upper middle class.

Palazzo delle Esposizioni on Via Nazionale

In this period, the large **Palazzo delle Esposizioni** was also constructed, at Via Nazionale 194 at the corner of Via Milano, (Tel. 06.3996 7500). http://www.palazzoesposizioni.it/. It was to be an alternative to the Biennale of Venice, but it was closed, restored, restructured and finally opened again in 1990. It now offers a variety of exhibitions of paintings, photographs, and multimedia. It is worth a look.

Saint Paul's Within the Walls, Via Napoli 58 at the corner of Via Nazionale, distinct from the Basilica of Saint Paul (outside the walls) on Via Ostiense, is the American Protestant Episcopal church. It was the first non-Catholic church to be built after the fall of the Pontifical State. Finished in 1880, the style is Romanesque-Gothic. The **mosaics** are by Edward Burne-Jones who belonged to a group of English painters who painted in the style of the Italian painters before Raphael (**pre-Raphaelites**).

A UPIM department store is at Via Gioberti 64 near Piazza Santa Maria Maggiore. The Flann O'Brien, Via Nazionale 17, is an Irish pub, patronized by Italians and foreigners. At Via Nazionale 71 is Castroni, a gourmet international deli. For fast food, there is a McDonald's at Via Firenze 58.

Continue down Via Nazionale and, just before Piazza della Repubblica, turn left onto Via Torino to go to Piazza di San Bernardo, the site of three churches: Santa Maria della Vittoria, Santa Susanna and San Bernardo.

6 Santa Maria della Vittoria,

at Via XX Settembre 17, is one of the greatest works of the Baroque style. Tel. 06 4274 0571. Construction was entrusted to Carlo Maderno and it was finished in 1626. The small church has a Latin cross plan with no side aisles. The name "*della vittoria*" or "of the victory" derives from the victory in 1620 of the Catholic army of Ferdinand II of Hapsburg over the "heretic" Protestants in the Battle of White Mountain for the conquest of Prague. The image of the Madonna above the altar, to whom the victory was attributed, is a copy of one found near the battle site. This church epitomizes the height of Baroque opulence through its abundance of marbles, gilded stuccoes, sculptures, paintings and elaborate decoration. Even though it contains works of Guercino and Domenichino, the main attraction is the *Ecstasy of Saint Theresa* that took Bernini two years to complete.

In the **Cornaro chapel**, deep relief statues of members of the family occupy the niches on the side walls, positioned to watch the spectacle of the Ecstasy of Saint Theresa, as if they were in a theater. (See left).

Some contemporary skeptics and Protestants were shocked - it seemed that Bernini went over certain limits. The reclining female figure, the expression on the face, the position of the foot, even though completely clothed, suggest how much the artist blurred the distinction between the sacred and the profane. Doubts fade when we see how the body disappears under the heavy robe next to the angel with the flaming arrow, and we remember the words of the Saint expressed in her autobiography: "God wished that I should see on my left an angel ... he had in his hand a long arrow with a flame coming from the point ... it hit the deepest reaches of my heart ... the pain was so strong that I moaned ... but together with such sweetness that I would have never wanted the pain to go away or to look for anything outside of God."

The vision of the saint celebrated Bernini's love of God through his enormous talent of identification and comprehension. The artist shows his immense capacity to express another's emotional state, capturing, in this case, religious ecstasy. This is one of the best examples of Roman Baroque.

Several secondary altars are decorated with colored marble inserts. In the transept on the right are sculptures by Guidi and Mannot. Paintings by Domenichino decorate the second chapel on the right, while those by Guercino and Guido Reni are in the third chapel on the left. The vault by Giovanni Domenico Cerrini in 1675 depicts Mary and the fallen, and is surrounded by sculpted angels. **151**

Santa Susanna. Across from Santa Maria della Vittoria, with the entrance at Via XX Settembre 14, is the church of Santa Susanna, which was for many years the Catholic church of the Americans in the city. (Now they attend Saint Patrick's at Via Boncompagni 31.) If you want to have an audience with the Pope and you are American, contact https://stpatricksamericanrome. org/ If you have little time, call the Vatican information office. (See Walk 5, The Vatican)

Situated just outside the perimeter of the Terme di Diocleziano (Baths of Diocletian), it dates from the fourth century and was built over two houses that belonged to the father and uncle of Saint Susanna. The façade is by Carlo Maderno, who is also responsible for the façade of Saint Peter's. The church has a single nave with a ceiling of large wooden coffers. The style of interior decoration is exemplary of Mannerism, which was a bridge between Renaissance classicism and the Baroque. Large wall frescoes depict the life of Santa Susanna and other martyrs, while frescoes on the sides are painted to suggest the texture of tapestry, soft and undulating. The nave contains statues of the four major prophets of the Old Testament: Jeremiah, Isaiah, Ezekiel, and Daniel. Through a glass inserted in the floor in the sacristy on the left side you can see some ruins of the early church, from 330 AD.

Early saint

Susanna was a member of a noble Roman family and niece of Pope Caius (283-296); she had embraced the Christian faith and decided to remain a virgin. Her resolve was secretly supported by Serena, the emperor Diocletian's wife, who had also converted. When Diocletian heard that Susanna declined to marry his adopted son, Maxentius, enraged, he entered her house, ordered her to worship an icon of the god Jupiter and, when she refused, had Susanna decapitated on the spot. The frescoes in the apse and along the nave recount both her story and that of Susanna of the Bible.

Via XX Settembre crosses Piazza San Bernardo. It was once called Piazza del Fontanone (piazza of the large fountain) because of the presence of the "mostra" of Acqua Felice, that is, the terminus of this aqueduct. The arched structure of the **Fountain of Moses** was built by Domenico Fontana in 1587 for Pope Sixtus V.

The dimensions and proportions are grandiose and pleasing enough. The Moses in the central arch, however, is attributed to Prospero of Brescia and has a grotesque form. With an ugly face and a fat figure, he is dressed in a toga that is too large, in a pretentious pose, and consequently has attracted scorn and sarcasm from the beginning. Legend says that the sculptor, because of the constant criticism, even by the Pope, became so depressed that he killed himself. But this is not very likely; in fact, it is thought that the statue of Moses was not even done by him but by Leonardo Sormani.

Take special note of the friendly lions that spout arched sprays. The two bas-reliefs in the side arches depict biblical episodes. On the left Aaron brings the Israelites to drink and on the right, Joshua leads the people toward the Red Sea.

The church of **San Bernardo alle Terme**, Piazza San Bernardo 104, Tel. 06.488 21 22, has a very original round shape. Without windows, as in the Pantheon, the only opening is in the center of the roof. The dome is 72 feet wide with octagonal coffers, which allow the weight on top to be reduced. Originally part of the bath complex of Diocletian, it has remained through the centuries, not surprisingly, substantially intact after being consecrated as a church.

From Piazza San Bernardo, take Via Emanuele Orlando, go left on Via Parigi and then right on Via Romita.

Feltrinelli International **bookstore** is at Via Emanuele Orlando 84. Trimani II Wine Bar, *Via Cernaia 37, between Via Goito and Via Castelfidardo, is a **wine bar** and **restaurant**.* At Via Goito 20 the shop Trimani *has a good selection of **wines, glasses**, and steins.*

7 The Aula Ottagona is an annex of the Roman bath complex and has

a separate entrance at Via Giuseppe Romita 8 a few steps away, between Via Cernaia and Via Parigi. Square from the outside, the interior has an octagonal form, and is one of the best preserved parts of the enormous Baths of Diocletian. The absence of heating and the existence of a large tub mentioned in the fifteenth century make us think that it was a hallway with a small *frigidarium* or cooling pool. As the inscription visible on the wall in Via Parigi explains, in 1609 the building was used as a grain silo. It is covered by a dome with an oculus in the center which led it to become a planetarium in the 1920's.

On display are some of the statues recovered from the huge imperial baths of Trajan, Caracalla, Diocletian and Constantine, copied or inspired by Greek masterpieces. Of note is a bronze statue, made around 315 AD, the *Greek Prince,* shown leaning on his lance. Most of the marble statues were done between 298 and 306 and come from the Baths of Diocletian. Among the statues of marble, the *Apollo Liceo* and *Aphrodite of Cirene* stand out. Note also the difference between the levels of the ancient floor and the modern one.

Coming out of the Aula Ottagona, continue on Via Romita up to Piazza della Repubblica.

8 Piazza della Repubblica. (M Repubblica) The Fountain of

the Naiads, in the center of the square, is the terminus fountain of the Acqua Pia Marcia. It provoked outrage and indignation on the part of the authorities when it was finished in 1901 because the four bronze nymphs seemed a bit too pagan. In fact, after its construction, barriers were erected around the fountain to hide it from the view of passersby, but they were torn down one night by a group of young men. Mario Rutelli designed the set of four reclining marine nymphs: the nymph of the ocean with a sea horse, the nymph of the lake with a swan, the nymph of rivers with a water snake and the nymph of underground water with a reptile.

The central figure, Glaucus, the god of the sea, was added in 1914; the fish that he holds spouts forth Rome's strongest jet of water with the exception of the fountains in Piazza San Pietro. The whole is even more impressive illuminated at night.

153

The present Piazza della Repubblica was created on an exedra, that is, a circular porticoed piazza, which was an open area for exercising as part of the Baths of Diocletian. In 1561 Pope Pius IV commissioned Michelangelo, by then 86 years old, to design a church utilizing part of the ancient structure. Thus, on the north side of the exedra, **Santa Maria degli Angeli** was created. The church contains the *calidarium* (hot pool) and the *tepidarium* (warm pool) of the ancient bath complex. The current transept was the central hall of the baths. It is almost as large as a football field and was then about 105 feet high, since the ancient floor was 15 feet lower.

The 8 red granite columns in the transept are original and the entire building was covered in mosaics, marbles, precious metals and statues. With truly monumental dimensions, it contains numerous tombs and paintings, and, in particular, the large sculpture of Saint Bruno by the famous French artist Jean Antoine Houdon, noted also for having sculpted George Washington.

Detail of the Fountain of the Naiads. The entrance to Santa Maria degli Angeli is visible on the right.

According to the Church, Easter must be celebrated the Sunday following the first full moon after the spring equinox. Pope Clement XI wanted a solar clock capable of verifying the calendar against the movement of the stars, to be able to check with precision the date for Easter. So, in 1702, he asked Francesco Bianchini to construct a meridian. Santa Maria degli Angeli was chosen because of its anti-seismic ground and its robustness, which guaranteed the stability of the clock.

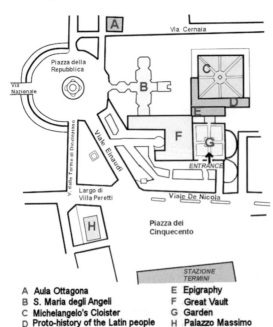

A Aula Ottagona
B S. Maria degli Angeli
C Michelangelo's Cloister
D Proto-history of the Latin people
E Epigraphy
F Great Vault
G Garden
H Palazzo Massimo

Map of Palazzo Massimo and the Baths of Diocletian

The **meridian** consists of a long stripe in the floor, oriented north-south and marked by numbers and the signs of the zodiac. A hole in the center of a large crest up high in a window permits a ray of sun to shine down and indicate on the strip the date at noon. During the summer solstice, June 21, the light hits number 33, near the Cancer symbol. Besides the verification of the date, this meridian served to regulate the clocks in Rome until 1846 when a shot from a cannon on the Janiculum hill began to announce noon every day.

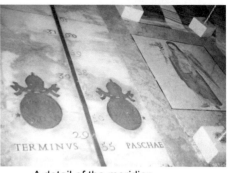

A detail of the meridian

McDonald's *is at Via Firenze 58, for* **fast food**.

From Piazza della Repubblica take Viale Einaudi and keep to the left until you get to Viale Enrico de Nicola. While you are walking, the ruins will be on your left.

The Fountain of the Naiads and Santa Maria degli Angeli

The **Museo Nazionale Romano** (Rome National Museum) is composed of four parts: **Palazzo Altemps** (see Walk 1), **Crypta Balbi** (see Walk 7), the **Baths of Diocletian** and **Palazzo Massimo**. The Aula Ottagona (Octagonal hall) is an annex to the Baths. A single ticket is valid for all 4 sites for several days. For tickets, https://www.coopculture.it/en/heritage.cfm?id=58.

9. The Terme di Diocleziano (Baths of Diocletian) have their

entrance at Via Enrico de Nicola 78, in front of the Termini station. This museum, part of the **Museo Nazionale Romano**, includes, besides part of the ancient bath complex, also **Michelangelo's cloister** and the area of the monastery constructed in the 1500's. The **epigraphy** section is dedicated to Latin writing while the proto-history area traces the culture of the region of Latium (Lazio, Rome's region), from the eleventh to the seventh century BC.

The baths were constructed from 298 to 306 AD and extended over many acres from the current Piazza dei Cinquecento, Via Volturno, Via XX Settembre and Via Torino. It was the largest bath complex in ancient Rome.

About 10,000 Christians were employed in its construction, a fact that was reported by the historians of the period and has been confirmed by finding numerous crosses incised in the bricks of the enormous construction. All the ancient baths were a cross between a spa complex and a campus. The baths could hold up to 3000 Romans at a time, where they could swim, exercise, receive massages, have a sauna or haircut, meet friends to chat, visit libraries, attend conferences or theatrical spectacles and shop. A moderate admission fee was usually charged, while some days access was gratis and open for all. (For more details about baths, see Walk 2, Terme di Caracalla).

Many archeological finds, taken from the complex, have been transferred to two other museums: the Palazzo Massimo nearby and the Palazzo Altemps near Piazza Navona. (Walk 1). The Baths have undergone centuries of plundering, neglect and the inexorable passage of time.

155

For the entrance to the baths, pass through the **open archaeological park** in front of the Piazza dei Cinquecento, where are displayed marble inscriptions, together with columns, capitals, architraves and various decorative elements. Many are funerary inscriptions and date from the late republic to the beginning of the empire (first century BC – first century AD).

The **epigraphy** section, dedicated to Latin inscriptions, includes vases, sarcophagi, tombstones and objects worked in metal. The several hundred on display were chosen from about 15,000 items that the Museo Nazionale Romano possesses. The ground floor includes the most ancient writings in Latin and in Greek in Italy. Among the most important are ceramic fragments with the writing REX (Latin for "king"), found near the Regia in the Roman Forum, and the dedications to Castor and Pollux found near Lavinio, a town near Rome.

Also on the ground floor are **inscriptions** which describe the popular **associations** in "colleges of occupations" which, according the historian Plutarch, go way back to the king Numa, that is, to the sixth century BC. There are traces of writing by merchants and artisans, freemen and slaves, butchers and sellers of flowers, flutists, and associations for actors and singers. The political importance of these associations grew until they had a significant role in organizing the plebeians during the unrest in the late republic. A series of laws led to the suppression of these "guilds" and subsequently they were rigidly controlled.

Associations

Today in the west we take for granted the existence of thousands of associations and organizations of various types and purposes. Guilds, or medieval artisans' associations, created to foster their common interests, spread across the whole of Europe. The proliferation of associations and a relatively greater tolerance of dissension in the west have facilitated the diffusion of power at various levels of society. This has been instrumental in the development of democracy. Many cultures, too often, have suppressed spontaneous attempts of individuals to organize, perceiving them as a threat to the existing authority. For example, the effects of two centuries of Mongol occupation on Russia resulting in greatly isolating it from Europe, and the harsh treatment of the Falun Gong spiritual movement by the Chinese government.

Michelangelo's Cloister is attributed to a design by the great artist. Together with the monastery, it is part of the transformation of the old Baths of Emperor Diocletian initiated by Pope Pius IV in 1561. Behind the church of Santa Maria degli Angeli, it occupies the most northern area of the perimeter of the baths. A fountain is centered in the 260 foot square and though it uses part of the bath's walls, the cloister has the typical structure of the monasteries of south central Italy.

The **proto-history of the Latin people**. This exhibit is on the raised floor around Michelangelo's Cloister. It analyzes the development of Latium (Lazio), the region around Rome, from the late Bronze Age to the Iron Age, that is, from about the eleventh to the seventh centuries BC. Modern graphics and charts illustrate the distribution of the population in the Alban hills, the coast and the interior and analyze the demographic development of the communities, the political and social structure, the technological level, relations with neighboring regions, religion and ideology.

Italy in the fifth century BC. Rome consisted of only a few square miles. At this time who would have bet on the Romans?

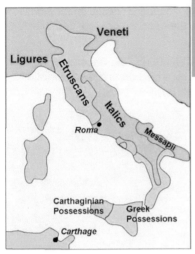

On coming out of the Baths of Diocletian, go to the right and Palazzo Massimo will be on the left side at the end of the piazza.

10 Palazzo Massimo at Largo di Villa Peretti 1, next to the Termini station, one of the four sites of the **Museo Nazionale Romano**, houses some of antiquity's best preserved mosaics and frescoes. The guided tour of the second floor is definitely worth the visit, which should be reserved as soon as you enter the museum for a timed visit or, better, reserve online at https://www.coopculture.it/en/heritage.cfm?id=58.

Main attractions

Due to the large size of the museum and the many works displayed, descriptions of the most important pieces will assist in providing an efficient and pleasant experience.

Ground floor

  Augustus as Pontifex Maximus
  Wounded Niobid
  Minerva

First floor

  Crouching Aphrodite
  Discobolo Lancelotti
  Sleeping Hermaphrodite
  Dionysus
  Girl of Anzio

Second floor

  Livia's villa garden room
  Three other complete frescoed rooms
  Mosaics on floors and walls

Basement

  Coins and artifacts

The building is bright and pleasant and, after the Vatican Museums and the Galleria Borghese, it is the most important museum of the city. Its **four floors** offer antiquities for everyone: Roman sculpture, statuary, frescoes, coins, mosaics and jewelry, organized thematically and by periods. In the basement you can see an extensive collection of Roman coins that reflect the political and military parabola of Rome. On the first floor there are sculptures from the first and second centuries removed from the Villa Adriana (Hadrian's villa), from Nero's villas and those of other emperors.

The exceptional recreation on the **second floor** transports you back in time to enter rooms from ancient Roman houses. Paintings and mosaics cover entire sections of walls and floors, some representing the mysterious cult of Dionysus. This Greek god of the forest and of wine was venerated at *"orgia,"* or mysteries of Dionysus, called also Bacchanalia. The celebrations connected, it is thought, to the return of spring, and constituted an occasion for promiscuity and drunkenness. Ever more extreme, the bacchanals were prohibited by the Roman Senate in 186 BC.

Palazzo Massimo was completed in 1887 and during the Second World War hosted some 30,000 wounded. The Palazzo is built around a courtyard and divided into *sale* (rooms) and *gallerie* (galleries).

From Republic to Empire

In the Republican period, the army was composed of citizen soldiers, mostly small land owners, the only ones who could afford to pay for and maintain their armaments. An army so composed was totally loyal to the State with which soldiers and officers identified themselves.

The gradual consolidation by large landowners, the use of slave labor and the consequent impoverishment of the middle class changed the composition of the Roman army. The proletariat began looking at a military career for social advancement. In the first century BC this new class of soldier began tying themselves to their own general rather than to the State. Their fortunes depended on the success of their general and vice versa. The personal success of Caesar assured land and a substantial amount of money to his veterans.

Julius Caesar was assassinated by a group of senators who wanted to maintain the Republic, which had lasted for about five hundred years. Augustus, Julius Caesar's adopted son, continued concentrating power, eliminating possible competitors and guaranteeing peace to a population tired of civil war. Perhaps Rome's territory had become too large to be governed in any other way.

Ground Floor

There are eight rooms and 3 galleries around a central courtyard. Near the entrance is a large polychrome statue of Minerva seated, in white marble, basalt and alabaster, found on the Aventine Hill. If the face seems strange it is because it was lost and has been replaced with a modern plaster cast of the same goddess.

In Room I (Sala I) is a **calendar** painted on plaster, which was found among the ruins of Nero's villa at Anzio. It dates from 84 to 55 BC and contains the twelve months of the year that we use today, the Roman feasts and a list of magistrates from the period 173 to 67 BC. This room also holds the statue of the so-called General of Tivoli, since it was found in this town, probably created by a Greek artist. The shield indicates he was a man of high standing in Roman society, perhaps a general.

Room IV allows you to see the faces of many of the **emperors** described in history books. Here are reunited representatives of the Julia-Claudius family: Octavian, the adopted son of Julius Caesar who, on becoming emperor, took the name of Augustus, his sister Octavia and wife Livia. Also on display are the princes who should have succeeded Augustus to the imperial throne, Germanicus and Druso, but who, either by destiny or intrigue, died prematurely. Finally the emperors Tiberius, Caligula, Claudius and Nero are also represented.

Room V is dedicated to the ideology of power. **Emperor Augustus** (27 BC – 14 AD) is shown dressed as Pontifex Maximus (below), the highest religious priest. Augustus defeated Antony and Cleopatra at Actium (Azio) in 28 BC, took the name Augustus, that is, "he who grows," and presented himself to the Senate and the people as the man who would end the civil wars. He succeeded and went on to oversee a period of peace and prosperity, but while his rhetoric featured him as a defender of the Senate and the republic, in fact he governed like a king, thus preparing the road for the emergence of the empire. He also tried to appear to his contemporaries as a new Romulus, the legendary founder of Rome, and at the same time he tried to restore the ancient moral values. (See Walk 4, Mausoleum of Augustus, about Julia) The Romans were changing; they were more affluent, always more permissive, young people didn't bother getting married, and the highly respected values of family devotion, duty and stoicism had become a notion of the past.

Augustus

Along Gallery III are numerous Greek personages, which give an idea of how much Roman society assimilated from the Greek; among these, *Alexander the Great* and *Socrates*. Busts of famous Greeks were often used in homes, libraries and schools. Note also a curious mosaic found in a villa from the first century that, in the central portion, depicts a cat attacking a bird, and in the lower portion two ducks.

Room VII displays several Greek originals from the property of the Roman historian Sallust, that previously were owned by Julius Caesar. These sculptures were brought to Rome after the conquest of southern Italy and Sicily, then Greek colonies, and from Greece itself, between the third and second century BC. Outstanding is a Greek original, *Wounded Niobid* (left), from about 440 BC, that shows one of the daughters of Niobe falling back while she tries to extract an arrow from her back. The myth of the children of Niobe, killed by Apollo and Artemis because of jealousy toward their mother, is a frequent theme in ancient art.

First Floor

Room I contains representations of the Flavian family, who, with Vespasian, the emperor who had the Colosseum built, and his sons Titus and Domitian, governed from 69 to 96 AD. The official portraits were often not only retouched, but the traits of the face idealized. Private portraits maintain, instead, a greater realism. Check in particular the different structures of the face in the portrait of the emperor Vespasian.

Room II is dedicated to Trajan (emperor from 98 – 117 AD) and Hadrian (117 – 138). From the time of emperor Nerva (96 – 98), the imperial succession was no longer seen as dynastic. The practical Roman mentality prevailed, recognizing that there were no valid reasons to limit the succession to the children, or   **159** even the adopted children, of the emperor. It was decided that the candidate should be the best of the senators. In an attempt to infuse new vitality into the institution, Trajan and Hadrian, again breaking with tradition, were both from the province of Spain. This was a period of peace and prosperity for all the citizens of the empire.

<u>Room V</u> expresses the theme of ideal sculpture of the country villas of the upper class. The *Girl of Anzio* was found in Nero's villa at Anzio. Perhaps a Greek original from the third century BC, it was made working two blocks of marble separately and then putting them together. The statue of *Apollo* from Anzio, from the first century, was inspired by an original from the fourth century BC. Observe the style of the wavy and elevated hair, which gives a feminine touch to the work. The statue of *Aphrodite Crouching* (right) caught the goddess while bathing. These sensual statues were frequently placed in imperial residences, in private and public gardens and baths.

When did they rule?	
Julius Caesar	46 – 44 BC
Augustus	27 BC – 14 AD
Tiberius	14 – 37
Caligula	37 – 41
Claudius	41 – 54
Nero	54 – 68
Vespasian	69 – 79
Titus	79 – 81
Domitian	81 – 96
Nerva	96 – 98
Trajan	98 – 117
Hadrian	117 – 138
Marcus Aurelius	161 – 180
Septimius Severus	193 – 198
Caracalla	211 – 217
Diocletian	284 – 305
Constantine	312 – 337

<u>Room VII</u> contains several marble and bronze statues of gods of human dimension or smaller: Apollo, Aphrodite, Artemis, Athena and Hercules. Of special interest is the bronze of *Dionysus,* which dates from the second century, discovered on the banks of the river during the construction of the levees. Here also is the *Sleeping Hermaphrodite.*

<u>Gallery II</u> contains female portraits and, as usual, the women of the imperial family are the trend-setters in matters of clothing and hairstyles.

Second floor
The semi-guided tour takes 45 minutes. Reserve at the entrance and you will be given a ticket for a timed visit. Incomparable paintings, mosaics, micro mosaics, inlaid decoration and plaster reliefs are displayed. This is a jewel you should not miss.

<u>Room II</u> shows a *triclinium*, a dining room, completely lined with frescoes of a **garden**, from Livia's villa. The writer Pliny described the villa of Livia, the emperor Augustus' wife, at the ninth mile of the Via Flaminia, which allowed an accurate identification when it was unearthed.

Greek and Roman gods		
Greek	*Roman*	
Zeus	Jupiter	King of all the gods
Hera	Juno	Jupiter's wife, goddess of marriage
Poseidon	Neptune	God of the sea
Apollo	Apollo	Sun god
Athena	Minerva	Goddess of war and wisdom
Aphrodite	Venus	Goddess of love and beauty
Ares	Mars	God of war
Dionysus	Bacchus	God of wine
Artemis	Diana	Goddess of transitions

Excavations done in the nineteenth century brought to light the walls of the villa, a statue of the emperor, and this fascinating room, reconstructed here in the museum.

In the villa of the empress, the room, used as a summer living room and for banquets, had a vaulted ceiling. Being partially underground, it was cool even in summer. On the fresco, beyond a wicker fence and a low wall, you are surrounded by a fantasy garden in full bloom, dotted by a variety of birds. Trees, both ornamental and fruit, and several types of plants and flowers are all painted at the height of bloom. Can you find the birdcage?

Galleries I and III. Along the corridors are **floor mosaics**, frequently of animals, Dionysian scenes and still lifes with bright colors and geometric designs, which date from the second century BC to the fourth century AD.

Gallery II, Rooms III, IV and V. These areas contain **frescoes** found during excavations of an ancient villa in the area of the Villa Farnesina. Facing the Tiber, it was built by Agrippa for the marriage between Marcello and Julia, the daughter of Augustus, later married to Agrippa himself. Only half of the ancient villa has been explored and this has allowed the recovery of the frescoes from nine rooms and some floor mosaics. The pictures in Gallery II were from a criptoportico, that is, a below ground gallery, painted white to increase the available light. The frescoes depict natural landscapes and a Dionysian atmosphere that is present also in Room III, with attractive urban and country landscapes on a black background.

Room IV has geometric floor mosaics also taken from the excavation of Villa Farnesina. In Room V three **bedrooms** have been recreated. Two of these, painted red, are for adults and contain some sensual elements. The other, painted white, is for children or women and is decorated mainly with religious symbols.

Room VIII contains **mosaics** found in Nero's villa by the sea at Anzio. The Nymphaeaum of Anzio used mosaic on the walls surrounding a fountain. The tesserae are diverse materials: several types of colored stones, shells, glass and pumice. In the large central niche is Hercules at rest. Marine frescoes detail dozens of fish, mollusks and crustaceans.

Mosaics
Mosaics are made by setting *tesserae*, small usually square pieces of stone, marble, glass or tile into a plaster or cement bed. The resulting surface is very durable and suitable even for floors as well as wall decoration. Many ancient floor mosaics in homes and public buildings have survived. The most common are black and white geometric designs. Sometimes delicate pictorial "emblems" were created with tiny tesserae called *vermiculatum*. Many fine examples are on the second floor of Palazzo Massimo. Mosaic has continued to be used through the centuries, especially in medieval churches such as Santa Maria in Trastevere and the Basilica of Santa Maria Maggiore. Most of the Renaissance "paintings" displayed in Saint Peter's basilica are actually mosaic copies. Some, of very large dimensions, decorate the inside of the dome where, because of the great height, the sizes of the tesserae are larger than a hand.

Room IX contains floors from the Villa di Baccano, on Via Cassia, belonging to the Severus imperial family. This complex was exceptionally large. The first floor was principally dedicated to the baths, while the second was used as a residence. Of particular interest are the four small beautifully preserved **mosaics**. Each picture depicts a chariot driver in his customary uniform at the side of his horse. The **four chariot teams** were easily recognizable at the games at the Circus Maximus by the colors of their clothing: the blue, the white, the red and the green. (See Walk 2, Circo Massimo). These were the standard colors of chariot races throughout the empire, as similar evidence has been found in Colchester, England.

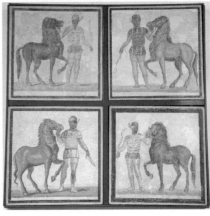

In Room XI there are some beautiful examples of **inlaid stone decoration**, called "*opus sectile*." This technique does not use small uniform squares as in mosaics, but stone, glass and colored marbles cut in the shapes and dimensions required by the design. This method permits more realistic curves and subtle shading as in the examples exhibited here.

What did the Romans eat?

It depended on the epoch. The many varieties of pastas were not yet invented and ingredients such as tomatoes, potatoes, coffee, rice and corn did not exist. Many writers like Pliny, Horace, Seneca and Juvenal enjoyed writing about cooking.

The Romans definitely used spices to keep their food tasty and safe. The well-off during the imperial period could afford delicacies and excesses such as boiled parrot, roast crane, nightingale tongues or camel heels. The early Romans had a much more frugal diet. The most popular dish was *puls*, a mush of cereal grains, then cheese, eggs, olives, nuts and a lot of vegetables.

Take a look at this sophisticated **recipe** for preparing duck, taken from the book *De Re Coquinaria* by Apicius, a culinary expert in ancient Rome during the first century AD.

   Duck with Hazelnuts

Take pepper, parsley, dried mint, mountain celery, and safflower, moisten with wine, add roasted hazelnuts or almonds, a little honey, mix with wine, vinegar and fish sauce. Add oil and heat while stirring; add celery and calamint (an herb still used in southern Europe). Make incisions in the meat and pour the sauce over it.

This mixture of sauce and nut flour gave the outside a crunchy texture while keeping it moist on the inside.

From Largo di Villa Peretti take Via del Viminale, go left on Via Torino, pass Via Cavour and you will find yourself in Piazza dell'Esquilino, which is at the rear of Santa Maria Maggiore. Walk around to the front entrance.

La Gallina Bianca, *Via Rosmini 9 is a* **pizzeria** *and* **restaurant** *with tables outside.*

The back of Santa Maria Maggiore, showing the semicircular apse and obelisk

11 Santa Maria Maggiore.

The sheer bulk of Santa Maria Maggiore is astounding. Looming in the center of open spaces, it can be encircled, in contrast with most other churches that nestle among other buildings, presenting only their facades. It is one of the **four patriarchal basilicas** of Rome. The others are Saint Peter's, San Giovanni in Laterano (Saint John Lateran) and San Paolo (Saint Paul's outside the walls). It is the first basilica in Rome to have been built by a pope, rather than an emperor, Pope Sixtus III, between 432 and 440.

On this hill, the Esquiline, women of the area visited the temple of the Roman mother goddess, Juno Lucina. The choice of this site by the pope for the construction of a church was not a casual one. The Council of Ephesus had affirmed in 431 as dogma the belief that Mary was the Mother of God, so the religious authorities had the intention of substituting the previous pagan cult with the veneration of the Madonna. The plan is characteristic of a fifth century basilica with a nave and two side aisles. It was enlarged

The facade

over the years and reconstructed in the thirteenth century. With the passing of time, many other churches were substantially altered according to the architectural style in vogue at the time, but in spite of all the additions during the centuries, Santa Maria Maggiore remains one of the best examples of the early Christian basilicas.

Architectural styles from several periods are present in the basilica. Early Christian and medieval elements are represented in mosaics and columns. Baroque is expressed mainly in the exterior of the apse from the 1600's and the façade, portico and loggia from the 1700's. It also contains numerous works of the Cosmati in mosaics, decorations and tombs, and elements from Mannerism and the Renaissance. We can even find Gothic, in the four windows of the apse and in the vault of the Chapel of Saint Michael.

The Romanesque bell tower, at about 245 feet, is the highest in the city. The two domes positioned over the chapels at the ends of the transept were added in the sixteenth and seventeenth centuries. The **chapel** in the left transept **(2)** contains the **tomb of the Borghese family** and includes Pope Paul V and Pauline Borghese, sister of Napoleon Bonaparte. (See Galleria Borghese).

NOTE: Numbers correspond to the diagram at right.

Forty ancient Ionic columns separate the nave and aisles. Although some have been restored, most of the **mosaics** on the architrave **(4)**, which date from the fifth century, are originals from the time of Sixtus III and illustrate scenes from the Old Testament. (This is another occasion where binoculars would be helpful.) A very early example of using interior decoration as a learning tool, the pictures tell the sacred narrative. On the left, eighteen panels relate stories from Genesis, including scenes depicting Abraham, Isaac, Jacob and Rebecca. Fifteen mosaics on the right feature Moses, the Ten Commandments, parting of the Red Sea, and Joshua and the siege of Jericho.

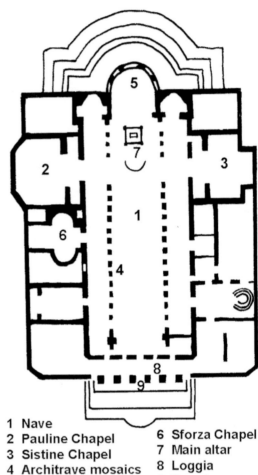

1 Nave
2 Pauline Chapel
3 Sistine Chapel
4 Architrave mosaics
5 Apse mosaic
6 Sforza Chapel
7 Main altar
8 Loggia
9 Facade

Madonna of the snow
According to legend, on August 5, 358, the Virgin Mary appeared requesting that a church be built on the spot where snow would fall the next day. The miraculous snow, rare even in Roman winters, fell on the Esquiline hill outlining the church, and a precursor to the current basilica was built by Pope Liberius (352 – 366). The event is commemorated in a service every August 5 with white petals raining down from above.

The mosaic in the **apse (5)**, dating from the thirteenth century, is considered among the best of the Roman tradition. It shows scenes from the life of the Virgin and culminates with Jesus crowning Mary, and is unusual in that it depicts Mary at the side of Jesus as his equal. As you can see the artist signed on the left lower part of the vault: IACOB TORRITI PICTOR H(OC) OP(US) FEC(IT). (The artist Jacopo Torriti made this work). The figures displayed in the Coronation of the Virgin are in the French style, similar to representations in the portals of the Cathedrals of Notre Dame, Sens and Strasbourg. Jesus' life is shown on the triumphal arch, and other mosaics in the apse include five scenes of Mary's life near Gothic windows, very rare in Rome.

The **Sistine Chapel (3)** (naturally not to be confused with the more famous one in the Vatican), on the right, is by Domenico Fontana and contains the tomb of Pope Sixtus V who began major urban redevelopment in the late 1500's.

The **Sforza Chapel (6)** on the left was designed by Michelangelo, but completed by Giacomo della Porta. We have seen the same two artists at work on the construction of the Basilica of Saint Peter as well. In the lively atmosphere created by Michelangelo in the Sforza Chapel, some experts have seen a precursor to the Baroque style which would explode a few years later.

The tomb of Pope Sixtus V in the Sistine Chapel. Four bronze angels hold a model of the chapel itself.

Dome of the Pauline Chapel

Behind the **altar (7)** and on the right is the tomb of Cardinal Rodriguez, perhaps one of the most beautiful done by the famous Cosmati family, experts in using polychrome marble. Nearby, a stone slab in the floor indicates the **tomb of the Bernini family**, where Gian Lorenzo Bernini is buried. It is ironic that the master of the Baroque and designer of so many exuberantly ornate monuments lies here in this very simple space.

Finally, once outside, at the front of the church, look up at the **loggia (8)** that contains the mosaics of the exterior façade from the thirteenth century. They are clearly visible from the piazza when the light is right, or even at night for they are illuminated. Binoculars would help.

One of the large Corinthian columns from the ancient Basilica of Maxentius in the Roman Forum was transferred in 1614 by Pope Paul V to the piazza in front of the Santa Maria Maggiore basilica. This column, also called the Column of Peace, 47 feet high, is the only one left from the ancient edifice. A bronze of the Madonna and

Gold from the Americas
The gilded coffered ceiling of the Santa Maria Maggiore basilica was done with gold from the first load brought back from America, which had just been discovered. Ferdinand and Isabella, sovereigns of Spain, donated it to Pope Alexander VI.

Child was added on top of the column in 1615. The **obelisk** now in Piazza dell'Esquilino, behind the basilica, came from the Mausoleum of Augustus. We have just seen its twin obelisk from Augustus' tomb on the Piazza del Quirinale, as part of the Fountain of Monte Cavallo.

The Druid's Den, *Via San Martino ai Monti 28, is an* **Irish pub**.

From Piazza dell'Esquilino, to get back to Termini station, head north (right) on Via Cavour.

Termini Station – the subway – shopping mall

A short distance away, under the Termini station, a shopping center has been built with a supermarket and many other shops. Subway stations and bus stops are in front of the station, in Piazza dei Cinquecento.

There are two **fast food** *McDonald's in the station, one on the upper gallery and one in the shopping center on the lower level. Numerous shops, cafes and eating establishments are in the Termini station.*

This walk is designed to take all day, or even more. It is about 3.5 km. (2.2 miles). The Quirinale and Via Nazionale would add about another mile, and this does not include the walking in Villa Borghese or the visits to the museums. If you have little time, do not miss the Galleria Borghese, Via Veneto, the Capuchin Cemetery, Piazza Barberini and Palazzo Massimo.

Walk Six - Baroque Rome
Additional Restaurants

Moma, Via di San Basilio 42, www.ristorantemoma.it. Restaurant with seasonal dishes. €€€

Massimo Riccioli Ristorante Bistrot, Via Veneto 50, Wonderful terrace. www.hotelmajestic.com. €€€

La Barrique, Via del Boschetto 41, Tel 06 4782 5953, Wine bar and restaurant. €€

Trimani Il Winebar, Via Cernaia 37, www.trimani.com, Multi-regional cooking. €€

Gioia Mia Pisciapiano, Via degli Avignonesi 34, Trattoria and pizzeria. www.ristorantegioiamia.it €

Ristorante Alessio, Via del Viminale 2G, www.ristorantealessio.it. Roman cooking. Near Piazza dei Cinquecento. €€

Amedeo Ristorante, Via Principe Amedeo 16, www.amedeoristorante. com. Modern decor. €€

Relative prices are indicated by the symbols € to €€€

Rival Geniuses Bernini and Borromini

Gian Lorenzo Bernini (1598 – 1680), born in Naples, spent his formative years at the workshop of his father, Pietro, a sculptor in his own right. Gian Lorenzo was not only a very successful sculptor and architect, the most important of the Baroque period in Rome, but also a painter, playwright and stage designer. His outgoing, charming personality and aristocratic manner was particularly suited for the life of society. The family transferred to Rome in 1605, where Pietro had commissions for sculptures and also for the Barcaccia fountain in Piazza di Spagna.

From an early age he enjoyed the support and patronage of Cardinal Scipione Borghese, nephew of Pope Paul V. Maffeo Barberini, who became Pope Urban VIII (1623-44), gave the artist the most important commissions in Rome. During Bernini's most mature years, from 1640 to 1660, he produced the **tomb of Urban VIII,** now in Saint Peter's (Walk 5, photo right), and he began to think about a form of art that would unify painting, sculpture and architecture. The Cornaro Chapel in **Santa Maria della Vittoria**, at #6 in this walk, is an attempt in that direction. Busts of the Cornaro family are housed as if in theater boxes, watching the scene of Saint Theresa's rapture.

Bernini excelled at creating sculpture that could be viewed from many angles. He designed the angels for Ponte Sant'Angelo to be viewed from 3 points of view, for people coming and going on the bridge (Walk 5). His David and Apollo and Daphne in **Galleria Borghese**, at #1 in this walk, are displayed so as to hold interest from all angles. This three-dimensionality is also reflected as you walk all around the baldacchino of Saint Peter's.

Later he, like Michelangelo, was drawn to architecture to interpret on a monumental scale his emotional and religious fervor, such as in the interior of Sant'Andrea al Quirinale (at #5), his idea of the mother church welcoming the faithful. His diplomatic and effervescent temper no doubt helped him in society and with the popes. He worked for every pope who was in power during his lifetime.

Some of **Bernini's masterpieces**: Palazzo Montecitorio, now the seat of the Chamber of Deputies, the façade of Propaganda Fide, Palazzo Barberini, Palazzo Odescalchi in Piazza SS. Apostoli, the church of Sant'Andrea al Quirinale. Fountains: Tritone in Piazza Barberini, Fountain of the Bees at the end of Via Veneto, The Fountain of the Rivers in Piazza Navona (Walk 1).

Bernini's baldacchino

In the Vatican (Walk 5): the *Baldacchino*, the *Tomb of Urban VIII*, statue of *Saint Longinus*, the *Tomb of Countess Mathilde*, the *Cathedra of Saint Peter*, the equestrian monument to Constantine in the portico and the *Colonnade*, and one of the fountains in Piazza San Pietro.

Galleria Borghese: *Rape of Proserpina, Apollo and Daphne, Bust of Paul V, Bust of Scipione Borghese*, model for monument to Louis XIV in terracotta, *David*, and *Truth Revealed by Time.*

167

Francesco Castelli Borromini (1599-1667) was from Bissone in the north of Italy and could not have been more different temperamentally. Withdrawn and melancholic, he epitomized the solitary artist. In spite of this, his many contributions are spread across Rome. Where Bernini's curves are showy, those of Borromini are geometrically grounded. His façades are a complex interplay of ellipses, ovals, rectangles, squares and precise calculations. His concave-convex rhythm reflects an increasing elasticity. This contrasts with Bernini's structures, which follow the classical Renaissance tradition of reflecting the proportions of the human body. Borromini's shapes almost seem to be flexible, or made of rubber. He merges architecture and sculpture in a way that must have shocked Bernini.

Undulating curves in San Carlo

The tiny jewel **San Carlo alle Quattro Fontane,** at # 5 in this walk (photo right), reflects his architectural vision. In fact, he worked mainly as an architect, and the sculptural quality of his designs also reflects the Baroque style. He could also create some amazingly original works, such as the spiral "beehive" steeple on the church of **Sant'Ivo** (Walk 1). Near the Farnese Arch on Via Giulia (Walk 1), a large sign lists all of his Roman works.

In a period of stress and depression, a self-inflicted injury, perhaps suicidal, perhaps unintentional, finally led to his death in 1667.

In spite of their rivalry, Bernini and Borromini worked together on some projects, such as Palazzo Barberini and the baldacchino of Saint Peter's.

Some of **Borromini's masterpieces**: San Carlo alle Quattro Fontane, Sant'Ivo (Walk 1), the perspective gallery in Palazzo Spada (Walk 1), Sant'Agnese in Agone in Piazza Navona (Walk 1), Palazzo Barberini (assisting Bernini), Palazzo Falconieri, Palazzo Spada, Sant'Andrea delle Fratte, and the Falconieri Chapel in San Giovanni dei Fiorentini, where he is buried, along with his relative Carlo Maderno.

The fanciful spire of Sant'Ivo by Borromini

WALK SEVEN - The Symbolic Center

Today, as two thousand years ago, if a Roman wanted to show the city to friends from out of town, where would he take them? Both a modern Roman and an ancient one would think of the **Campidoglio**. The symbolic center of ancient Rome was the site of the most important ancient temple to Jupiter and home of the earliest Senate. The piazza was transformed into a Renaissance jewel by Michelangelo's genius. Showing off the city, our friend 1900 years ago would stop also at the Forums, especially **Trajan's Forum**, the last to be built and the most spectacular.

The growth of the city and its political climate in the first and second centuries compelled all-powerful emperors to build forums. (See the *Ancient Origins* Walk 2 and The Roman Forum in the *Imperial Rome* Walk 3). **Trajan's Market,** the first multilevel functional complex, was one of the wonders of the ancient world, and the concept was rediscovered in the last century with the construction of modern shopping centers. In the center of the city, it boasted shops selling all sorts of products, administrative offices, multi-level streets and many fountains and terraces.

The medieval flavor of Rome is recalled during a walk in the picturesque streets of the **Monti** neighborhood and the **Jewish quarter**. The suggested **alternate route** takes you away from the noise and traffic of Via Cavour and Via dei Fori Imperiali. Coming out of the subway station, following our tour, the tourist will have a quieter, more intimate and fulfilling experience.

In this walk ...

1. Michelangelo's **Moses** in the church of **San Pietro in Vincoli**

2. The **Suburra**, an ancient violent, but today quiet, neighborhood, an optional walk

3. The **Imperial Forums** of Augustus and Trajan

4. **Trajan's Market**, an amazing ancient multi-level commercial center

5. **Palazzo Venezia** in historic **Piazza Venezia,** a hub in the center of the city

6. **Monument to Vittorio Emanuele II** with the **Museo del Risorgimento,** a museum dedicated to the Italian unification in the 19th century

7. The **Campidoglio** with Michelangelo's beautiful piazza, the **Capitoline Museums** and the panoramic view over the Roman Forum

8. The medieval church of **Santa Maria in Aracoeli** and the nearby ruins of an *insula*, second century apartments

9. **Crypta Balbi,** remains of an ancient courtyard, a recent addition to the Roman National Museum

10. The **Fountain of the Tortoises**, a lighthearted Baroque fountain

11. The **Jewish quarter**, the oldest Jewish community in Europe, offers typical culinary specialties

Below: view from the Palatine hill, with the Roman Forum in the foreground, the Campidoglio's Palazzo dei Senatori, and the white Monument to Vittorio Emanuele II in the background.

Because the Capitoline Museums are open also in the evening, the description of this walk is in the direction of Via Cavour to the Campidoglio. Some tourists stop for dinner at nearby restaurants or pizzerie and come back later to enjoy the special lighting on the Campidoglio and the fantastic view of the Roman Forum at night. There is everything to pass an exciting day and an unforgettable evening.

Instead, if you find yourself going in the opposite direction, once past Piazza Venezia, taking Via dei Fori Imperiali, the Colosseum appears at the end of the street. Walking straight down, the monument is continually in view in the background and as you are getting closer, everything else is dwarfed.

Begin by taking the subway to the Via Cavour stop. At the exit, to visit the church of San Pietro in Vincoli proceed briefly downhill on Via Cavour to a stairway on your left, Via Franceso di Paola, which takes you up to the church. (If you come out in Piazza della Suburra, a stairway will take you rapidly up to Via Cavour.)

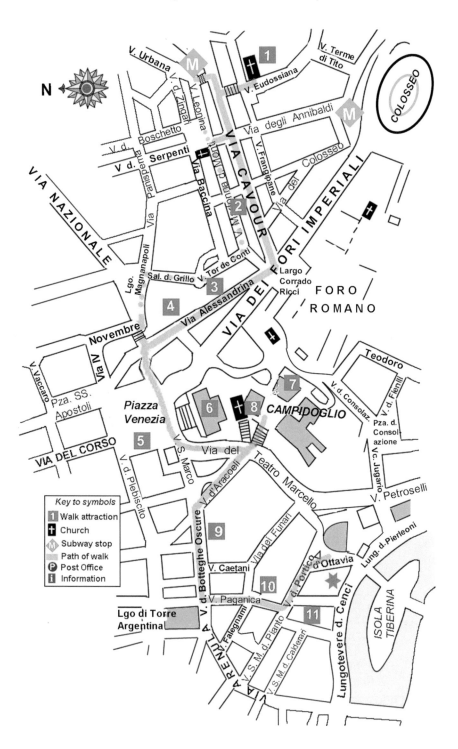

1 San Pietro in Vincoli. (M Cavour)

This church, Saint Peter in Chains, according to legend, contains the chains used to imprison Saint Peter, on display at the altar. Nearby was the site of the main Roman prison. During the persecutions of the Christians by Nero around 67 AD, the Apostles Peter and Paul lost their lives. But the church merits a visit especially for the statue of **Moses** by Michelangelo. Originally the artist planned a huge monumental tomb adorned with over 40 sculptures for Pope Julius II, but the pontiff interrupted the project to have Michelangelo work instead on the Sistine Chapel. The statue of Moses would have been higher up and the observer's point of view at a lower level than the current position. Meditative and wise, holding the ten commandments under his arm, but also powerful and capable of leadership, Moses projects a sense that the contemporaries of Michelangelo called *"terribilità."* This characteristic belonged to the artist and to the pope and led to some famous clashes between the two strong personalities. The tomb was never finished, thus Michelangelo referred to it as "that tragedy of a tomb."

Is it lunch time yet? The area around San Pietro in Vincoli, the streets behind Via Cavour, like Via Leonina, Via dei Serpenti and Via della Madonna dei Monti are good places to find a snack or lunch.

If short on time, continue down Via Cavour, skip number 2, the Suburra, and go to #3, the Imperial Forums.

*Continue down Via Cavour to Largo Corrado Ricci. Keep to the right and take Via Alessandrina, which borders on the Imperial Forums. Going left on Via dei Fori Imperiali, on the left is a **Visitor Center** with exhibits and information on the Forums.*

*La Vecchia Roma is a **pizzeria** at Via Leonina 10. Finnegan's Irish Pub is at Via Leonina 66. At Via Leonina 82 is La Bottega del Cioccolato for **chocolate** specialties. Pizzeria Leonina has **pizza** by the slice at Via Leonina 84. The trattoria Da Valentino at Via Cavour 293 has good meals at moderate prices. Stop at the **wine bar** Cavour 313 (the name is the address).*

***The alternate route**: An additional interesting area to explore is the picturesque Monti neighborhood: Piazza della Suburra, Via Leonina, Via dell'Angeletto, Via degli Zingari, Via dei Serpenti, Via Clementina, Via Cimarra, Via Boschetti and Via Baccina. This is an alternate way to visit this area and reconnect with the rest of the walk: continue on Via Leonina, Via Madonna dei Monti, Via Tor dei Conti, Piazza del Grillo, Salita del Grillo and Largo Magnanapoli from where, going down Via IV Novembre, **you can pick up the walk skipping to number 4**, Trajan's Market.*

2 The Suburra.

The name comes from the Latin "sub urbe," under the city, that is, it indicated the lower part of the neighborhood, located on the right of Via Cavour going toward the Forums. It extended around Piazza della Suburra and it was one of the less desirable and ill-famed areas in ancient times. The buildings of diverse styles and periods guarantee diversity.

The itinerary along Via Tor dei Conti and Salita del Grillo passes quickly from the **ancient classical period** to the **medieval** and then to the **Baroque**. These are quiet streets, in marked contrast with the crowded and noisy Via Cavour and Via dei Fori Imperiali, and they offer a peek at the Forum and Trajan's Market.

At the Cavour subway station, go down Via Leonina.

At Via dei Serpenti, on one side the buildings are perfectly lined up, while on the other they are sinuous and irregular, from which the word "serpenti" (serpents).

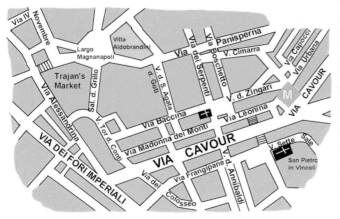

The houses are of different heights on both sides. These irregularities, together with the Colosseum in the background and the Madonna dei Monti church, make a unique composition.

Past that intersection, continuing on Via Madonna dei Monti, note the isolated rustic house on the left, out of place, and, at the end, the imposing **Tor dei Conti** (below). Named for this noble Roman family that produced many cardinals and popes, the tower, of medieval origin, is only a third of its original height. The whitish marble and the dark basalt were taken from the Forums nearby. Hardwearing basalt was used extensively for flooring in ancient Rome.

On Via Tor dei Conti, the heavily guarded Arco dei Pantani was the principal passage between the high-crime area of the Suburra and the Forums in ancient Rome. The term "pantano" means marsh, referring to the frequent flooding of this area, the lowest of the city.

In Piazza del Grillo, between Palazzo del Grillo and the ancient wall, is the House of the Cavalieri di Malta, which is part of the Sovereign Military Order of Malta (SMOM), the smallest state in the world. (See Walk 4).

Going up the hill, on the left is the imposing Roman wall, made of large blocks of peperino, a gray rock of volcanic origin, which in ancient times separated the Suburra from the Forums.

Finally at Largo Magnanapoli, one of the **prettiest urban landscapes** stands out. In the center of the piazza the ancient stones remaining were part of the Servian Walls from the fourth century BC that protected the young city. Arranged on the side of a hill in step-like fashion are the Torre delle Milizie, the Villa Aldobrandini, and the façade of a church. Largo Magnanapoli forms an **exceptionally artistic urban composition**. Looking on the other side, on Via XXIV Maggio, you can see the ancient obelisk of the Fountain of Monte Cavallo in front of the Palazzo del Quirinale, home of the president of the Italian Republic. (Walk 6).

Continue downhill on Via IV Novembre and skip to number 4 Trajan's Market.

3 The Imperial Forums.

The growth of the city and the affirmation of Rome as a commercial and administrative center rendered the older Forum, from the republican age, ever more crowded. This pushed the emperors to

successively build other forums, each seeking to leave his stamp on Rome, with new basilicas, temples, and porticoed piazzas adjacent to the old ones. In these newer and more comfortable environments, business-men had their meetings, assemblies convened, trials were held, arrest warrants issued, fines levied and religious services were attended. While the buildings in the original Roman Forum were constructed over time in a haphazard manner, these new Forums were systematically planned. Thus, in a continuum, next to the Roman Forum, and under the area of the current Via dei Fori Imperiali and Via Alessandrina, grew the Forums of Caesar, Augustus, Vespasian, Nerva and Trajan. Columns from Basilica Ulpia, part of Trajan's Forum are shown above.

The original Roman Forum assumed a more ceremonial function, with the Curia (the senators were much less powerful during the empire), the nearby temple of Jupiter Capitoline, the Temple of Concord, the Via Sacra, the Rostrums and the Temple of Vesta. (See Walk 3 - Imperial Rome)

All activities happened in the open so that public officials were under constant scrutiny. On their way to the Forums these officials had to walk the streets and be in close contact with the Roman citizens who did not hesitate to express their opinions forcefully. The orator who drew the biggest crowds and the highest number of important people listening had the most influence.

The ubiquitous SPQR signs (Senatus Popolusque Romanus) refer to the relationship between the Senate and the people. The amorphous crowd turned into the "populus" in the Forums, and not many politicians dared to go against the will of the Roman people for too long. In granting, or not, life to the combatants in the games at the Colosseum, wise emperors usually sided with the crowd.

The **Foro di Augusto** (Augustus' Forum), finished in 2 BC, contained a large arcaded piazza dominated by an enormous statue of the emperor. "I found Rome in wood and bricks and I left it in marble" is a famous expression of Augustus.

The locations of the ancient forums, with the modern streets' positions

Julius Caesar	- 44 BC
Augustus	27 BC - 14 AD
Vespasian	69 AD - 79 AD
Nerva	96 AD - 98 AD
Trajan	98 AD - 117 AD

Mercato di Traiano

Via Alessandrina

Colonna Traiana

Foro di Traiano

Foro di Augusto

Via Cavour

Foro di Nerva

Foro di Vespasiano

Via del Fori Imperiali

Foro di Cesare

Foro Romano

Today there are only 3 columns left of the Temple of Marte Ultore (Mars the Avenger) that Augustus, the adoptive son of Julius Caesar, had built to commemorate the battle of Phillipi in 42 BC. Brutus and Cassius, the conspirators against Julius Caesar, were defeated and led to suicide. With Augustus, Rome reached the natural boundaries of the great rivers of the Rhine and Danube in the north, Euphrates in the east, the Atlantic Ocean in the west and the Sahara desert in the south.

Populus power

A determined individual could effect political changes when he was able to captivate and bring the *populus* to his side. An anecdote of the fourth century BC tells of an old skinny, filthy man with a long beard and hair, entering the Forum. He told his story to a group of citizens that gathered around him. He recounted that he was a Roman citizen and that during the recent wars with the Sabines his farm was destroyed. He had to borrow money to pay the taxes and then, unable to pay it back, he was tortured and imprisoned by his creditors.

Soon similar stories arose from other people. More and more people joined the protest, and the outrage built until the Senate was forced to repeal the laws that put debtors at the mercy of their creditors.

Augustus (statue at right) ordered expeditions to the Arabian Peninsula and to the area between the Rhine and Elba rivers, following the spirit of expansion of his republican predecessors. But he decided wisely against invading other territories. Instead, he paused, consolidated his empire, and advised the next emperor Tiberius against the rush to conquest. The rise of Augustus ushered in the Pax Romana, a period of unmatched peace and prosperity that lasted about 2 centuries. However, it cemented the end of the republic and

the beginning of the empire. Augustus listed his own accomplishments in a document called *Res Gestae*, posted in public places all over the empire and read in the Senate upon his death:

- Doubled the size of the empire
- End of the Civil War and beginning of a period of peace and prosperity
- Construction of three new aqueducts in Rome
- End of the military draft
- Made Rome safer by establishing a permanent police force and fire brigade that worked also as night police
- Accepted the title of prince but refused that of king or emperor and proclaimed that he wanted to maintain and invigorate the republican traditions
- Reduced the number of senators from 1000 to 600

His list is of course selective since he ignored the destruction of life and property during the 14-year civil war, of which he was the winner. There is no mention of his dead rivals: Brutus, Cassius, Lepidus, Antony and Cleopatra. He refers to the battles with Sextus Pompey, (the son of Pompey Magnus, the main enemy of Julius Caesar), as clashes with "pirates." No mention of the defeat at the Teutoburg Forest in Germany (9 AD) or of his increasing control that allowed him to extend his power at the expense of the republican institutions he repeatedly claimed to uphold.

175

The first firemen

The fire brigades were conceived in 6 AD during Augustus' reign. A special militia of 3500 men called "vigils" was set up, not only to put out fires but to prevent them. A necessity, considering that most of the densely packed homes and apartments were made of wood. Even today Italian firemen are called "vigili del fuoco."

According to a law of the emperor Tiberius, freed slaves could become firemen and after 6 years had the right of Roman citizenship. Firemen had at their disposal pumps, ladders, ropes, poles, blankets, vinegar and naturally the abundance of water of the city.

Continuing on Via Alessandrina, you can see part of the Foro Traiano on both sides of the street.

The **Museo del Vittoriano**, Via di San Pietro in Carcere, just on the other side of Via dei Fori Imperiali, offers a variety of art exhibits. See number 6.

Foro Traiano (Trajan's Forum), the last to be completed, was the most spectacular. Why did the emperor build yet another forum? Even though emperors were not elected, they were wise to consider the desires of the upper class, and the growing need for more public spaces was one of these. Trajan's conquest of Dacia (now Romania) was very expensive, but, with the spoils, the emperor sponsored the construction of this project that represented also a grandiose example of political propaganda.

The **forum** contained a large piazza with porticoes, an enormous basilica, two libraries, a temple, the famous column and an exceptional multilevel covered complex. At the entrance, you were greeted by a portico 388 feet by 292 feet, with a statue of the emperor on horseback in the center. The nearby Basilica Ulpia, used as a court, was also enormous, 559 by 197 feet. Designed with five aisles on two floors, functional and yet splendid for the abundance of precious marbles, it was the largest covered space in the city. Two libraries, set next to Trajan's Column, one in Greek and the other in Latin, contained the knowledge of the western world. Unfortunately, very little remains, making it difficult to imagine the former glory.

The most visible and best-preserved monument is **Trajan's Column**, shown here flanked by two Baroque churches. Formed by 18 cylindrical blocks set on one another with tiny openings to let some light in, it has a spiral stairway inside. Like scenes from a film sculpted in stone, 2500 figures in bas relief describe the most important phases of the two campaigns of Trajan against the Dacians, now Romania, in 101-102 and 105-106 AD. Booty from the victory consisted in 225 tons of gold, 500 tons of silver and 50,000 slaves. Besides the forum, this wealth provided funds for the construction of other buildings in Rome and roads in Italy and provinces.

Right above one of the small windows, the emperor Trajan on horseback, followed by the cavalry, is reunited with other troops at a fortified encampment. The soldiers bring with them a sacrificial bull and 3 standards. In the panel below, the Roman auxiliaries on the left fight the bearded Dacians on the right. In contrast with the heavily armored legionnaires above, the auxiliaries, foreign troops often from local tribes, wear only a fringed shirt and neckcloth.

Deciphering the events on the column today is very difficult but it was not always this way. In fact, originally it was painted, projecting a different effect than the uniform gray color. In addition, its setting was between 2 libraries, whose windows allowed viewing the action up close.

Trajan's ashes were deposited at the base of the column, the first time anyone had been buried inside the confines of the *pomerium*, the sacred perimeter of the city. His statue was on top of the column until 1587 when Pope Sixtus V replaced it with one of Saint Peter.

Details of Trajan's Column

The Romans were in Dacia from 106 to 270. The Latin language was introduced, Roman-style cities constructed, and the mines developed. Dacia became a flourishing province of the empire. Romanians speak a romance language and at the beginning of the 21st century, after joining the EU, Romanians formed the largest immigrant group in Italy.

On the right of Via Alessandrina you can see, from the outside, the **Mercati di Traiano**. *For the entrance, go down Via Alessandrina and on until you find a stairway on the right, Via Magnanapoli, that takes you up to Via Quattro Novembre (or Via IV Novembre). Continue on the right uphill and the entrance is at number 94.*

4 Mercati di Traiano (Trajan's market).

Built at the beginning of the second century, it soared up to 6 levels, contained up to 300 spaces and was considered one of the wonders of the ancient world. A central street, **Via Biberatica**, going uphill in a south-north direction, separated the complex into two parts. It was a **multi-functional center**. On the ground floor there were activities associated directly with the Forum: commercial, religious and social.

As a rich and cosmopolitan city, Rome imported and sold products all across the empire. In particular, a vast section was reserved for spices from the east that were in high demand. On the lower levels there were also shops for fruit, vegetables, flowers, fish, oils and wines. A section was reserved for the distribution of food to the poor. Finally, the upper levels were dedicated to managerial, administrative and legal functions.

Before beginning the work for Trajan's Market, the architect Apollaro of Damascus had much of the hill between the Quirinal and Campidoglio removed. The surface of the hill had been as high as the top of Trajan's Column. The excavation created the level space that we now see in the forum.

The raised northern part of the market, that is, the area around Via IV Novembre, permitted an easy access to the upper floors, by means of arches and elevated streets. The entire complex was crossed by streets on several levels and contained an abundance of fountains and terraces. Today the entrance is on the third level. On the ground floor there are remains of the pavement. Complete shop walls are well-preserved in the building, while some maintain the original mosaic flooring. The upper floors have been reconstructed in different periods.**177**

Amazing complex
Trajan's market contained up to 300 spaces, elevated streets, and an abundance of terraces and fountains. In the words of a Roman journalist of the time, Ammianus Marcellinus, describing the reaction of the emperor Constantine during a visit to Trajan's market, " ... he stopped amazed, while his mind tried to comprehend the grandiose complex, which cannot be described in words and can never be replicated by common mortals."

The curved portico with two levels of shops

Two unusual buildings just outside the market stand out. The tall one, on the northeast side, is the **Torre delle Milizie** that dates from the thirteenth century. The massive white building on the other side of Via dei Fori Imperiali, to the east, is the modern **Monument to King Vittorio Emanuele II**. (See number 6).

Frequently, **art exhibitions** are held in the main hall of Trajan's Markets.

Fresh fish
In an age before refrigeration, keeping fish alive was the best means to guarantee their freshness. The upper class took great pride in their ability to offer fresh fish to their guests. They even had ponds to keep and breed fish.

*Continue down Via Magnanapoli, which takes you to Piazza Venezia. The Antica Birreria Peroni at Via di San Marcello 19, the continuation of Piazza SS. Apostoli, formerly a traditional beer and sausage place, now offers a **variety of dishes.** Scholars Lounge Irish Pub, Via del Plebiscito 101b, frequently has live music.*

Trajan's Market with the remains of Trajan's Forum in front. The Torre delle Milizie rises above it all.

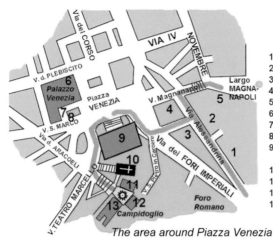

1 Foro di Augusto
2 Foro di Traiano
3 Foro di Cesare
4 Colonna Traiana
5 Mercati di Traiano
6 Palazzo Venezia
7 Madama Lucrezia
8 La Pigna
9 Monumento a Vittorio Emanuele II
10 Chiesa di Aracoeli
11 Palazzo Nuovo
12 Palazzo dei Senatori
13 Palazzo dei Conservatori

The area around Piazza Venezia

5 Palazzo Venezia, built in 1455, was one of the earliest creations of the Renaissance. It has been the residence of the pope, the embassy of Venice, then it passed to France and to Austria from whom the Italian government

confiscated it in 1916 during the First World War. In the Great War, Italy was on the side of the allies in opposition to Germany and the Austrian-Hungarian Empire. Against the latter it fought three wars of independence, which led to the unification of Italy with the capital at Rome in 1870. Later the palazzo became a museum, and from 1929 to 1943 it was also the headquarters of Benito Mussolini and the Gran Consiglio of the fascist period. Some will

remember seeing black and white newsreel clips of the time with "Il Duce" inciting the crowd congregated in Piazza Venezia. From this balcony facing the piazza Mussolini made many of his speeches. The museum houses paintings from the XIII to the XVIII century, sculptures, and terracottas. Before the recent restrictions, Piazza Venezia had some of the most traffic in Europe.

Walk around Palazzo Venezia in a southerly direction, pass under the balcony and, on the inside corner, is an ancient Roman statue. This is **Madame Lucretia** (photo right), one of the famous "talking statues." In Rome, during the time of the popes, political opposition or simply free expression was not possible. The Romans, however, found a way to have their voices heard. They left notes with satirical comments on contemporary subjects attached to certain statues spread around the city, which became the talking statues. (See # 7 and Walks 1 and 4 for more).

About 40 yards further, right at the corner between Piazza San Marco and Via San Marco is the unusual fountain **Pigna** (pinecone), frequently a place for meeting friends in the city. The water, like that of all the other fountains and "fontanelle" (street drinking fountains) spread over the city, runs continuously and is perfectly drinkable. (This is also the starting point for Walk #1.) **179**

On the other side of the piazza is the enormous white Monument to Vittorio Emanuele II, commonly called the "Vittoriano."

6 Monument to Vittorio Emanuele II.

This enormous construction, started in 1911 and finished in 1927, is dedicated to the unifier king of Italy and to the Italian Risorgimento, which is the 19th century movement that led to Italian unification. At the base of the Rome goddess statue is the "Altare della Patria" or the Altar of the Nation. Two sentinels guard the tomb of the Unknown Soldier, containing the remains of an unidentified fallen soldier from the First World War. The glaring whiteness is due to the special kind of marble (calcare di botticino), very white, that contrasts with the typical travertine more often used in other monuments. Visible from the top of the steps are, among other things, at the other end of Via del Corso, the obelisk in Piazza del Popolo.

There are two museums inside; the **Museo del Risorgimento** can be accessed from the stairs or, with a shorter climb, accessed from behind from the Campidoglio (see #7).

Napoleonic ideas and the secret societies of the Masons, Carbonari and the Young Italy of Mazzini awakened nationalism. Cavour, as Prime Minister of the House of Savoy, with international alliances and a second war with Austria, gained part of northern Italy. Then Garibaldi, with his landing in Sicily and a series of regional plebiscites, made the unification possible in 1861. Finally, in 1870, Rome was taken away from the Papal States and became the capital of the new nation.

Displayed are documents, paintings, prints, sculptures and arms to document the historical period, especially as related to the main protagonists, from Mazzini's pen to Garibaldi's sword. A section is also dedicated to the First World War.

The **equestrian statue** in the center is of grandiose proportions. The figure of the king is 16 times life size; the hoof of the horse is more than 20 inches wide. Right after the trip from the foundry, a dinner was held inside the belly of the horse and 21 people were served.

The other, the **Museo del Vittoriano**, has occasional rotating exhibits, including artistic, historical or cultural exhibits on Rome itself. The main entrance is just off Via dei Fori Imperiali at Via San Pietro in Carcere. The art exhibits will usually require an entrance fee, but there is free admittance to the other halls. Outside, on the upper level of the Vittoriano, you can admire **panoramic views** of the city.

Go around the monument to the right until you get to the stairs for the Campidoglio.

7 Campidoglio.

The Campidoglio or **Capitoline Hill** is one of the seven hills of Rome and in ancient times consisted of two peaks. The southern area was the site of the Temple of Jupiter Capitolino, the most ancient and venerable place in Rome. Some of the ruins of the temple can be seen at the base of Villa Caffarelli and under Palazzo dei Conservatori. Here, after walking down the Via Sacra, was the end point for religious processions, and those of victorious generals who came to offer thanks to the gods. (It was a tradition that the general be followed by a slave who whispered continually "remember that you are only a mortal.")

Here, in republican times, consuls were sworn in after being elected. The northern peak, in the earliest times, was the seat of the Senate consisting of a fortress, difficult to conquer, where the Romans retreated in case of a siege.

Archaeologists tell us that from the eighth to the sixth century BC, in the area around the Campidoglio, the Romans who had lived in simple huts began to build houses with stone foundations and to erect monumental temples like that of Jupiter Capitoline.

What we see today is the stupendous Piazza del Campidoglio designed by Michelangelo. Leaving the traffic behind to walk up the ramp-like low steps, called the *cordonata*, two statues, called the **Dioscuri**, that is, Castor and Pollux, the twin sons of Jupiter, flank the top of the stairs. The piazza strikes the visitor as a harmonious and comfortable room in the open.

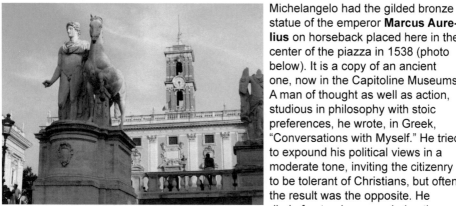

One of the Dioscuri statues, with the Palazzo dei Senatori in the background

Michelangelo had the gilded bronze statue of the emperor **Marcus Aurelius** on horseback placed here in the center of the piazza in 1538 (photo below). It is a copy of an ancient one, now in the Capitoline Museums. A man of thought as well as action, studious in philosophy with stoic preferences, he wrote, in Greek, "Conversations with Myself." He tried to expound his political views in a moderate tone, inviting the citizenry to be tolerant of Christians, but often the result was the opposite. He died of natural causes during the Germanic campaign in 180 AD at Vindobona, today Vienna, defending the borders.

Palaces delineate three sides while the beautiful floor of stone in a striking design of intersecting arcs is slightly convex. During the last 30 years of his life, Michelangelo was mostly occupied with architecture, his real passion. The Pope gave him the commission to redesign the Campidoglio, which was the symbolic center of ancient Rome. He had to deal with the existing limitations: the gentle hill, the **Palazzo dei Senatori** (the center building which today is the city administration) and the **Palazzo dei Conservatori** (the building on the right), which were at an angle of 80 degrees instead of 90. He had the **Palazzo Nuovo** built on the left, facing the Palazzo dei Conservatori, and designed identical façades for the two.

181

The dramatic focal point is the façade of the Palazzo dei Senatori in the center, which, because of the convergence of the other two, seems even larger and dominates the piazza. All three of the façades express a vigorous scheme of horizontal and vertical elements, which reflect the sculptural genius of Michelangelo.

At the foot of the Palazzo dei Senatori, Michelangelo designed the **double staircase**. Below, he had installed two ancient statues, the Nile on the left and the Tiber

on the right. To depict a river, the Romans used a figure of a mature bearded man, leaning on a symbol of the river's region. In this case, the **Nile** leans on a sphinx and the **Tiber** on Romulus, Remus and the she-wolf. In the center, in the niche is a statue of Minerva, goddess of wisdom and art, holding a ball. The palace has been the seat of the city administration since the twelfth century.

Stoicism

Admiral James Stockdale, the highest ranking naval officer held as a prisoner of war in Vietnam, said that it was the Stoic teaching of Epictetus which enabled him to endure 7½ years of captivity after he was shot down.

Just as we today may enlist the aid of religion or self-help programs, Marcus Aurelius, a student and a writer of Stoic philosophy, used it to search for guidance and to help him in the daunting responsibility of governing. Some of his writings that emphasize an accepting attitude to the difficulties of life and the need to maintain personal standards of conduct in an imperfect world defy their time: "Every moment, think steadily as a Roman … with simple dignity, feeling of affection, freedom and justice … perform every act of your life as it were the last …"

Since we are all part of the same whole, he recommends that our attitude toward others be love. "It is a special characteristic of man to love even those who stumble. …." "Begin the morning by saying to yourself, 'Today I will meet with the ungrateful, the arrogant, deceitful, envious, selfish. This will happen because of their ignorance of what is good and evil.' … but I cannot be angry, … nor hate them, … for we are made for cooperation." His nobility, intelligence and stoic devotion to duty is quite transparent and it shows that, at least during his reign, Roman society was more civil than commonly thought.

On the left side, right behind the corner of the Palazzo dei Senatori, is a column with, at the top, a copy of the **Capitoline Wolf,** the symbol of Rome, the wolf suckling Romulus and Remus. The wolf tops a column to the left of the Palazzo dei Senatori. Rome's mayor enters the Palazzo dei Senatori by this stairway, a standard shot on Italian TV news. The original is in the Palazzo dei Conservatori. Walking around the Palazzo dei Senatori, both to the left and the right, you reach terraces where you can get a spectacular **view of the Roman Forum**. Admire the imposing ruins, developed from the seventh century BC and in use for more than a thousand years.

In the evening, the evocative illumination penetrates the darkness revealing the remains of the most important buildings, such as the Temple of Saturn, the Curia (Senate), the arch of Septimius Severus and the three standing columns of the Temple of Castor and Pollux

Almost at the foot of the hill, on the southeast side, is the **Mamertine prison** where, among other things, those condemned for political reasons were strangled. According to legend, Saints Peter and Paul were imprisoned here and were able to escape after converting their guards.

In earliest times, on the southwest side of the Campidoglio, a place called *Rupe Tarpea* (Tarpaean Cliff), was where traitors and criminals were executed by throwing them off the cliff that faces Via di Monte Caprino and Via del Tempio di Giove. The cliff is visible from Piazza della Consolazione.

The Palazzo dei Conservatori and the Palazzo Nuovo form the **Capitoline Museums** where incomparable classical works are displayed. http://en.museicapitolini.org. The **Palazzo Nuovo** contains mainly sculptures of the Roman imperial period. In the courtyard is **Marforio** (photo at right), one of the famous "talking statues" (like Madame Lucretia at # 5). Among the more interesting works: the original statue of Marcus Aurelius, two Roman copies of Greek originals, the Dying Gaul and the Capitoline Venus, the Room of the Philosophers with statues of famous ancient personages such as Socrates, Homer, Cicero, and Sophocles, and the Room of the Emperors.

From the Palazzo Nuovo you can descend to an **underground gallery** connecting to the Palazzo dei Conservatori. The underpass is evocative, wide and well illuminated, with numerous classical works on display: statues, capitals, inscriptions, sarcophagi and amphorae. Helpful signs explain the route. The massive blocks of stone were the **foundation of the Tempio di Giove** (Temple of Jupiter) built 2500 years ago, the oldest and most sacred site in ancient Rome.

One corridor on the left leads to the **Tabularium** (right), with high, well-preserved vaulted ceilings. From its monumental arches you get a beautiful comprehensive view of the Roman Forum. The Tabularium, erected in 78 BC was the state archive. The documents were conserved on wooden boards, papyrus, stone, or engraved on bronze tablets. The Tabularium became the foundation for the Palazzo dei Senatori.

Royal limits
Excavations on the Campidoglio confirmed what the ancient historians had said about the construction of the Temple of Jupiter Capitoline (Tempio di Giove Capitolino), in the seventh century BC. The king Tarquinius Priscus chose the site for its dominant position over the surrounding area. It was recorded that the king started the work but never saw it completed. Now we know that much time was spent removing 15 feet of silt to get down to the solid bedrock (tufo lionato) on which to prepare the foundation.

The **Palazzo dei Conservatori** houses the **first public art collection**, donated in 1471 by Pope Sixtus IV, and exhibits other sculptures from the classical period.

Among its principal works, on the first floor are splendid frescoes of the history of Rome and ancient bronzes: The Capitoline Wolf; the Spinario, a boy captured at the moment of removing a thorn from his foot; Brutus, the adopted son and one of the assassins of Julius Caesar; and the gilded bronze statue of Hercules. The **Pinacoteca Capitolina**, on the second floor of the Palazzo dei Conservatori, contains 240 paintings from the XIV to the XVIII century, including works by Titian, Rubens, Caravaggio, Tintoretto, Velasquez, Guido Reni, and Guercino among others. In addition there are tapestries and a porcelain collection.

After entering a courtyard, pieces from the colossal statue of Constantine stand out. The head, the hands, feet and knees were incorporated into a torso made of wood and bronze Pieces of the colossal statue of Constantine flank the door that leads to a **panoramic cafeteria** on the second floor of the Palazzo dei

Conservatori. To access it, enter through the door in the **courtyard** near the hand of Constantine. The sign says "Terrazza Panoramica Café Capitolino." From there by the stairway or the elevator, go to the second floor. (Or if you are not planning to go into the museum, you can walk around to the right of the building where there is another stairway to go up to the café.) The terrace faces Teatro Marcello and you can easily make out the dome of Saint Peter's, the distant hill Monte Mario, and, looking the other way, San Giovanni in Laterano and closer, the square tower of the Palazzo dei Senatori. Both the museums and the Pinacoteca are open in the evenings. The Campidoglio, as well as the Colosseum and other monuments, are to be visited at night as well as the daytime, for the beautiful effects of the lighting on the buildings.

8 Santa Maria in Aracoeli.

When you walk up the **cordonata**, the ramp-like steps are almost effortless. Notice the contrast with the steps, almost parallel, that lead up to the church Santa Maria in Aracoeli. The high difficult staircase brings to mind the medieval idea that sinners needed to repent and take a painful route to salvation. From Piazza del Campidoglio between Palazzo Nuovo and Palazzo dei Senatori, a few steps lead to a stairway called the Scala dell'Arce Capitolina. Straight up the steps leads to the Museo del Risorgimento; go off to the left to enter the church by a side entrance.

Rebuilt in Romanesque-Gothic style in the 1300's, it was first erected in the sixth century. Gone are the original mosaics and frescoes that adorned the façade. Only a massive display of bricks is left. The hole in the center is what is left of the first public clock in Rome, installed there in 1412 and later moved to the tower of the Palazzo dei Senatori

The church contains precious marbles and columns salvaged from the forums in the valley below.

On the third column on the left is an inscription "A Cubiculo Augustorum" that indicates it came from the bedroom of the emperor Augustus. The floor is of the cosmatesque type, that is, made with pieces of colored marble and glass set in geometric designs. The pulpits are similarly decorated. On the columns, note how each capital is different, and the abundance of cande- labra. The gilded coffered ceiling was built to remember the victory of Marcantonio Colonna in the naval Battle of Lepanto against the Turks in 1571 that stopped their advance west- ward. In the Middle Ages, the church was used as a popular assembly, and came to be called the "church of the Senate." When the medieval neighborhood nearby and the sacristy itself were demolished to make room for the Vittoriano, the basilica itself barely escaped destruction.

In the chapel of the Holy Child, left of the altar, next to the bookshop, is a copy of the **Santissimo Bambino** (right). The 15th century original, said to be made from olive wood from the Garden of Gethsemane, was stolen in 1994 and never recovered.

At the foot of the stairs that go up to Santa Maria in Aracoeli are the remains of an **insula,** which dates from the second century (photo below). This is an example of the buildings, 2 to 6 stories high, used as rental apartments for the common people. Even 19 centuries ago, when the city was growing to stabilize at around a million, people found it convenient to live in the center. Like today, there was not sufficient housing for the ever-increasing population.

This led to building as high as possible, to construction speculation and to an excessive population density. Ancient Rome had to deal with **urban problems** similar to those of a modern city: furnish decent housing, regulate traffic, pro- vide adequate public services such as water distribution, and removal of trash. We know that the height of the apartments was controlled and the limit lowered

repeatedly by Julius Caesar, and reduced even more, to not more than 20 meters (about 65 feet) during the reign of Trajan. Even with that, the quality of construc- tion was not always the best and they could simply collapse. Numerous aqueducts were built to make water available by means of pipes in the houses of the rich and those who lived on the ground floor, storeowners or tenants who could afford the rent. The others, the majority, lived in less desirable upper floors and had to use the public fountains.

To avoid complete chaos, wheeled traffic was not permitted during the day. So at night the city was overrun by carts transporting all sorts of goods. The noise from the wheels clattering over cobblestones at night must have been unbear- able to many people. The first-century writer Martial wrote: "In Rome most sick people die of insomnia, because which rental home allows you to sleep?"

Between the Palazzo Nuovo and the Palazzo dei Senatori, the stairs on the left lead to Santa Maria in Aracoeli, but on the right a staircase leads up to the **Museo Centrale del Risorgimento**, (described earlier), in the Vittoriano.

Go back out of the church the same way, and down the steps. **185**

Follow the signs for the museum. They will lead to a terrace with a **wonderful view** over Trajan's Market and part of the Forum. There is a large bar cafeteria here. Continue up to another terrace where the view is even better. From here can be seen Trajan's Column, The Quirinal, the Colosseum and the Farnese Gardens, with explanatory signs indicating the various periods in history (medieval, modern, Renaissance, Baroque). .

From the other side of the terrace, the domes of Il Gesù, Sant'Agnese in Piazza Navona, San Pietro and others can be seen. Again, the period of construction is identified for the major monuments. Upon leaving the terraces, you may enter the museum

Go down Via dell'Aracoeli, turn left on Via delle Botteghe Oscure and one of the four parts of the Museo Nazionale Romano is on the left.

Enoteca Corsi, *Via del Gesù 87, offers an inexpensive meal. It is only two blocks from Via delle Botteghe Oscure, going up Via Celsa.*

9 Crypta Balbi is at Via delle Botteghe Oscure 31. http://archeoroma. beniculturali.it/en/museums. It is part of the Museo Nazionale Romano together with the Terme di Diocleziano (Baths of Diocletian), Palazzo Massimo and Palazzo Altemps. There are numerous objects and artifacts that highlight the life and economic activity between the ancient period and the Middle Ages. The Crypta was a large ancient courtyard with porticos attached to a theater, dating from 13 BC, which Lucius Cornelius Balbo had built. On the first and second floors of the museum, the evolution of the city from the fifth to the tenth centuries is exhibited. Thousands of objects have been brought to light that demonstrate how Rome produced and exported luxury goods in exchange for other merchandise from all over Europe.

Constructions from the first, second, fourth, eleventh, twelfth, thirteenth and sixteenth centuries have been found. The most modern are from the twentieth. Toward the end of the second century, a large room was transformed into a mithraeum, to worship the god Mithras. After the fifth century it was abandoned and only recently excavated. In the seventh century twenty feet of debris filled the buildings, as the result of an earthquake.

Continue on Via delle Botteghe Oscure.

At Via di Torre Argentina, at the corner of Largo Argentina, is <u>Il Del-fino</u>, a **tavola calda** *where you can get something to go or sit. Right in front, <u>Pascucci</u> prepares many flavors of* **fruit shakes***, fresh and cool, very desirable especially in summer.*

At **Largo di Torre Argentina**, four of the oldest temples from the republican period, from the fourth to first centuries BC, have been brought to light. The

ruins are several meters below the current level of the street in the center of this large piazza. In fact, in many places around the city you will notice that the ruins are at a lower level. This allows the numerous **cats** that live here to be undisturbed by the traffic above. An association keeps them well fed; yet it is not unusual to see local people bring food to the cats who sometimes stuff themselves with pasta.

Take a left on Via Paganica, and you come to Piazza Mattei where you can see one of the most joyful fountains ever built.

10 Fontana delle Tartarughe (Fountain of the Tortoises) was designed

by Giacomo della Porta and executed by Taddeo Landini in 1585. Four bronze youths each push a turtle over the edge of a marble basin above their heads, while balancing one foot on dolphins, which also joyfully spout water. Note the lightness, the relaxed and easy movement. It seems that the artist wanted to immortalize the carefree lightheartedness of youth, reminding us that once we were capable of such free and natural action. The turtles have been stolen and retrieved repeatedly. The four that we see today are copies of the three originals that were recovered. They are conserved in the Museo Capitolino (see # 7.).

Take Via Reginella from Piazza Mattei to Via Portico d'Ottavia.

11 The Jewish quarter consists of the area between Via Arenula, Piazza Mattei, Via del Teatro Marcello and the Tiber. Jewish people have lived in the city for more than two thousand years, forming the oldest Jewish community in Europe. An attitude of discrimination was often fomented by papal pronouncements, only intermittently enforced, starting at least with Innocent III in 1291. Until 1555 they lived relatively free and fairly integrated also into the highest levels of Roman society, occupying positions as bankers, merchants and even doctors to the pope. **187**

This all changed during the papacy of Paul IV. Consumed with the struggle of the Counter Reformation, he reorganized the Inquisition, and published the index of prohibited books After 1555, laws were passed that legally restricted what Jews could do. Among other things, they could not hold land, the choice of careers was limited to some of the less attractive ones, such as street sweepers and rag-pickers, and they were forced to wear a yellow shawl when they ventured out of the ghetto. In the panorama of Europe they were not treated the worst, but certainly not as well as in Amsterdam where they found a greater tolerance. Several Saturdays a year the Jews were required to go to the local churches and hear sermons that tried to convert them. Those who did not go had to pay a fine. Among the restrictions, probably the worst was the hated curfew. In the evening, the three gated entrances to the ghetto were closed, so people could neither come in nor leave. During the seventeenth century, nearly 9000 inhabitants were forced to live in only 30 acres, in dreadful sanitary conditions.

The area around the Jewish quarter

The walls and houses that constituted the barrier were knocked down on the Jewish Passover of April 17, 1848, however numerous restrictions remained until 1870, the year of the unification of Italy. As happened in other European cities, even after the removal of the borders of the ghetto, most preferred to remain in the same area, where they had lived for so many centuries. Unfortunately, later, this facilitated the actions of the Nazi SS. During Fascism, initially the Jews did not suffer discrimination. Laws were enacted under German pressure just before the Second World War, but they were for the most part ignored by the people. However, during the German occupation of Rome, more than a thousand Roman Jews were arrested and sent to concentration camps.

Portico d'Ottavia, at the bend in Via Portico d'Ottavia, was a cultural complex erected in 146 BC that contained libraries and halls for concerts or spectacles. Augustus had it rebuilt and dedicated it to his sister Octavia. Since the eighth century it has been part of the church of Sant'Angelo in Pescheria (*"pesce"* means fish). Five columns are visible on the left of the church and, behind it, an authentic medieval house.

Since antiquity, and up to the end of the nineteenth century, the city's main fish market was held here. An inscription on the right-hand pilaster of Portico d'Ottavia, from the fifteenth century, recorded a curious form of taxation. The head of any fish longer than the length of this stone plaque (1.13 meters) was to be given to the Conservators, that is, members of the Capital Council. This usage was abolished only after the French Revolution in 1789. The small streets and the piazzas of the quarter are attractive and distinctive.

The Roman synagogue

The ghetto is one of the zones that have maintained much of the atmosphere of the Rome of years past. There are shops selling typical confections and restaurants that offer Roman-Jewish cuisine. Among the specialties: *artichokes alla giudia* and *coda alla vaccinara* (oxtail). The most well-known are: Giggetto, Via del Portico d'Ottavia 21 (Tel. 06.686 11 05), and Al Pompiere, Via Santa Maria dei Calderari 38 (Tel. 06.686 83 77).

> *On Via Portico d'Ottavia there are two **pastry shops**.* La Dolceroma *at number 20 is an Austrian pastry shop.* Pasticceria Boccione, *at Portico d'Ottavia 1, is a traditional **Jewish bakery**, popular with locals.* Yesh Sheni, *Via S.M. del Pianto 65, is a **tavola calda** with Italian and Jewish dishes. At Via Arenula 85 is a stationery store,* Cartoleria, *since 1896. The southern end of Via Portico d'Ottavia leads to Lungotevere near Isola Tiberina and reconnects with Walk 2 - Ancient Origins.*
>
> *To revisit the Campidoglio after dark, go back toward Piazza Venezia by walking along Via delle Botteghe Oscure and go right, slightly uphill, on Via dell'Aracoeli.*

The entire walk marked on the map is about 3 kilometers (2 miles). If time is short, do not miss the Campidoglio, Trajan's Markets and the Fountain of the Tortoises.

Walk 7 - Additional Restaurants

Trattoria Da Valentino, Via Cavour 293, Tel. 06.488 13 03. Closed Friday. Simple and good food. Near Via dei Serpenti. €

Cuoco&Camicia, Via di Monte Polacco 2. www.cuocoecamicia.it. Near the Cavour Metro station. €€

Baires, Corso del Rinascimento 1, Tel. 06.686 12 93. Argentine cuisine. €€€

Alle Carrette, Via Madonna dei Monti 95, Tel. 06.679 27 70. Roman style pizza, with tables outside. €

Angelino ai Fori, Largo Corrado Ricci 40 at Via dei Fori Imperiali, www.angelinoaifori.com. Classic and Roman cooking. View of the Forum. €€

Abruzzi, Via del Vaccaro 1, Tel. 06.679 38 97. Roman cuisine with Abruzzese accents. €€

La Taverna del Ghetto - Kosher, Via Portico d'Ottavia 8, www.latavernadelghetto.com. Real kosher restaurant where you can taste typical Roman-Jewish cooking. In a palazzo from the 1300's. €€

Al Pompiere, Via S. Maria de' Calderari 38, www.alpompiereroma.com. Roman cuisine and Jewish specialties such as artichokes alla giudia (photo above). In the historic Cenci Palazzo in the center of the ghetto. €€€

Open Baladin, Via degli Specchi 6, www.openbaladinroma.it. Birreria with a good variety of beers. €€

The Medieval Landscape
The Watchtowers – Friend or Foe?

What was Rome like during the Middle Ages? Around the year 1000, according to tourist guides of the period, Rome was a city "in which so numerous are the towers they resemble sprigs of wheat." A pilgrim approaching the city saw a spectacle similar to the town of San Gimignano in Tuscany today. Why the change?

Tor dei Conti, only half its original height

From a population of a million people in the second century, Rome during the Middle Ages descends to mere tens of thousands. They inhabit especially the Suburra, the area around Teatro Marcello, and Trastevere, around the old churches. The ancient buildings are abandoned, except for those transformed into churches, and they degrade. People for centuries have been removing construction materials, melting the metals and pulverizing statues to produce lime. The flood of the river, earthquakes and centuries of neglect leave the ancient buildings half buried. The once "*caput mundi*" is a shadow of itself. The ground of the Palatine, Campidoglio and the Forum, the center of the ancient power, are cultivated for grapes or held for pasture.

Everybody steals; the Roman people to survive, millions of pilgrims take whatever they can as a souvenir, and even emperors do. Charlemagne, after his coronation as Holy Roman Emperor by Pope Leo III, going home, takes away carts full of marble columns, bronze statues, and other artifacts.

A multitude of people, ignorant, poor and undernourished, experience religion mixed with superstition and idolatry. The houses, at most two stories, are spare, and with no water and no bathrooms. The rich Roman families and some high priests live in luxury after plundering jewels, mosaics and every sort of ornament from the ancient buildings.

The election of a pope has become a private affair of the noble Roman families, fought over without qualms or conscience. Being able to become pope allows supremacy over the other families, legitimates the use of violence, and guarantees wealth for the entire clan. The Frangipane, Crescenzi, Conti, Tuscola, Pierleoni, Savelli, Annibaldi, and Orsini families unite in temporary factions, pro popes or pro emperors, only to then start feuding again amongst themselves. The word "nepotism" was born later in the 1400's in this atmosphere as a way to grant high-office positions to relatives, without regard to merit, from "*nipote*" which means nephew or grandchild.

Torre degli Anguillara in Trastevere

A custom in tune with the times starts to develop in the Middle Ages: the sacking of the residence of the dead pope. After his demise, like clockwork, a mob invades his home and takes away everything that is not nailed down. A dead pope does not have any authority, and a new one has not been elected yet, so no family is in control.

One example will give an idea of the horrifying degradation of the period. At the end of the tenth century, Pope Giovanni XIII of the Crescenzi family plundered without moral scruples to enrich his family. At his death, the emperor Otto I favored the election of Benedict VI. The Crescenzis, not happy with the wealth accumulated up to that point, imprisoned the pope and elected the antipope, Cardinal Francone, who took the name Boniface VII, called the "monster" by his contemporaries. Boniface VII had Benedict VI immediately imprisoned and strangled, and when the son of the emperor, Otto II, approached Rome with his army, the pope escaped to Constantinople with the entire treasure of the church.

Another typical tower, cut to size

The lookout towers were a necessary evolution of the building in Rome. From a higher standpoint it was easier to detect a possible attack and defend a fortified home. Not only the powerful Roman families fortified their homes but also anyone who exercised some sort of authority was wise to incorporate an observation tower in his home.

Here are some of the towers that you may encounter on the walks.

Torre dei Conti at the end of Via Cavour (this walk) is perhaps the easiest to envision, in that it stands fairly alone. Built in 1200 by the Conti family it was part of a fortified area. Next to Trajan's Market, the square Torre delle Milizie, the largest in Rome, was also once owned by the Conti family. After an earthquake in the fourteenth century it began to lean. Others in the area are the Torre dei Margani in Piazza Margana, (this Walk) which served also as a residence. The bell tower of San Franceso di Paola, next to San Pietro in Vincoli (this Walk) is another tower of the Margani family.

The Torre degli Annibaldi is said to have given the Annibaldi family a good spot to watch over the Frangipane family who had taken up residence nearby and fortified the Colosseum. Near San Clemente (Walk 3) on Via dei Santi Quattro Coronati, the church of Santi Quattro Coronati's fortress tower dates to the ninth century

Other notable towers are the Torre degli Anguillara in Trastevere (Walk 2), the Tor Sanguigna, now built into the corner of a building in Piazza Sanguigna (Walk 1), and Torre dei Frangipane in Via dell'Orso (Walk 4).

Torre delle Milizie, above Trajan's Markets

SHORT VISITS

If you have only two days in Rome, we suggest the following parts of the walks.

First day of two, or if you only have one day, use this list.
Concentrate on parts of Walk 3, Walk 1 and Walk 5.

Begin at the **Colosseum**, the greatest ancient amphitheater. (Walk 3, #2). Proceed down Via dei Fori Imperiali. You will pass the **Roman Forum** on the left, described in Walk 3, and some of the Imperial Forums on the right, described in Walk 7. You can observe some of the ruins without going in.

When you get to Piazza Venezia, curve around the large white Monument to Vittorio Emanuele II and climb to the **Campidoglio**, Michelangelo's splendid square. (Walk 7, #6). Come back and take Via dell'Aracoeli, continue to Piazza del Gesù to visit the **Gesù** church with Baroque decoration. (Walk 1, #1) Continue on Via del Gesù, turn left on Via di Santa Caterina and continue to Piazza Minerva to see the Elephant obelisk by Bernini. (Walk 1, #6). Visit the **Pantheon**, the most admired and intact ancient building. (Walk 1, #5).

Take Via della Palombella to **Piazza Navona,** the most lively piazza in Rome, with Bernini's Fountain of the Four Rivers. (Walk 1, #10).

From the north end of the piazza go straight north on Agonale to Piazza Tor Sanguigna, and then go left on Via dei Coronari. Continue all the way down Via Coronari to Piazza de Coronari and take Via di Panico which goes off on an angle to the right and leads to Ponte Sant'Angelo. Cross **Ponte Sant'Angelo** (Walk 5, #10) with Bernini's statues of angels and a good view of **Castel Sant'Angelo** from the outside. When you get to the other side of the bridge, go to the left and take Via della Conciliazione which goes straight to Saint Peter's. Walk through Bernini's elliptical colonnade and visit **Saint Peter's Basilica** (Walk 5, #5). The nearby medieval Borgo neighborhood offers a variety of restaurants.

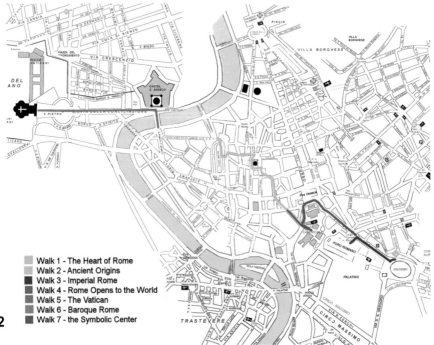

Walk 1 - The Heart of Rome
Walk 2 - Ancient Origins
Walk 3 - Imperial Rome
Walk 4 - Rome Opens to the World
Walk 5 - The Vatican
Walk 6 - Baroque Rome
Walk 7 - the Symbolic Center

Day Two concentrates on parts of Walk 4, Walk 7 and Walk 2.

Visit the **Spanish Steps**, (Walk 4, #5) (there is a Metro stop).

Walk down Via del Babuino, past the "talking statue" Babuino fountain, (Walk 4, #6) to Piazza del Popolo (Walk 4, #7). Visit **Santa Maria del Popolo**, containing Caravaggio paintings and works by Bernini.

Walk back on Via Margutta, the street of the artists, (Walk 4, #9) to Piazza di Spagna and the Barcaccia fountain. High fashion shops are on the nearby streets. From Piazza di Spagna go through Piazza Mignanelli and take Via Propaganda which becomes Via S. Andrea del Fratte. Continue on Via del Bufalo and turn left on Via Poli, cross Via del Tritone and Via Poli leads into the **Trevi fountain** (Walk 4, #1).

Go back on Via Poli, turn left on Via del Tritone to Via del Corso, turn left and pass Piazza Colonna with the column dedicated to Marcus Aurelius (Walk 1, #4). Walk down Via del Corso to **Piazza Venezia** (Walk 7, #5). Along the way, peek to the right at Via Lata to see the Facchino fountain. (Walk 1, #2)

Piazza San Marco is to the right of Piazza Venezia. Here is another talking statue, Madama Lucrezia. At the corner is the **Pigna fountain**; here take Via di San Marco, continue on Via delle Botteghe Oscure, turn left on Via Paganica to Piazza Mattei and the **Fountain of the Tortoises** (Walk 7, #10).

Continue on Via Paganica and turn left on Via Portico d'Ottavia to visit the Jewish quarter and the ancient ruins of Portico d'Ottavia. (Walk 7, #11). Continue on Via Portico d'Ottavia to Lungotevere and cross the Isola Tiberina (Walk 2, #9).

Proceed into Trastevere (Walk 2, #10) and visit the rest of this charming neighborhood, including #11 the **Church of Santa Cecilia**, the patron saint of music, and #12 **Santa Maria in Trastevere**, with an example of a medieval façade, while appreciating the local shops and restaurants.

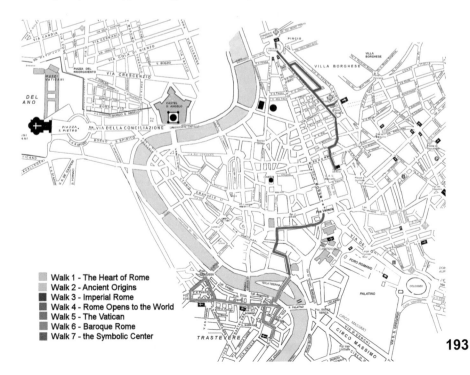

Walk 1 - The Heart of Rome
Walk 2 - Ancient Origins
Walk 3 - Imperial Rome
Walk 4 - Rome Opens to the World
Walk 5 - The Vatican
Walk 6 - Baroque Rome
Walk 7 - the Symbolic Center

Although we checked all of the information, in a complex city such as Rome, over time, things change: restaurants close or change names, and visiting times of monuments may vary. Try to be alert and flexible.

Admission tickets. It is possible to buy tickets online for multiple attractions ahead of time. Try sites such as https://www.coopculture.it/en/colosseo-e-shop.cfm, or for multiple sites, http://www.roma-pass.it/en/the-cards/

Otherwise, try to buy a pass at one of the less crowded venues.

Museums (*museo*) usually have continuous hours, opening at about 9. Closing time may range from 5 to 7 PM or even later, especially in summer. Check the individual times online whenever possible. Some are open later in the summer and others are not open at all in afternoons during winter. Several of the museums and other attractions are closed Monday, except the Vatican Museums. Unfortunately there is no standard, so check before going.

Stores. Most stores are open from 9:30 AM to 7:30 PM, especially in the center. Some smaller stores can be closed during the lunch break of 1:30 PM to about 3:30 PM, when they reopen until about 7:30 PM. Hours for some categories of stores may vary.

Pharmacies, (*farmacia*) noted by a green cross, are not all-purpose stores as in the US, but mainly sell medicinal products. They keep the same hours as stores, but some will be open later and on Sundays on a rotating basis. Look for the list posted out front. A few in the center are open all night.

Money. When you need cash, use the ATMs, called Bancomat. They are easy to find.

The prices that you see advertised in the stores already include sales tax. They use a system of value-added tax (IVA).

Churches are often closed for a couple of hours in early afternoon, from about noon or 1 PM to 3 or 4 PM when they usually reopen until about 6 or 7 PM. Check the times online when possible. Many churches, right inside the entrance, have detailed information about the building and works of art that they contain. Naturally you are expected to dress modestly and walk around quietly, since there may be people there to pray.

Tourist Information Points
There are numerous tourist kiosks, called Tourist Information Points (TIP), around the center, which have lots of information, free maps, brochures, and info  about current exhibits. Feel free to use them to ask any questions you might have and to check on opening times of stores, attractions. Some are:

> Via del Corso near Via di Pietra (Walk 1)
> Piazza di Spagna (Walk 4)
> Piazza Navona (Walk 1)
> opposite the Roman Forum (Walk 3 or 7)
> near Castel Sant'Angelo (Walk 5)
> near Santa Maria Maggiore and at the Termini train station, both (Walk 6).

Maps
In addition to our maps, it is useful to get one of the whole historic center. One of the best is called "Streetwise Rome" – it is plasticized and practically indestructible, and folds accordion style – very convenient. Free paper maps are available at the tourist kiosks.

Public transportation

Rome has three **subway** lines, Linea A, Linea B, and Linea C. Metro stops are designated by a sign with a big **M**. Fare cards are bought at a ticket machine or newsstand or a "tabacchi" store, situated near bus stops. The "tabacchi" are identifiable by a dark rectangular sign with a

large white capital **T** outside above the store.

Buses also cost the same and use the same tickets as the Metro. You do **not** buy tickets on the bus. When you get on the bus (at the back, not the front), you stick the ticket into a slot on a ticket reader. It will stamp the time. Tickets allow you to get off one bus and on another without buying another ticket for a period of time, (currently 90 minutes). Many locals have passes so you won't see them sticking their tickets into the machine very often. Bus stops have tall rectangular signs with the numbers of the buses that stop there. They list all of the places they stop as well. The end of the line is called "*capolinea*." A lot of buses start and end from around Piazza Venezia and around Termini station.

There were a number of convenient electric mini-buses in use in earlier years but at this writing they have not been reintroduced.

Of course there are taxis, too, usually found at taxi stands around the city.

Electricity

Electricity is usually 220 volts. Occasionally there are some sockets that are 125 volts, so it is best to verify first. The plugs have round pins but are not all standard, especially in older buildings, so you will need an **adapter**, perhaps a variety. If your charger or appliance does not have dual voltage you will also need a transformer. It's best to buy this at home before traveling. Travel stores and AAA offices sell packs of adapters in various sizes and transformers.

Bathrooms

Most bars have them, but will expect you to buy something. There are bathrooms in museums too of course. Ask for the "gabinetto." Sometimes the sign will say W.C. or "toilette." Men are "uomini" or "signori"; women are "donne" or "signore." For the faucet handles, **F** (*freddo*) is cold; **C** (*caldo*) is hot. It's a good idea to carry tissues in case toilet paper is not available.

Internet

There are some internet cafés which may also offer fax and phone. Public wi-fi is increasingly available, but rules seem to be changing. Check on the internet before you go for suggestions.

American Embassy and Consulate, Via Vittorio Veneto   Tel. 06.46741
Canadian Embassy   Via Salaria 243   Tel. 06 854441
Canadian Consulate....Via Zara 30   Tel. 06 854441
U.K. Embassy   Via XX Settembre 80A   Tel. 06 4220 0001

Food

Style of cooking. Regarding the style of cooking available in the capital, you will be pleasantly surprised by the variety. Italian restaurants in the US initially reflected the cooking of Italian immigrants, who were in large measure from the south of Italy, especially Sicily and Campania (Naples). Although they have evolved over time to offer a greater variety, in Italy there are at least a dozen regions, each with its rich and distinct culinary tradition. Many restaurants offer the traditional Roman cuisine with its own unique dishes, but you will also find menus from other regions, such as Emilia-Romagna, Tuscany, Abruzzo, etc, and an increased selection of international choices.

Pizza. Roman style pizza has a thin and rather crunchy crust, while the Neapolitan style is thicker, softer and similar to "New York" pizza. They have other kinds as well. Many places offer the characteristic "*forno a legna*" (wood-fired oven) which may yield a slightly burned crust. It is often served as an individual pizza; some places, especially outside the city center, only serve pizza at night. Toppings traditionally are *margherita* (simple mozzarella and tomato sauce) or with *funghi* (mushrooms), *prosciutto* (cured ham), or *prosciutto cotto* (cooked ham). (*Peperone* means peppers, not what Americans call pepperoni.) *Capricciosa* indicates a lot of toppings but can vary from place to place.

In Italy **bars** are more like cafés; they have alcohol, but they are mainly a place to get coffee and non-alcoholic drinks. Frequently there will also be something to eat, as sandwiches or ice cream. In short, they are very convenient. At a bar you **pay first at the cashier's**, who will give you a receipt, which you then hand to the person behind the bar who will get your ice cream, drink or coffee. If you want something but do not know the name, try English first with a cashier, if that doesn't work, walk toward the counter and raise your hand to grab attention. Through words or by indicating, communicate to the counter person what you want. He will speak to the cashier who will charge the right amount. A tip (typically 20 or 30 cents) while handing over the receipt is pretty common for locals and will attract the server's attention, but it is not necessary. Another popular venue is the *enoteca* (wine bar) which also serves light fare.

"Fast" food. A *tavola calda* or a *rosticceria* (sometimes called snack bar too) will have quick meals, sometimes cafeteria style, or just order a few items at the counter and either eat them at small tables or on the go. They usually have *pizza al taglio* (by the slice), sometimes calzones, potato crochette and *suppli* (fried rice balls with a bit of mozzarella or meat inside), vegetables, and sometimes chicken. Pricing is by "*etto*" or 100 grams, about 3 ½ ounces. Many bars also have sandwiches, called "*panini*" or "*tramezzini.*" Some people buy them and then go and eat outside, finding a picturesque spot, like the steps of a fountain or monument.

Restaurants. As a rule of thumb, be wary of places too close to the main attractions frequented only by tourists. Since tourists come and go and there is an endless supply, owners have less incentive to maintain quality. The best establishments are those frequented by both tourists and locals. Usually a "*hosteria*" or "*trattoria*" will offer simpler food than a "*ristorante*" and often is less fancy, less expensive and just as good.

At the end of each walk a **list** of nearby restaurants is available.

A Tip – buy a small bottle of water at a bar or deli to drink while walking around. When you finish it, just fill it up at a street fountain. One bottle will last a long time!

A quick lunch
You can stop at an *alimentari* (grocery store) and buy in one section cold cuts and cheese and bread in another. Often they will make the sandwich for you if they are not too crowded. Choose the bread and the cold cuts you like and ask, "Mi può fare un panino?" Can you make me a sandwich? If you want ham and cheese: "Mi può fare un panino con prosciutto cotto e formaggio?"

197

The Legacy of Rome

Rome has a rich and long history that goes back 2800 years to the Etruscans and the Greeks and it has been the center of Christianity for the last 2000 years. Since 1870 Rome has been the seat of the Italian government and contains the Vatican State. It was the first city to reach a population of about a million people at the apex of the territorial expansion in the third century AD. We had to wait until the industrial revolution and nineteenth century London, founded by the Romans, to reach again a population of one million. Imagine a single political entity covering Europe, the British Isles, North Africa and the Middle East with long periods of peace, one language and one currency. Rome is called the eternal city as one of the great cities in history and for its vast contribution to western civilization.

The **alphabet** that we use today is the Latin alphabet. During the Middle Ages, Latin, the language used by the Romans, developed into the Romance **languages** like Italian, French, Spanish and Portuguese, but also influenced English, where a majority of words are of Latin origin.

Julius Caesar instituted the **calendar** that we use today, perfected 1600 years later by Pope Gregory XIII with the introduction of the leap year. Finally in the 1900's also Japan, China and others adopted it. The names of the months are of Roman origin. August comes from Augustus.

The **Roman republic**, with divided powers that balance each other and elections every year lasted 500 years. The American founding fathers were avid readers of Latin classics and wrote the American constitution, basing it on the experience and ideals of the Roman republic. Words such as constitution, president, vote, veto, congress, senate, representative, founding fathers and many others derive from the Roman experience. The Capitol comes from *capitolium*, the ancient political and religious center.

Roman **architecture** has been copied all over the world from triumphal arches like the Arc de Triomphe in Paris, the Jefferson Memorial in Washington and neoclassic buildings for governments and universities. The **arch** was the Romans' most important development in architecture. With ensuing experience, their engineers pushed forward to create the vault and the dome. These elements were used extensively, combining stone and **concrete** for construction of bridges, aqueducts, basilicas, stadium and palaces all over the empire. The **Pantheon** represents the apex of this evolution with its dome 43 meters in diameter, the largest unreinforced solid concrete dome in the world. Some bridges and aqueducts built with this technology are still functional, such as the famous Alcantara Bridge in Spain, 600 feet long with six arches, 148 feet high. Only after the eighteenth century, with the Industrial Revolution and the production of steel, was the stone arch surpassed with the use of new material and technical advances. Arch, column, vault, and capital have Latin roots.

Many ancient structures like the Pantheon, the Colosseum and the Roman Forum are still standing thanks to the invention of **concrete**. Its formula was lost in the Middle Ages, later rediscovered and widely used all over the world. Modern concrete exposed to salt water corrodes within decades. Instead, this ancient concrete used also for seawalls and harbor piers is stronger today than when it was first mixed 2000 years ago. The reason, scientists have determined, is that the chemical reaction produced tobermorite crystals.

Passion for the games is another legacy. The Colosseum could hold up to 70,000 spectators and, by means of 80 wide exits and a series of well-planned corridors and stairways, could empty in only 12 minutes. It has represented the standard for **sports arenas** constructed all over the world. The Circus Maximus, an **oval track** with bleachers for over 300,000 people was the largest stadium of all time, where horse races and all sorts of spectacles were held for more than 1000 years. Chariot races produced spirited private **betting**.

Roads, using different sizes of gravel and granite three feet deep, were built all over the territories, initially to promote military conquest. They extended to 50,000 miles of paved roads across the empire and also facilitated trade and travel in Europe for centuries. Some of these also became the base for the construction of modern roads. The word street comes from the Latin *strata*.

Rome developed ideas of **justice** into a system of law that we now take for granted. The magistrates defined and interpreted the laws using the Twelve Tables, established precedents, resolutions by the Senate and later pronouncements of the emperor. The state prosecuted matters of criminal law. The right of appeal was granted by law, higher and lower courts were organized, and for the first time professional jurists were created. In 529 AD Justinian, Roman emperor of Constantinople, decided to simplify and systematize the **body of laws** in the Justinian code. After the Dark Ages, from the twelfth century on, the economic and social development in Europe led to the rediscovery of Roman law which was then incorporated by many European countries. Still today we use terms like *modus operandi*, *habeas corpus*, *ipso facto* and more.

Rome itself, in the second century AD, boasted 11 **aqueducts** that allowed the construction of enormous **public baths**, and underground sewers promoting public health and hygiene. Some are still in use today. The baths were a mix of a mall, library, gym and spa. For a fee, homeowners could have potable running water in the pipes of their homes.

The Romans invented many surgical tools and pioneered the use of the caesarian section, but their most valuable contributions to **medicine** came on the battlefield. Under the leadership of Augustus, they established a military medical corps that was one of the first dedicated field surgery units. They were even known to disinfect instruments in hot water prior to use, pioneering a form of antiseptic surgery that was not fully embraced until the 19th century. Latin is also frequently used in medical terminology, such as "bacterium," "umbilicus," "cerebellum."

Newspapers called "*acta diurna*" were written on wood or papyrus and posted on heavily trafficked areas like the Roman Forum. They included important government affairs, proceedings of the Senate, but also results of gladiatorial combat, gossip and as in our time, sensational news for all to see. The words "journal" and "journalism" come from *diurna*.

A brief overview of Rome's artistic periods

The churches, piazzas and palazzos of Rome have been subject to constant modifications over the centuries. This is one of the delights but it also means that there are few structures that completely represent one particular style. Many churches, even if initially built in ancient, medieval or Renaissance Rome, were restructured (some would say ruined) at the end of the sixteenth and during the seventeenth century. That was the height of the Baroque style in architecture and painting. These modifications are particularly evident in the façades and the interior decoration.

Ancient Roman art

The Etruscans and Greeks who inhabited parts of Italy influenced early Roman art and architecture greatly. The Romans imitated their styles. Columns with Greek capitals abounded and many sculptures were made as copies of highly prized Greek originals. Classical sculpture was very lifelike, and paintings, which frequently covered walls, were fairly realistic and included a measure of perspective. The greatest building phase was during the imperial period from the first to the fourth centuries. With Constantine and the legalization of Christianity in the fourth century, churches were built, usually as basilicas, the same format that had been used for Roman courts and meeting places.

Although there is something ancient in every corner of the city, the best examples of ancient Roman art and architecture can be seen walking these paths:

Walk 2 (Ancient Origins): the area where the city was originally founded, Circus Maximus, which was continuously modified over many centuries, the ancient city walls, the Baths of Caracalla and one of the earliest churches, Santa Sabina.

Walk 3 (Imperial Rome): Roman Forum and the Colosseum, the most emblematic monuments, and ancient buildings under the church of San Clemente.

Walk 7 (The Symbolic Center): the several imperial Forums created during the centuries, plus the most ancient temples on the Campidoglio.

Walk 1 (The Heart of Rome): the Pantheon. **Walk 6 (Baroque Rome):** the many ancient objects and sculptures in the Palazzo Massimo museum and Diocletian's Baths.

The medieval period

Art became more stylized and less realistic. Mosaics were frequently used in church interiors and also on façades. Not many new buildings were erected, but the effort was on renovation, especially of interiors. The Cosmati family, working from about 1150 on, created many beautiful floors in churches, using small geometric shapes of colored marble. It is difficult to point out buildings that still completely retain the medieval aspect since most have incorporated later styles. However, the general atmosphere and buildings in the Trastevere neighborhood are the clearest examples.

200

Walk 2 (Ancient Origins) strolls through Trastevere where several areas such as Piazza in Piscinula, Vicolo dell'Atleta, Piazza Santa Cecilia and Piazza Sonnino exhibit some medieval buildings. The mosaic façade of Santa Maria in Trastevere is perhaps the closest to the original appearance. The ancient church of Santa Sabina on the Aventine hill has been restored close to its original appearance.

Walk 3 (Imperial Rome) includes the medieval remains under the church of San Clemente. Walk 7 (The Symbolic Center) has an example in Santa Maria in Aracoeli. Finally, in Walk 1 (The Heart of Rome), Santa Maria sopra Minerva and the area between the Pantheon and the Tiber display a general medieval atmosphere.

The Renaissance
The classical antiquities of Rome and Greece were rediscovered. The emphasis on earthly matters and the discovery and use of **perspective** produced realistic depictions freed from the mysticism and religiosity of the medieval period.

The high Renaissance from about 1500 is characterized by a **true classical revival** with artists studying ancient masterpieces, and frequently utilizing classic motifs such as columns in their paintings. Inspiration for artists was provided by the excavation of the newly discovered Domus Aurea as well as the beginning of the Vatican art collection of ancient sculptures in 1506. Work began on Saint Peter's by Bramante, Sangallo and **Michelangelo** and on the Stanze di Raffaello in the Vatican by **Raphael** (1508 –11).

The best examples are:

Walk 5 (The Vatican) contains the most complete gathering of Renaissance art. Michelangelo is most prominent with the Pietà, the design for the dome of Saint Peter's, frescoes on the ceiling of the Sistine Chapel, and the Last Judgment. Other artists contributing to the chapel were Perugino, Ghirlandaio, Botticelli, Luca Signorelli, Cosimo Rosselli and Pinturicchio. The Vatican Museums contain works by Raphael, Titian, Giotto and Perugino as well as sculpture from ancient Rome which served as inspiration for these artists.

Walk 1 (The Heart of Rome) meanders through areas built up by the popes during this time. Via Giulia was the most important street, with many palazzos from the 15th and 16th centuries. **Walk 4 (Rome Opens to the World)** boasts Santa Maria del Popolo, which contains works by Raphael, Bramante, Pinturicchio, Sebastiano del Piombo and others.

Michelangelo appears again in **Walk 7 (The Symbolic Center)**, with Piazza del Campidoglio, the facades of the two facing palazzos and the double staircase of the Palazzo dei Senatori plus the statue of Moses in the church of San Pietro in Vincoli. Although **Walk 6 (Baroque Rome)** is overwhelmingly Baroque, Michelangelo's Santa Maria degli Angeli, built over ancient baths, and the nearby cloister show that art from all periods can be found in any of the walks.

Baroque Rome

The Protestant threat appeared to wane in the late sixteenth century after the Counter Reformation and the ensuing relief brought a new exuberance to the arts. Papal patronage was still all-important but new religious orders, such as the Jesuits, also began commissioning works of art. This is the **Baroque** period, most characterized in Rome by the great sculptor and architect **Bernini**. There was much rebuilding and renovation of church exteriors, as well as sumptuous interior decoration and construction of fountains. In fact, so much embellishment was added that later there have been attempts to remove much of it in order to restore the older medieval churches to their original appearance. An example is Santa Sabina. Architecture used more interplay of curves, greater depth and movement than earlier work. The greatest architects include **Borromini** and **Carlo Maderno**. Sculpture became more expressive and showed dramatic movement as in Bernini's David and his Ecstasy of Saint Theresa. Painting is represented by many of Raphael's pupils and the dramatic chiaroscuro of **Caravaggio**.

The best examples are in **Walk 6 (Baroque Rome)**: Bernini's sculptures in Galleria Borghese, his fountains of the Bees and the Tritone, and his church of Sant'Andrea al Quirinale. Equally outstanding are the many works of Borromini, such as San Carlo alle Quattro Fontane. Various other churches with Baroque façades and interiors include Santa Susanna, Santa Maria della Vittoria and Santa Maria Maggiore.

Walk 5 (The Vatican) is also the showcase for Bernini in the colonnade of Piazza San Pietro, the baldacchino inside Saint Peter's and the statues lining Ponte Sant'Angelo.

Various other baroque artists are featured in **Walk 1 (The Heart of Rome)**. Besides the interiors of il Gesù, Sant'Ignazio and Palazzo Spada, the façades of Sant'Agnese, Sant'Andrea della Valle and Palazzo Pamphilj, there are Borromini's spire of Sant'Ivo and several stunning paintings by Caravaggio adorn San Luigi dei Francesi. Bernini appears in the Elefantino in front of Santa Maria sopra Minerva and the spectacular Fountain of the Rivers in Piazza Navona.

Walk 4 (Rome Opens to the World) features more Caravaggio paintings in Santa Maria del Popolo, the **Late Baroque** Trevi fountain and the Spanish Steps. There was an increasing tendency to return to antiquity, which would later result in the neo-classic period.

A short history of Rome

Republic

Legend tells us that **Romulus** founded Rome in 753 BC on the slopes of the Palatine hill. In fact, excavations have ascertained human occupation on most of Rome's famous hills from at least as early as the tenth century BC. For the first 250 or so years, **kings**, some of them Etruscan, ruled Rome. Then, in 509 BC the king was overthrown and the **Roman Republic** was created which boasted many democratic elements such as an advisory council that evolved into the **Senate**. In assemblies called "comitia," citizens voted for legislation and for government officials who served for one year, including two co-consuls, representing the executive branch, also serving one year terms and each having veto power over the other.

Although the ruling classes were solidly entrenched, in 494 BC the lower classes obtained someone to look after their interests with the creation of the position of **tribune of the plebeians**. The year 450 BC brought the Twelve Tables, codifying the existing laws of the Republic on bronze tablets displayed in the Forum, formalizing basic equality for all citizens, whether patrician or plebeian.

During the third century BC, aqueducts were built to bring water to the increased population of Rome, and major roads such as the Appian Way were constructed both to foster trade and to move troops. Rome expanded, conquering and incorporating much of Italy and later, as a result of the Punic Wars with Carthage, Sicily, Corsica and Sardinia, the western Mediterranean and part of Asia Minor. Greece and Macedonia were annexed after the fourth Macedonian War.

Empire

Politics in Rome were divisive between reformers and vested interests in the Senate, rife with assassinations and increasing military power. When **Julius Caesar**, after conquering Gaul, defied the Senate by bringing his army back over the Rubicon river, civil war broke out and in 48 BC he became the absolute ruler. During his reign, some peace was attained but after his assassination in 44 BC, full civil war broke out again between the conspirators Brutus and Cassius and his adopted son Octavius. When finally Octavius came to power, (27 BC – 14 AD), he took the name **Augustus Caesar** and ushered in a peaceful productive time known as the Augustan Age, where military expansion gave way to the arts and public works, especially building. Although Augustus declared he was returning to republican rule, in fact, the Republic was dead and the imperial period started. Gradually the Senate became ever less powerful while imperial power and excess flourished.

Emperor **Constantine** legalized Christianity in 313 AD and split the empire into East and West, transferring the capital to Constantinople.

Over the next centuries of frequent barbarian invasions, the West began to wane until the commonly accepted date of the fall of the last western emperor in 476 AD. Although the eastern empire continued for a thousand years, developing into the **Byzantine empire**, Rome fell into decline and decay. Its aqueducts cut off, its splendid monuments neglected and covered in vegetation, the population went from its height of around one million during the period of maximum expansion, in the third century, to a mere 30,000 people. The history of Rome from the Middle Ages on is intertwined with the ascendancy of the papacy and the artistic achievements that it fostered.

Center of Christianity

Rome quickly became the center of Christianity with the martyrdom there of **Saints Peter and Paul**, and it was in Rome that their successors, **the popes**, lived. When Christianity began to edge out pagan cults to be the favored religion, the early churches, such as Santa Sabina, were built. Since the emperors were now distant, in Constantinople, the pope assumed temporal duties for the administration of the city. In the later Middle Ages the Church's larger bureaucracy, political power and autonomy led to conflict with kings and emperors across Europe. Starting around 1450, popes began a conscious effort to beautify the city, building or renovating churches and commissioning frescoes and sculptures. The greatest project of all began, a replacement for the original **Saint Peter's**. This task would take 120 years and employ most of the greatest architects and artists of the time.

The Protestant Reformation begun by Luther in 1517 and the Sack of Rome in 1527 by German and Spanish mercenaries dealt an initial blow. But the reaction, the Counter Reformation, brought reform and new vigor to the church, including the creation of the Jesuit order. New church buildings and exuberant embellishment of existing ones make **Baroque art** the most visible style pervading Rome.

Capital of Italy

Italy, until the mid nineteenth century, remained a collection of separate city-states, with the Papal States occupying much of the central part of the peninsula. The groundwork laid by the French Revolution and other independence movements led to the **Risorgimento**, or revolution, pushed forward by Mazzini and Garibaldi. After one failed attempt to create a republic, the rebellion continued, pressed on by the Piedmont State and Cavour, until in 1861 most of Italy was united in a kingdom. The Pope in Rome, however, aided by French troops, resisted until 1870, when Rome was finally freed and became the capital of the country. The Pope was sequestered in the Vatican until 1929 when a concordat was signed to formalize relations.

Serious economic problems and social unrest after World War I, when Italy fought on the side of the Allies, brought Mussolini to power with his march on Rome and began 2 decades of Fascist rule. Rome was spared major destruction during World War II and, after the liberation, the democratic **Italian Republic** was established by referendum. Prosperity ensued especially in the 50's and 60's in spite of frequent changes in governments, corruption and the presence of the largest communist party in the west. Immigration increase crowded new suburbs into the surrounding areas.